COPYRIGHTI

Copyrighting Creativity
Creative Values, Cultural Heritage Institutions and Systems of Intellectual Property

Edited by

HELLE PORSDAM
University of Copenhagen, Denmark

Routledge
Taylor & Francis Group

LONDON AND NEW YORK

First published 2015 by Ashgate Publishing

2 Park Square, Milton Park, Abingdon, Oxfordshire OX14 4RN
52 Vanderbilt Avenue, New York, NY 10017

Routledge is an imprint of the Taylor & Francis Group, an informa business

First issued in paperback 2020

Copyright © Helle Porsdam 2015

Helle Porsdam has asserted her right under the Copyright, Designs and Patents Act, 1988, to be identified as the editor of this work.

British Library Cataloguing in Publication Data
A catalogue record for this book is available from the British Library

The Library of Congress has cataloged the printed edition as follows:
Copyrighting Creativity: Creative Values, Cultural Heritage Institutions and Systems of
  Intellectual Property / edited by Helle Porsdam.
    pages   cm
  Includes bibliographical references and index.
  1. Cultural property – Law and legislation. 2. Copyright. 3. Intellectual property.
  I. Porsdam, Helle, 1956- editor.
  K3791.C67 2015
  346.04'8–dc23   2014048314

ISBN: 978-1-4724-3165-3 (hbk)
ISBN: 978-0-367-59865-5 (pbk)

Contents

List of Figures

List of Contributors

Balázs Bodó is Marie Curie Research Fellow, Institute for Information Law, University of Amsterdam.

Lucky L. Belder is Assistant Professor at the Centre of Intellectual Property Right (CIER) of the Molengraaff Institute for Civil Law, University of Utrecht and a co-PI of CULTIVATE.

Martin Fredriksson is Associate Professor at the Department for Culture Studies, Linköping University.

Valdimar Tr. Hafstein is Associate Professor of Folklore/Ethnology University of Iceland and one of the PIs of CULTIVATE.

Fiona Macmillan is Corporation of London Professor of Law at the School of Law, Birkbeck, University of London and one of the PIs of CULTIVATE.

Darryl Mead is Deputy National Librarian at the National Library of Scotland.

Fred Saunderson is Intellectual Property Officer at the National Library of Scotland.

Peter Schneck is Professor (Chair) for American Literature and Culture, University of Osnabrück.

Martin Skrydstrup holds a PhD in Cultural Anthropology from Columbia University. He is currently a Postdoctoral Fellow, Department of Food and Resource Economics, Faculty of Science, University of Copenhagen.

Stina Teilmann-Lock is Associate Professor, Department of Design and Communication, University of Southern Denmark.

Kim Treiger-Bar-Am teaches Law at Bar Ilan University, Israel.

Introduction

Helle Porsdam

Is copyright the 'elephant in the room' these days?[1] Do issues concerning intellectual property (IP) protection come up in an ever-increasing number of both discourses and popular practices involving culture and cultural heritage? This volume of essays argues that this is indeed the case. Its contributors are scholars from both the humanities and the social sciences – from cultural studies to law – as well as cultural practitioners and representatives from cultural heritage institutions who share an interest in the contribution of IP to the role of these institutions in making culture accessible and encouraging new creativity.

The move from cultural theory and innovation to cultural practice inevitably involves legal protection and, historically, IP has often lagged behind new technological breakthroughs. This is true not least in the digital age and has led to various problems concerning the impact of new technologies and digital media on knowledge production on the one hand, and contemporary modes of production of cultural goods, the reception and safeguarding of cultural heritage and the dissemination of knowledge about culture on the other.

Digitisation expands the horizon of creative possibilities and in so doing puts pressure on the viability and applicability of legal regimes that were constructed for an analogue world. New forms of collaboration emerge in internet-based fan communities as well as in the arts, sciences and humanities. These developments are at the very core of contemporary culture and have an impact on individuals as well as institutions.

The incarnation of creativity and innovation in practice, cultural heritage institutions are significant stakeholders in the new digital information infrastructures. For the past two decades, they have accordingly involved and engaged themselves actively in various debates – scholarly as well as public – concerning copyright and cultural heritage. The same cannot be said for humanities scholars who, though recognising the seminal role of these institutions in the presentation of culture, as the collective memory of society and in stimulating new creativity and innovation, have too often allowed cultural heritage institutions to remain on the periphery of scholarly debates concerning copyright.

---

1 I owe this wonderful suggestion to Professor Evelyn Welch, Vice-Principal for Arts & Sciences and Professor of Renaissance Studies at King's College London. At a conference a couple of years ago, she mentioned how copyright issues keep coming up in relation to her own research focus on material culture, early modern consumption and the social and economic dynamics of fashion in Europe between 1500 and 1700.

With this volume of essays and with CULTIVATE we hope to change this. The name given to 'Copyrighting Creativity: Creative Values, Cultural Heritage Institutions and Systems of Intellectual Property', CULTIVATE is/was a three-year research collaboration (2010–13) between the universities of Copenhagen, Uppsala, London, Utrecht and Iceland. I was the Project Leader and my partners were: Professor in Library and Information Science Eva Hemmungs Wirtén from Linköping University (formerly Uppsala University); Professor of Law Fiona Macmillan, Birkbeck School of Law, University of London; Professor of Intellectual Property Madeleine de Cock Buning and Assistant Professor Lucky Belder, both at the Centre of Intellectual Property Right (CIER), University of Utrecht; and Associate Professor of Folklore/Ethnology Valdimar Tr. Hafstein, University of Iceland.

A project under HERA (Humanities in the European Research Area which is a partnership between Humanities Research Councils across Europe and the European Science Foundation), CULTIVATE is/was part of the first HERA Joint Research Programme for the theme 'Humanities as a Source of Creativity and Innovation'. Our common research question was this: 'What is and what ought to be the relationship between creativity, cultural heritage institutions and copyright?'

In order to get the best possible advice on how to answer this research question we invited relevant experts to the Tate Modern, London (one of our external partners) in late April 2013 for our final conference. The present volume is based on the talks given at this conference as well as on the work done within CULTIVATE.

Like CULTIVATE, the volume is European focused. We made the deliberate choice, while writing our application for HERA, that we wanted to target our research specifically towards Europe (and European concerns). Beyond the obvious fact that HERA concerns humanities in the European research area, this also had to do with the many recent publications that address issues relating to the historical and contemporary anxieties of authorship and ownership for indigenous collections. As the great interest in these anxieties shows, they are pressing and need our attention. We do therefore address them in this volume – especially in the introduction and in the first part, but also in some of the later parts – but they do not form the centre of attention, as they are covered so convincingly elsewhere.[2]

There is a large amount of literature out there on each of our three core themes: copyright/IP, creativity and innovation, and cultural heritage (institutions). Our volume is different from the majority of this literature in that it attempts to link these areas – and to discuss and analyse the relationship between them. Culture, cultural heritage and cultural rights are the crux of this relationship. Often referred to as 'the poor cousin' of human rights, cultural rights are an area of human rights in which people – scholars as well as the general public – are becoming more and more interested. Human rights and IP is one of the most challenging topics to emerge within human rights debates, moreover – a reflection, in our current

---

2   See e.g., Coombe, Wershler and Zeilinger (2014) which especially deals with the Canadian context, but whose authors address a broader set of issues too.

knowledge societies or economies, of the importance of cultural issues, especially as these relate to identity and cultural pride. 'Human rights and intellectual property', writes Paul Torremans in the Foreword to his edited volume *Intellectual Property and Human Rights* from 2008, for example, 'is clearly a field in full expansion and development' (Torremans, 2008: xxiv).

The present volume may be viewed as a part of this recent trend – but it also looks at the cultural issues involved from a non-legal perspective. Reflecting the fact that both the CULTIVATE team and the contributors to our volume come from different academic disciplines, our volume is very much an interdisciplinary endeavour – and as such may also say something important about what each one of our particular disciplines can add to the general picture.

The Major Issues and the Nine Chapters

In addition to this introduction, the volume consists of nine chapters and an epilogue, and is divided into three thematically different, yet overlapping parts: (I) *Who owns culture: Cultural heritage institutions and copyright*; (II) *The Arts, Literature, Design and Copyright*; and (III) *Creativity, Authorship, Copyright and the Public Domain*.

Part I: Who Owns Culture: Cultural Heritage Institutions and Copyright[3]

When it comes to cultural heritage – to the legacy of physical artefacts and intangible attributes of people and groups – it is interesting to note that whereas 'Transnational studies' are currently very popular within both the humanities and the social sciences, the policies of most source nations and the international dialogue about cultural property are becoming ever more regional and/or nation-oriented. This calls into question the (transnational) principle of cultural artefacts as the legacy of all humankind that is expressed in numerous UNESCO documents.

Most often, since the 1970s when restitution of cultural heritage started to become a very hot international political issue, the debate was concerned with antiquities or the stolen treasures of the ancient world. As former colonies sought independence, they would try to reclaim their own history by asking to have the artefacts returned that physically tie them to it. The core question is: Whose culture is it? And the underlying issue is one of identity and of the right to reclaim the objects that are its concrete symbols. Are cultural artefacts the common heritage of us all in an interconnected world? Or do encyclopaedic museums such as the

---

3   I wish to thank my CULTIVATE partners for allowing me to draw on their respective contributions to the Pecha Kucha we performed at the Tate Modern conference in London in April 2013.

British Museum that embody this idea of the oneness of humanity only pay tribute to Western ways of thinking?

In the European context, the demand for the 'repatriation' of cultural objects has been expressed in sometimes very strange ways. One example is the nationalistic Danish People's Party and its fight to have one of the earliest Danish laws, the so-called Jutlandic Law from 1241, repatriated from the Swedish Royal Library. Modern historical research has shown that this old manuscript was either purchased or given to the Swedes in the 1720s. But such historical fact has not interested the Danish People's Party who has invented its own story of the Jutlandic Law as spoils of war and has used a postcolonial discourse to argue that these Danish artefacts contain an invaluable part of Denmark's history and identity and therefore really do belong in Denmark.[4]

For indigenous peoples and other minorities something slightly different, though in many ways related, is at stake: the distinctive rights to their intangible cultural heritage. These communities are increasingly concerned with the misappropriation by, for example, international companies of their traditional knowledge, and they have seized on IP as the forum in which to protect their cultural heritage. Their claims for IP are voiced in terms of identity politics, cultural survival and human rights and 'these new claims for intellectual property understand rights not just in the familiar terms of incentives-for-creation, but also as tools for both recognition and redistribution' (Sunder, 2006: 273). These claims force the international legal and political system to pay more attention to potential violations of the cultural rights of minorities and indigenous peoples as well as to articulate the principles through which traditional knowledge and traditional cultural expressions may best be recognised and protected.

There is something ironic about the fact that, today, there are basically two groups who are interested in copyright (and IP) *expansion*: exploiters (companies and corporations) who use copyright expansion as a mechanism to protect investment, and indigenous peoples who seek to protect their traditional knowledge. These are strange bedfellows – the more so as everyone else works towards *limiting* IP extension. Future IP fights will be about finding the right balance between these different claims. In and of itself, each one of the claims is legitimate and understandable enough; in practice, however, they cannot be seen in isolation, but must be weighed against each other so that a fair solution can be found for everyone involved. Cultural rights of one kind or another will be invoked both by the 'free culture' and 'access to knowledge' proponents and by those who have the best interest of indigenous groups in mind – the problem being that these rights sometimes work against each other.

The protection and promotion of cultural diversity is an issue here. The European Treaty specifically mentions respect for cultural and linguistic diversity, for example, just as it states that Europe's cultural heritage should be safeguarded and enriched. The promotion of *Europeana*, the European Digital Library, is one

---

4   I talk about this case in Porsdam (2012b).

way to achieve this. *Europeana*'s aim is to reach full disclosure of the European cultural heritage by 2025. The estimated costs are a hundred billion Euro – one reason being the costly nature of copyright.

Cultural contents to which no rights apply is in the public domain. Public domain contents may be digitised and disclosed online without legal obstacles, but content protected by copyright is in the private domain. The process of finding rights holders and clearing copyright is both expensive and time consuming. The legal framework for the protection of cultural contents in the EU is the *Acquis Communautaire* which consists of nine directives harmonising the national laws of the 28 EU Member States. One of the most important of these directives is the *Information Society Directive* from 2001 which is sadly outdated at this point – being inefficient and waiting to be revised. It states, among other things, that *reproduction* and *communication to the public* are exclusive rights of copyright holders, that digitisation is reproduction, and that disclosing digital material online constitutes a form of communication to the public. The *Information Society Directive* furthermore states that such disclosure may not be undertaken by cultural institutions without permission, unless an exception applies which is implemented in national law.

The EU *Acquis* lists one mandatory and twenty-one optional copyright exceptions. These latter allow for instance 'private copying', certain forms of reproductions by cultural heritage institutions as well as the use of works for educational or scientific purposes, but they do not provide a blanket exception for digitisation and online disclosure of cultural contents. This creates a major challenge for institutions who are confronted with the responsibility to seek permission for digitisation and online disclosure of cultural contents. It is but one example of the fact that the *Acquis* is not keeping pace with all the new technological developments of our information society.

It is interesting to note, furthermore, that non-EU rules can also be relevant for the digitisation of cultural heritage in the EU. For example, digitisation and disclosure of heritage in Dutch cultural heritage institutions, stemming from Indonesia – a former Dutch colony, now part of the emerging ASEAN Union – may be subject to Indonesian rules. Thus, according to the Indonesian Copyright Act 'commonly owned' cultural content is copyright protected perpetually, and the State is the copyright holder. Foreign users must ask permission from the State in order to reproduce and publish these works. These provisions seem to implicate both that EU heritage institutions may not digitise and disclose online Indonesian heritage which is part of their collections, and that these digital reproductions are intended to be accessed in Indonesia.

Part I consists of Chapters 1, 2, 3 and 4. Chapter 1, 'Two Doctrines of and for Cultural Property: How Europe and America Are Different', concerns the resurgence within the past three decades of national and native claims to artefacts held by heritage institutions in Western metropolises. Martin Skrydstrup asks what form of property museum objects embody, how we should understand the coming into being of the institution of 'cultural property' and the contemporary praxis of 'retention', 'return', 'restitution', and 'repatriation'? Or, to slightly rephrase the question at the centre of this volume of essays: What is and what ought to be the relationship between cultural/artistic productions past and present, museums and cultural property?

In his doctoral research, Skrydstrup interrogated these interrelated questions vis-à-vis two distinct cultural property polities: the American NAGPRA regime, which is renowned for its uniform legalistic approach, and the Danish ad hoc ethical modality, which has come to be known under the rubric of UTIMUT. His archival and ethnographic research focused predominantly on the 'experts' of each regime trusted to make findings and deliberate disputes. What emerged was two distinctively different technologies of recognition of claimants; where NAGPRA grappled with definitions of indigeneity, specifically with regard to Hawaii, UTIMUT circumvented this question and only recognised other metropolitan museums as legitimate claimants. Skrydstrup found that the undergirding doctrine of NAGPRA was restoration of 'prior possessions', whereas in UTIMUT the operating modality was 'patrimonial partage', i.e. a form of division of collections, according to curatorial criteria of preservation and display. In this chapter, he juxtaposes and elaborates on these different concepts of cultural property in the US vs. Europe and argues that the gateway to their understanding goes through the nature of transactional orders within each polity. Furthermore he argues that such transactional orders simultaneously expose the guilt and consciousness of the postcolonial nation-state and offer prospects for State legitimacy by way of redeeming colonial legacies.

Chapter 2 offers a discussion by Lucky L. Belder on 'Museums Revisited: The Position of the Museum in the New Governance of the Protection of Cultural Heritage and Cultural Diversity'. In general, Belder notes, the European Union aims for an ever-closer EU and for more welfare for all. The Lisbon Treaty specifically talks about respect for cultural and linguistic diversity, just as it states that Europe's cultural heritage should be safeguarded and enriched. The plan for Europe 2020, the EU's growth strategy for the coming decade, is to support new information *technologies* that may in turn support sustainable growth, competitiveness and social development (http://ec.europa.eu/europe2020/index_en.htm).

But what is information technology without CONTENT, Belder asks? What is the role of museums, archives and libraries in providing sustainable access to cultural heritage? And what does Unity in Diversity mean considering the modest nature of European cultural politics? What is the relation between EU politics on the single market, on the one hand, and the mainstreaming of the support for cultural diversity, on the other? And why is it that at one and the same time, cultural diversity is considered a strength that will support the dynamics of our societies, but also as something that is under siege and urgently needs protection?

In Chapter 3, 'Libraries, Creativity and Copyright', Darryl Mead and Fred Saunderson argue that by holding and giving access to everything that has gone before, our cultural heritage institutions, especially our national libraries, will have an increasing role in supporting future creative work. National libraries are the institutions with the capacity to collect (from) the worldwide web; they have already collected the world's printed output for more than 300 years, as well as sound and vision for over a century. Most extraordinarily, they can help you find virtually anything and then give all of us access to it for free.

Libraries have much larger collections than other cultural heritage institutions, Mead and Saunderson remind us. Library collections include both fact and fiction. Most of the material in a library has been interpreted, and the present has been built from past creative processes. The library provides a map of nearly all ideas from all of history. The library is the holder of all of the publicly available information in the world – in patent terms, it is the holder of all prior art. Everything in the library is available as the basis of future creative work. The biggest constraint for the vision of delivering a creative future is not a lack of funding, it is copyright, according to Mead and Saunderson. Chapter 3 explores the intricate relationship between creators' rights, our collective heritage and the future role of libraries in supporting and enabling creative endeavour to flourish.

Moreover, in the digital era where the book, thanks to ubiquity of electronic copies is not a scarce resource anymore, libraries find themselves in an extremely competitive environment, where several different actors are in a position to store and provide low cost access to a large number of documents. One type of these competitors is shadow libraries, piratical text collections which by now have amassed electronic copies of millions of copyrighted works and provide access to them usually free of charge to anyone around the globe. While such shadow libraries are far from being universal, they are able to offer certain services better, to more people, under more favourable terms than most public or research libraries. In Chapter 4, 'Libraries in the post-scarcity era', Balázs Bodó offers insights into the development and the inner workings of one of the biggest scientific shadow libraries on the internet to understand what kind of library people hack together for themselves if they have the means, and if they don't have to abide by the legal, bureaucratic and economic constraints that library innovation usually faces. He argues that one of the many possible futures of the library is hidden in plain sight in the shadows, and those who think of the future of libraries can learn a lot from book pirates of the twenty-first century about how texts in electronic form can be stored, organised and circulated.

Part II: The Arts, Literature, Design and Copyright

One of the questions pervading the relationship between copyright law and the 'arts' (including, for present purposes, literature and design) is that of constitution and authorisation. Does some generally accepted definition of what amounts to the 'arts' constitute and authorise the subject matter of copyright or, on the other hand, does copyright law constitute and authorise concepts of what are the 'arts'? It increasingly appears that copyright law defines, controls or affects the meaning of 'arts' in the broader social and cultural spheres. This very effect is evident in the way in which arts festivals, for example, tend to brand themselves according to copyright categories as literary festivals, film festivals, music festivals, theatre festivals, dance festivals, despite the fact that almost no arts festivals confine themselves to only one artistic form.

Both tangible and intangible cultural heritage are objects of protection under international law, yet as a concept, they remain notoriously difficult to define precisely. Copyright is a private property right whereas cultural heritage rights are enjoyed in community. The international conventions on the protection of intangible cultural heritage do not seem to envisage the need for any limitation on the extensive private property rights wielded by copyright owners, though. If there is any point to cultural heritage rights, it must be to limit the privatisation of cultural heritage through copyright. But, in reality, copyright suffocates cultural heritage since it is a formalised technique of private appropriation of intangible cultural property. All the rules here seem to be set by the copyright regime, which has spawned the idea of the public domain in order to explain its relationship to everything else that exists in intellectual space. When IP rights are used as a technology to appropriate intangible cultural heritage then, so far as copyright is concerned, what it consequently privatises is taken from the IP domain. Under these circumstances, much depends upon the geography and architecture of this public domain.

The public domain has been invented by IP scholars in order to attempt to explain and understand the limits on IP's colonisation of intellectual space. But the basic problem with the public domain (apart from the fact that it is an imaginary space) is that it is more or less lacking in any legal architecture. It has been imagined only as the place where there are no IP rights, only as a place defined by absence. So, if we pull the arts, literature and/or design out of the propertised zone of intellectual space on the basis that cultural heritage as a community right does not belong there, then this may have the effect of leaving their contents completely unprotected. Instead of being a suspension in time and space, their contents simply become a free-for-all for all time.

Legally speaking, what is needed therefore is a kind of legal architecture in the public domain that: (a) recognises that some things can never be privately owned because of their cultural (heritage) significance; and, (b) develops the concept of group and communal rights, belonging to less than the public as a whole, bounded by property on the outside, but inside promoting freedom and space for creativity, innovation, and cultural conservation. This concept of the bounded creative community would recognise a legal suspension of the copyright regime that mirrors the temporal and spatial suspension of the arts, literature and/or design while preserving the incentive for creativity through the exercise of rights against those outside their temporal and spatial boundaries. In the end, then, this is not just an argument about suspension, but also one about balance: balance between the community rights in cultural heritage and the private rights in copyright; and balance between the regular order of life and the rupture inherent in the 'collective effervescence' (Durkheim, 1912/1954, quoted in Sassatelli, 2008: 18–19) of the arts, literature and design.

Part II consists of Chapters 5, 6, and 7. As the title of Chapter 5 implies, 'Arts Festivals as Cultural Heritage in a Copyright-Saturated World' concerns the way in which many of the activities that occur as part and parcel of arts festivals can be mapped onto existing categories of copyright works. Indeed, argues Fiona Macmillan, so powerful is the rhetoric of these categories that there is a question about the extent to which they have constituted the very idea of 'arts' in this context, so that festivals typically identify themselves as film festivals, musical festivals, theatre festivals and so on, even if in fact empirical research reveals that almost no festivals confine themselves to only one form of 'artistic' output (Macmillan, 2013c). It would, therefore, be tempting to treat festivals as being just like any other form of distribution of copyright protected works. Turan, for example, argues that film festivals, at least, are an alternative form of distribution for films that have failed to find the usual commercial outlets for distribution (Turan, 2002: 7–8). This observation might also hold good for musical festivals given that there are particular constraints on commercial distribution in both the film and music industries which, like all constraints, are likely to produce a drive for alternative means of fulfilling desire.

However, maintains Macmillan, limiting our understanding of festivals to being merely another means of distribution is really limiting our understanding of the nature of arts festivals and their social, political and economic significance. While it is undoubtedly true that arts festivals, particularly some arts festivals, produce economic value for the entertainment industries, they also encompass a range of other values that are less easily measured but nevertheless present. Chapter 5 argues that arts festivals should be recognised as a form of cultural heritage. If this case can be made out, then it raises a problem: that the public and communal values of arts festivals as forms of cultural heritage appear to be in potential conflict with the intellectual property rights that saturate the arts festival environment.

Stina Teilmann-Lock is the author of Chapter 6, 'The Artfulness of Design: Copyright and the Danish Modern Inheritance'. She discusses a 1961 Danish Supreme Court ruling which said that a set of cutlery was an original work protectable by copyright, notwithstanding its being 'neither unique nor innovative'. The 'low' originality requirement for design must have as its concomitant a narrow scope of protection. Hence, to this day, only a 'close imitation' of a design would amount to copyright infringement. In this way, Teilmann-Lock explains, Danish law resolves the problem that arises from the fact that in any design the form is always conditioned by its function. Too rigid an interpretation of protection – and too broad an interpretation of copying – might have the undesirable effect of creating a monopoly on, say, stackable chairs, soup spoons or toothbrushes.

The Danish solution is now in jeopardy, however. Case C-145/10 Painer (2011) does not allow for inferior protection of any type of original work. In her chapter, Teilmann-Lock considers what may be the effect of such a change on design law in

Denmark and how, more broadly, the evolution of Danish design in the twentieth century may serve as an indicator of shifting relationships between copyright, creativity and cultural heritage. Shifts in these relationships affect the formation and dissemination of art and culture in society. Copyright law regulates creative expression by either promoting or restricting it: the copyright rules thereby also come to contribute to the shaping of a cultural heritage.

Chapter 7, 'Who Owns *Uncle Tom's Cabin*? Literature as Cultural Property', concerns the historical dimension of cultural heritage. As a living tradition to be continued into the future, this historical dimension arguably finds one of its most obvious manifestations in literary history claimed by a community or a culture, a region or a nation, or even transnational or global communities (e.g., in the idea of world literature). According to Peter Schneck, this modern idea of literary history as an essential aspect of cultural identity and heritage is essentially connected to the increasing legal definition and protection of literary property in the form of copyright regulation.

Using a specific example from nineteenth-century US-American literature, Harriet Beecher Stowe's *Uncle Tom's Cabin*, Chapter 7 addresses some essential ambiguities and problems that beset our conventional understanding of literature (and its history) as a form of cultural property since it remains fundamentally defined by the struggle between conflicting notions of individual and collective ownership. The major question is how our ideas about the future of literary property as cultural heritage may benefit from the historical debates and struggles surrounding the cultural acknowledgment and legal definition of literature as property.

Part III: Creativity, Authorship, Copyright and the Public Domain

To a large extent traditional Romanticist notions of authorship still inform copyright law – national rules on authorship and copyright ownership are based on the author as an autonomous agent operating in isolation. In reality, however, in our age of file sharing and peer-to-peer networking, of social software and Web 2.0, of mashups and remixes, Wikipedia and YouTube, authorship is predominantly a collective endeavour. Multiple authorship – as well as the recognition of art forms and practices that value process as much as end product – are a challenge to traditional views on authorial control, both in relation to the economic rights and to the immaterial interests (or 'moral rights') of the author. It is no wonder, therefore, that approaches questioning the viability of the 'original work of authorship' as a legal object as well as the traditional relationship between the three hermeneutic elements of Author, Reader and Text inform a number of research projects on copyright today.

Historically, folklore and traditional culture offered an alternative to authorship. Folklore, by definition, is everything that works of authorship are not. It is peer-to-peer, it is collaborative and collective. The concept of folklore emerged alongside norms of authorship in the eighteenth century, and like authorship, it had its heyday in the nineteenth century. A critical genealogy allows us to understand folklore as a constitutive outside of authorship. It is the remainder of the author concept – a product of its limitations. Folklore is the non-authored – or even anti-authored. It imagines creative agency differently than through the dominant understandings given force in copyright; it thinks in alternative terms about creative processes as collaborative, incremental, and distributed in space and time. Such creative processes are in fact all around us today – they have become the norm, not the exception.

Going back into history makes it possible to relate some of today's paradoxes and problems back to the emergence of the dichotomy between authorship and folklore, between copyrighted works and the public domain, and between the universal individual subject (which finds its ultimate expression in the figure of the author) and the collective subaltern subject (also known as the folk). The creation of the *Berne Convention for the Protection of Literary and Artistic Works*, usually known as the *Berne Convention* (1886), and its subsequent revisions are the key to understanding this dichotomy. The different developments that copyright underwent in the United States and Europe, are also important. Whereas in the Anglo-American system copyright has been viewed as a divestible property right that can be freely traded – the author normally does not hold this right for very long, the name of the game being to find a publisher who can exploit the work and make it profitable in the market – mainland European law has defined authors' rights as inalienable (and non-economic) human rights, as moral rights that are intimately connected with the integrity of an author and his/her creation and therefore cannot be freely traded (Porsdam, 2014).

There is an entirely different philosophical approach to copyright at stake here – one that also surfaces when it comes to the issue of whether IP rights are human rights or not. From a perspective that owes a great deal to the Anglo-American view of copyright as a piece of property, the argument has been made that the protection of the moral and material interests of authors cannot be equated with IP protection, because IP rights are not fundamental and inalienable entitlements of the human person. IP rights lack the fundamental characteristics of human rights as they are established by legislative acts, limited in time and can be bought, sold or revoked. By contrast, it has been argued by a more European *droit d'auteur* inspired group of scholars and activists that IP rights are implicit in the right to the protection of moral and material interests of authors and the right to property in the UDHR (Ovett, 2006).

Part III consists of Chapters 8 and 9. In Chapter 8, 'Pirates, Librarians and Open Source Capitalists: New Alliances in the Copyright Wars', Martin Fredriksson relates how, since the closing down of Napster in 2000, questions of copyright and piracy have been increasingly politicised, giving birth to an ideological pirate movement that takes its most concrete form in the formation of Pirate Parties. Over the last years this movement has come to frame piracy and filesharing as practices and technologies to revitalise the public sphere and promote wider access to a common cultural heritage. The pirates stress how an expanding intellectual property rights (IPR) regime limits the public access to culture and knowledge and privatises the cultural heritage. This is a concern that they share with many actors and participators in the cultural sector, such as libraries and archives, as well as with members of academia for whom open access is becoming the new publication paradigm.

The protests against the American Stop Online Piracy bill (SOPA) in 2011 and 2012, where major tech companies like Google joined forces with the digital rights movement to oppose more restrictive IP-laws, implies that there are not only cultural but also business interests involved in the cult of cultural accessibility. Chapter 9 explores how issues of cultural accessibility versus IPR in the knowledge society seem to create new, and sometimes contradictory, intersections between apparently disparate actors such as the digital rights movement, cultural institutions, academia and the technology industry. Eventually, it raises the question of what this can tell of the meaning of the public sphere and the cultural commons in the twenty-first century.

In the last chapter of the volume, Chapter 9, 'Copyright, Creativity, and Transformative Use', Kim Treiger-Bar-Am looks at how authors and artists are influenced by and respond to the cultural heritage. As such their creativity relies upon copying and changing elements of prior works. Despite copyright's purpose of fostering creativity, copyright law restricts copies of prior works, and changes to them. The distribution right prevents the production of *copies*; the integrity right prevents *changes* to works; and the right to derivative works prevents *copies with changes*. Yet copyright doctrine provides a defence to authors whose work makes transformative use of prior expression. Under US copyright law transformative use is often seen to satisfy the requirements of the fair use defence, and developments in UK law may be seen to support such a defence as well.

Chapter 9 explores the transformative use defence, in particular with regard to appropriation art. Treiger-Bar-Am shows that in analyses of the transformative use defence courts utilise a hermeneutic analysis used in free speech case law and in the art world as well, relying on the Reader's understanding of the meaning of the use of prior works. She puts forward that this method of analysis enables courts to accept transformativity in appropriation art, and to further copyright's goal of encouraging and promoting creativity.

Finally, in his last Words, Valdimar Hafstein comments on the previous nine chapters as well as offering a few remarks of his own regarding the themes of this volume and his own research within CULTIVATE. We ought to re-think the concept of creativity, he argues, and proposes a revised understanding of creative agency on the model of the collector-editor, indexed to adaptation rather than to the threshold of originality. Creativity is collective, incremental and distributed, and this ought to be reflected in the relationship between cultural heritage institutions and copyright. Hafstein's 'Last Words' form an attempt to address the 'how it ought to be' part of the double question that frames the book – '*What is and what ought to be the relationship between creativity, cultural heritage institutions and copyright?'*

What will the future bring? For cultural heritage institutions, what Madhavi Sunder has called IP3 – the convergence of Identity Politics, the Internet Protocol and IP rights – will increasingly come into play (Sunder, 2006). Working towards both preserving cultural artefacts and making culture accessible through exhibitions (both analogue and digital), these institutions will be confronted not only with claims for the repatriation of cultural artefacts, but also with demands for making public certain artefacts that may be under copyright protection. The fight for 'free culture' and for access to knowledge will become even more intense as they – and people in general – worry about the privatisation of the public domain by IP rights holders, corporate but also private ones, that will result, they claim, in the loss of creativity and of all the visions for free and accessible culture and education for everyone that accompanied the rise of the internet. Future IP fights – and their successful resolution – will be about finding the right balance between all these different cultural claims.

Select Bibliography

Belder, L.P.C. (2011). 'Friends or foes? Two ways of thinking on the relation between the tasks of cultural heritage institutions and the protection of copyright', in Estelle Derclaye (ed.) *Preserving and accessing our cultural heritage*. Cambridge University Press.

Blake, J. (2000). 'On Defining the Cultural Heritage', *International and Comparative Law Quarterly* 49, 61–85.

Connolly, A.J. (2014). *Cultural Heritage Rights*. Ashgate Publishing.

Coombe, R.J. (1998). *The Cultural Life of Intellectual Properties*. Durham/London: Duke University Press.

Coombe, R.J., Wershler, D. and M. Zeilinger (eds.) (2014). *Dynamic Fair Dealing: Creating Canadian Culture Online*. University of Toronto Press.

Cuno, J. (ed.) (2009). *Whose Culture?: The Promise of Museums and the Debate over Antiquities*. Princeton University Press.

Derclaye, E. (ed.) (2011). *Copyright and Cultural Heritage: Preservation and Access to Works in a Digital World*. Edward Elgar.

Hafstein, V.T. (2004). *The Making of Intangible Cultural Heritage: Tradition and Authenticity, Community and Humanity*. Berkeley: University of California Press.

Hafstein, V.T. (2004). 'The Politics of Origins: Collective Creation Revisited', *Journal of American Folklore* 117: 465, 300–315.

Hafstein, V.T. (2009). 'Intangible Heritage as a List', in *Intangible heritage* 2009/1/26. Taylor & Francis US.

Hafstein, V.T. and M. Skrydstrup (2012). 'Europe at the Crossroads of Rights and Culture(s)', in *A Companion to the Anthropology of Europe*, vol. 41. Wiley-Blackwell.

Helfer, L.R. and G.W. Austin (2011). *Human Rights and Intellectual Property: Mapping the Global Interface*. Cambridge University Press

Macmillan, F. (2008). 'Human Rights, Cultural Property and Intellectual Property: Three Concepts in Search of a Relationship', in C. Graber and M. Nenova (eds), *Intellectual Property and Traditional Cultural Expressions in a Digital Environment*. Cheltenham: Edward Elgar.

Macmillan, F. (2012). 'Rights, Culture, Property: In Search of a New Design for Intellectual Space', in Helle Porsdam and Thomas Elholm (eds.), *Dialogues on Justice: European Perspectives on Law and Humanities*. Berlin/Boston: de Gruyter.

Macmillan, F. (2013a). 'The Protection of Cultural Heritage: Common Heritage of Humankind, National Cultural "Patrimony" or Private Property?' *Northern Ireland Legal Quarterly* 64: 3, 351–64.

Macmillan, F. (2013b). 'Arts Festivals: Property, Heritage or More?' in K Bowrey and M Handler (eds.), *Law and Creativity in the Age of the Entertainment Franchise*. Cambridge University Press.

Macmillan, F. (2013c). 'A Taxonomy of Arts Festivals: Mapping Issues in Cultural Property and Human Rights', Working Paper 2, HERA 'Cultivate Project', http://www.cultivateproject.dk/

Ovett, D. (2006). 'Intellectual Property and Human Rights – Is the Distinction Clear Now?', Maison des Associations, Switzerland, Policy Brief, No. 3, October [previously available at: http://www.3dthree.org/pdf_3D/3D_GC17_IPHR.pdf]

Porsdam, H. (ed.) (2006). *Copyright and Other Fairy Tales: Hans Christian Andersen and the Commodification of Creativity*. Cheltenham: Edward Elgar.

Porsdam, H. (2009). *From Civil to Human Rights: Dialogues on Law and Humanities in the United States and Europe*. Cheltenham: Edward Elgar.

Porsdam, H. (ed.) (2012a). *Civil Religion, Human Rights and International Relations: Connecting People Across Cultures and Traditions*. Cheltenham: Edward Elgar.

Porsdam, H. (2012b). 'Cultural Heritage and Law: The Case of Cultural Looting', in Porsdam, H. and T. Elholm (eds), *Dialogues on Justice: European Perspectives on Law and Humanities* (Law & Literature). Berlin and Boston: De Gruyter, 219–36.

Porsdam, H. (2014). 'H3) Chapter 48: Property Rights', Entry in the SAGE Reference project *The SAGE Handbook of Human Rights* (2014 – in print).

Porsdam, H. and T. Elholm (eds.) (2012). *Dialogues on Justice: European Perspectives on Law and Humanities*. Berlin and Boston: De Gruyter.

Sassatelli, M. (ed.) (2008). *European Public Culture & Aesthetic Cosmopolitanism* (EURO-FESTIVAL Project: European Arts Festivals and Public Culture,

Deliverable 1.1, WP1 Main Report, October 2008; http://www.euro-festival.org/publications.html), 15–40.

Sunder, M. (2006). 'IP3', *Stanford Law Review* 59: 2, 257–332.

Torremans, P. (ed.) (2008). *Intellectual Property and Human Rights: Enhanced Edition of Copyright and Human Rights (Information Law)*. Kluwer Law International.

Turan, K. *Sundance to Sarajevo: Film Festivals and the World They Made*. Los Angeles: University of California Press, 2002.

Wirtén, E.H. (2004). *No Trespassing: Authorship, Intellectual Property Rights and the Boundaries of Globalization*. Toronto: University of Toronto Press.

Wirtén, E.H. (2008). *Terms of Use: Negotiating the Jungle of the Intellectual Commons*. Toronto: University of Toronto Press.

Wirtén, E.H. (2011). *Cosmopolitan Copyright: Law and Language in the Translation Zone*. Uppsala: Uppsala University.

Yu, P.K. (2008). 'Cultural Relics, Intellectual Property and Intangible Heritage', *Temple Law Review* 81, 433–506.

PART I
Who Owns Culture: Cultural Heritage Institutions and Copyright?

Chapter 1

Two Doctrines of and for Cultural Property
How Europe and America are Different

Martin Skrydstrup

A New Order of Things?

In March 2008, a group of international experts on cultural property were invited
and flown to Greece at the expense of the Greek Ministry of Culture to contribute
to the conference 'Return of Cultural Objects to their Countries of Origin', which
met at the New Acropolis Museum in Athens.[1] Before its official inauguration,
these experts were allowed a first peek into the New Acropolis Museum, where
one of its principal architects Prof. Dimitrios Pandermalis explained that the
proportions of the concrete core and the rectangular glass box of the gallery at the
top floor mirrored the exact dimensions of the perimeter of the Parthenon: 'That
way, visitors will get a sense of the scale of the sculptures in relation to the mother
temple. The idea is that the visible facades of the Parthenon and the sculptures
that once adorned it unite in your imagination, allowing you to picture the temple
as it was in Periclean Athens'.[2] This frieze was a single long depiction of what is
presumed by most classicists to be the Panathenaic procession, which once ran
around the perimeter of the inner walls of the temple. Our guide told us that the
panels lost to antiquity would be left blank and those that remained in London
would be reproduced in plaster covered by a special mesh to make clear that
they were not the originals. Pandernalis explained that: 'the idea is that the fine
veil will make the missing sculptures look like the ghosts of the missing pieces.

---

1   The formal invitation card read: 'The Conference will bring together high profile
experts such as law specialists, archaeologists, academics, journalists, museum professionals
and others'. (Letter of Invitation issued by Hellenic Ministry of Culture; Directorate of
Prehistoric & Classical Antiquities; Athens; Greece; February 2008)

2   The Parthenon – the centrepiece of the Acropolis, today referred to as the 'sacred
rock' in the heart of Athens – was commissioned by Pericles, at the height of Greek power.
The result was a meticulously self-contained and perfectly proportioned marble temple
enclosed by 46 fluted Doric columns. The building had been abandoned when the seventh
Earl of Elgin shipped many of its sculptures to London in 1801, triggering a controversy
that has rumbled on for more than two centuries. It has been a church, a mosque and even a
gunpowder store, depending on who held Athens at the time. Partly destroyed by a Venetian
mortar in 1687, the Parthenon began to matter again politically after the Greeks won their
war of independence over the Ottoman Empire (Turkey) in 1821.

We want these ghosts to haunt the visitors and make them wonder where these artefacts are. This is going to be the most eloquent way to present the problem of the Parthenon sculptures'.[3] With 'problem' Pandermalis referred to the fact that currently, Greece possesses 36 of the 115 frieze panels, and 39 of the 92 metopes that ran above the exterior colonnade and showed scenes from Greek legend. By fusing sculpture, architecture and the ancient landscape into a unity, these top-floor galleries delivered a mesmerising message. This was about showing the concepts of *genius locus* and *in situ context* for the many visitors. It was a tangible aesthetic argument about the Parthenon, which evoked a powerful narrative about loss and belonging – and ultimately ownership.

The next day, the conference hosted by the New Acropolis Museum was officially opened by the Greek Minister of Culture Michalis Liapis in the presence of the President of the Greek Republic Karolas Papoulias and a number of dignitaries, VIPs and experts flown in from across the globe. Liapis opened the inauguration with the following words:

> We find ourselves in a Museum that relates dialectically with the Sacred Rock of Acropolis that integrates in perfect harmony with the archaeological and natural surrounding environment. We want people to consider that this Museum is their own museum, every Greek person's museum, every citizen of the world's museum. The construction of the New Acropolis Museum is the best possible conjuncture for the return of the Parthenon marbles, the masterpieces of classical antiquity. The claim for return is not only a Greek demand; it is a universal demand, and a global debt, so to say, having to do with culture. A request comparative to the requests for peace in the world and for the protection of human rights. The best supporters of this demand are the thousands of visitors that will be coming to see the marbles, will see the voids there, and will be thinking that some pieces of these artefacts are 4000 miles away from their destination point.[4]

With Greek pathos the Minister continued to speak about the 'dismemberment of the Parthenon temple by Lord Elgin' and the 'necessity of the reunification of the Parthenon sculptures'. Towards the end of his discourse, he recalled the top-floor gallery of the new Museum, which 'stands as a constant reminder of the unfulfilled debt to world heritage', which is currently 'in exile', but 'British authorities can reunify the sculptures of the Parthenon for this and subsequent generations'. The Minister closed on a sentimental note, evoking a quote from his predecessor, Melina Mercouri (1920–1994), who originally raised the issue in UNESCO back in 1982: 'I hope to see the marbles back home before I die, but if they come later I shall be reborn'.[5]

---

3 Transcribed from the author's fieldnotes, 16 March 2008.
4 Transcribed from the author's fieldnotes, 17 March 2008.
5 Transcribed from the author's fieldnotes, 17 March 2008.

Following the address of the Minister of Culture, Ambassador and Permanent Delegate of Greece to UNESCO, George Anastassopoulos, took the podium:

> We, as an international community of stakeholders, must explore all paths that lead us to the most appropriate solutions for all, in accordance with internationally agreed norms. The examples you will be studying today will uncover some effective strategies in this direction. These are so-called success stories that have been resolved in and out of the realm of the Inter-governmental Committee and hence offer invaluable insights into the resolution of diplomatic, legal and ethical dilemmas associated with the return of cultural property.[6]

Commenting on these six precedents for the return of cultural property, George Bizos – a Greek expatriate and prominent human rights lawyer who has campaigned against apartheid in South Africa – spoke with pathos and poetics about the natural light of Attica under which rationality was born and that no one at the foot of the sacred rock should refer to the Acropolis as being in ruins, since it embodied *paidea* – the spirit of Greek learning. In 1963, Bizos reminded the audience that the law of the Trustees of the British Museum was not 'written in stone'. It could be changed, just as Cecil Rhodes's apartheid laws were changed, because they prevented a nation-state from 'doing the right thing'. Observing quite rightly that most of the six case studies were in fact so-called 'exchanges' or 'loans' and not transfers of legal title, Bizos powerfully argued that: 'loan is a four letter word that obstructs justice'.[7]

Did this highly orchestrated event taking place at a site of singular significance signal a new order of things? Did it mark something akin to a contemporary shift in the meaning of 'legitimacy' and 'justice' in the question of the Parthenon Sculptures and by implication the global debacles of ownership of cultural artefacts?

A year later, in June 2009, when the New Acropolis Museum was officially inaugurated, the British Queen, the Prime Minister Gordon Brown, as well as Directors and staff from the British Museum, politely declined the invitation

---

6 Transcribed from the author's fieldnotes (17 March 2008). The first day of conferencing was devoted to the presentation of the following six cases:

I) The transfer of the Axum Obelisk from Italy to Ethiopia (2003).

II) The transfer of the Stone Birds of great Zimbabwe from Germany to Zimbabwe (2003).

III) The transfer of human remains from the Royal College of Surgeons in the UK to the *Ngarrindjeri* Aboriginal group in Southern Australia (2003).

IV) The transfer of more than 35,000 cultural objects from Denmark to Greenland (1984–2001), a project that will be dealt with in detail in Chapter 5.

V) The Reunification of a Neo-Sumerian Alabaster figure implemented by The Louvre (Paris) and Metropolitan Museum of Art (New York City) in 2002.

VI) The long-term loan of a *Kwakwaka'wakw* transformation mask from the British Museum (London) to the U'mista Cultural Centre, Alert Bay, British Columbia, Canada (2005).

7 Transcribed from the author's fieldnotes (17 March 2008)

extended to them by the Hellenic Ministry of Culture to participate in the opening ceremony. In its aftermath, the impending Greek state bankruptcy and bailout in 2011 has perhaps transposed the scene of the argument about the cultural debt which the world owes to Greece, into the unpaid economic debt which Greece owes to the world.

Why Compare Nation-States?

My purpose in writing this rather lengthy description of the 2008 event in Athens is to make three introductory arguments. Firstly, what was at stake in Athens in March 2008 was a contest between different moral-ethical-legal regimes competing for recognition of global status. The audiences of this event were left to judge which institutional regimes handled the question of cultural property in the most ethical and most morally convincing manner. Secondly, it seemed that the nations and natives taking on the role of claimants vis-à-vis metropolitan museums were all to some degree involved and embroiled in self-conscious projects of nation-building, or perhaps more accurately, projects of re-imagining what nationhood might mean in a globalised postcolonial world. The institutions of 'cultural property' are remarkably productive sites for observation of different and at times competing ways of national imaginations. My third argument is that this event in Athens invites a comparative project: How can we account for the fact that some nation-states are positively inclined to return cultural objects in their museums to claimants in far-away institutions, whereas others are not? To undertake such a comparative project seems full of modernist illusions and pitfalls. It reinforces stereotypes of nationhood, reifies boundaries and overlooks heterogeneity, i.e., that Hawaii and Rhode Island are not America, and Denmark and Greenland are not Europe. Such critiques have merit, but they miss the virtue of comparisons: bringing into sharper relief the fundamental principles or in a legal sense the *doctrines* which govern the political life of cultural property in particular nation-states vis-à-vis their subaltern claimants. Moreover, given my second argument, it makes sense to retain the nation-state as a unit of comparison. My aim in this article is to explore the expertise of modern nation-states in their dealing with claims for cultural property and in so doing chart the main contrasts between American and European approaches. A comparative project works best when the entities to be compared are different enough to present stark differences of a common phenomenon and yet similar enough for the variations to be consistent. I claim to meet this standard by choosing one of the 'success stories' mentioned in Athens, namely the transfer of more than 35,000 objects from Denmark to Greenland (1984–2001) entitled UTIMUT (the term designates 'return' in Greenlandic) and the American repatriation regime NAGPRA (Native American Graves Protection and Repatriation Act), which significantly was not mentioned as a model of amelioration in Athens. These two regimes are similar in so far as they offer different responses to the same problem of cultural property within the broader realm of a nation-state[8] and they are different enough to offer a perspective on one another.

Over the past 40 years, nation-states, or as I prefer to call them, metropolitan property regimes, have converged on how to curb illicit traffic in cultural property, which the number of signatories to the UNESCO 1970 Convention shows.[9] However, if there is consensus on *restitution*, there is much less uniformity on the question of *return* or *repatriation* of cultural property, that is transfers of cultural objects which took place before 1970 and which are currently claimed by the nations and natives from where they originated. Thus, we are dealing with a type of claims, where there often is no direct evidence of criminality, but where the vicissitudes and circumstances of history have transported cultural artefacts away from the places where the objects were made and which are now claimed back with recourse to restorative justice by the descendants of those who once held the objects. The case of the Parthenon Sculptures is the archetype of this sort of claim.

We might argue that nation-states challenged with such claims have met them in two distinctive ways. Their responses reflect the pragmatic and strategic needs of their institutions and the historical predicaments they find themselves in as nation-states, be that couched as post-nationalism or post-colonialism. Most generally, these responses can be divided into two basic forms: rights-based regimes cast as legal formalism, versus debts-based regimes cast as situational ethics. The first type of regime is prescriptive, the latter subscribes to the ideology of voluntarism. This contrast is systemic and does not correspond to actual societies or nation-states, which may have adopted one approach internally and another externally, or may have blended them in various hybrid assemblies. How can we account for these differences? In this chapter, I intend to draw out and juxtapose the stark contrasts of two cultural property regimes and by doing so hopefully arrive – albeit by a somewhat indirect route – at an answer to this question. However, before I begin to depict the salient features of a property regime gravitating towards a rights-based approach, namely the American NAGPRA polity, and one which comes closer to a debts-based morality, namely the Danish UTIMUT framework, which has come to be known under that rubric – through its conspicuous returns to Greenland – I would like to begin with my ethnographic inroads to each regime.

Sites of Cooperation and Complicity

Among the first problems with which a comparative anthropological project on cultural property is confronted, is where to conduct fieldwork and what might constitute its ethnography. As an anthropologist, I would argue that doctrines

---

8   In the case of UTIMUT, the Danish Commonwealth (*Rigsfællesskabet*).

9   There are currently (May 2014) 126 State parties or signatories to the *Convention on the Means of Prohibiting and Preventing the Illicit Import, Export and Transfer of Ownership of Cultural Property*, adopted by UNESCO in Paris, 14 November 1970.

cannot be gleaned from canonical texts, but have to be sought at varied sites and in successive episodes of enactment and performance, rather than in codified regulatory traditions. Trained in cultural anthropology, I am generally inclined towards descriptive thickness of situations, places and persons in the tradition of Clifford Geertz. More specifically, I would choose to follow the trajectories and itineraries of specific objects involved in controversial disputes, which were thought to challenge the regime in which they were embedded, taking my methodological cues of multi-sited ethnography from Bruno Latour (2005), George Marcus (2000) and Arjun Appadurai (1986). However, whereas much contemporary anthropology is interested in material objects on the move, their agentive potentialities and the flux and instability of their materiality, I am more interested in the self-perpetuating normative and moral commitments that give regimes of expertise their coherence, authority and legitimacy. Thus, I have singled out 'case studies' on the basis of their capability of provoking substantial arguments, which usually drew forth a discernible policy response at the national level. In other words, case studies, which gave rise to new institutional arrangements, altered existing terms of normative discourse and were associated with a sense of novelty and challenge to the state of affairs. However, what happens when an anthropologist enters this politically and morally charged terrain through a mode of inquiry that remains close to the micro-politics and social practices on the ground?

To answer this question, I would like to render my initial field experiences from trying to access and open each regime up through an in-depth study of an extended case. The entry point to NAGPRA was a most contested dispute relating to what the claimants conceived as a *Kii Aumakua* and the holding institution in Providence, Rhode Island, saw as a 'utilitarian spear rack mounted on a canoe'. The gateway to the UTIMUT regime was singled out as a pair of talking drums/ *fontomfrom*, which was claimed by the Akuapem Kingdom in Ghana from the National Museum of Denmark. By offering some glimpses from my field diary, I hope to show that the ethnographic approach to cultural property might render some generality, but through significant events it nevertheless remains more acute and adroit.

Early in September of 2006, I arrived at the Bishop Museum (BM) in Honolulu, Hawaii, on a multi-sited fieldwork itinerary following the single most contested material object within NAGPRA. The record stated that the artefact – a *kii aumakua* – had been repatriated jointly to *Hui Malama* and the Office of Hawaiian Affairs (OHA) from the Museum of Natural History in Providence (RI) in 1998; however, nobody knew where the object currently was. In Hawaii, I contacted the Bishop Museum (BM), asking if they knew the whereabouts of the piece. An employee at the Museum responded that the object in question was currently sitting in the basement of the BM, on loan from OHA. However, the employee told me that if I wanted to see the object for research purposes, a request for access was necessary and this was made conditional upon the premise that I was accompanied by representatives from the Native Hawaiian community, more specifically OHA representatives. As I later arrived at the museum with a whole delegation of OHA representatives, the employee noted my entourage with the comment: 'You brought the right people with you! Wow, a whole delegation! Let's first see the exhibition on Native Hawaiian Featherwork and then we can go to the basement and see the *kii aumakua*.'[10] Within the NAGPRA regime, access to objects and information on part of the BM was made contingent upon cooperation with the Natives.

Change of scene from Honolulu to Copenhagen: Late in May of 2004, I arrived at the National Museum of Denmark (NMDK) in Copenhagen on a multi-sited fieldwork itinerary following a pair of talking drums claimed by the Akuapem Royal Kingdom in 1996 and again in 1998. I was scheduled to work with archival materials at the Ethnographic Collection (EC) concerning an Arctic repatriation case. The employee at the NMDK had pulled out part of the file I had requested in advance and arranged the material in her office. She instructed me that she was responsible for the surveillance of my work and throughout the morning, she watched me closely. At noon, she asked me to break, since no staff could be assigned to watch me during lunch break. During the lunch break, I made my way to the canteen and began to make conversation with a couple of employees, whom I knew were involved in NMDK's so-called 'Ghana Initiative' (2004–10), which aimed at identifying and conserving the so-called 'common heritage' of Denmark and Ghana, when Denmark built fortifications and plantations on the Gold Coast (1659–1850). Discussing my research on cultural property, one of the employees challenged me in a harsh, almost aggressive tone: 'As I understand your research you travel around the world and talk with people who want to file repatriation claims to museums. And you call it fieldwork! Do you know what they call people who do that in the U.S.? They call them "cultural brokers". Brokering is a risky business. So, now you have been warned!'[11] To stress the seriousness of the warning, the employee then told me a story from Alaska, which some Canadian colleagues had told him, which involved repatriation of artefacts, archaeologists, gunfire and natives in the wild.

In both Honolulu and Copenhagen, it would seem that the nature of ethnographic inquiry triggers institutional (dis)-comfort zones, which render the success criteria of conventional ethnographic fieldwork – rapport and collaboration – complicated with holding institutions. However, beyond the triviality of ethnographic encounters, the stark contrast between the two regimes is that within NAGPRA, access to the holding museum was made conditional upon cooperation and rapport with the natives, whereas within UTIMUT access to and communication with the holding museum seemed compromised by an imagined complicity with the natives. Thus, it would seem that what counts as native and the entitlements it confers, that is, the technology of recognition of claimants – who has standing to

---

10   Transcribed from the author's fieldnotes (September 2006).

11   The employee spoke in Danish, but did use the English word 'cultural broker' for lack of a similar term in the Danish language. Transcribed from the author's fieldnotes (May 2004).

make a claim for cultural property – differed radically in each regime. NAGPRA seemed all about reclaiming and restoring nativeness, whereas within UTIMUT, the native was circumvented.

NAGPRA and UTIMUT

Now, after having set the stage for a juxtaposition of NAGPRA and UTIMUT I want to dwell a little on the history of each regime and their more formal features. With the adoption of The National Museum of The American Indian Act (NMAIA; 1989) and The Native American Graves Protection & Repatriation Act (NAGPRA; 1990) the United States took a comprehensive, totalising and systematic legal approach to the repatriation of cultural property to indigenous communities. The magnitude of these two legal instruments is difficult to overestimate. The NMAIA requires the 19 separate museums under the Smithsonian Institution – the world's largest museum complex – to comply with repatriation provisions inscribed in the law. NAGPRA demands every agency, repository, or department receiving federal funding in every corner of the US to make inventories, consult with Native tribes and repatriate certain objects. Significantly, private collectors and private institutions, which do not receive any federal funds, are exempt from NAGPRA.

The most compelling political motif behind NAGPRA is to return human remains and funerary objects to the lineal descendants of Native communities. If the men who penned the Constitution afforded equal rights under the law for every citizen, why should Native American burials and skeletal remains not enjoy the same protection under the law as the graves and remains of other religious minorities? 'For decades', Representative Morris Udall (D) stated at the passing of NAGPRA,

> the skeletal remains of American Indians were removed from their burial sites, studied, catalogued, and relegated to the bins of museums and science. This legislation is about respecting the rights of the dead, the right to an undisturbed resting-place … What we are saying to American Indians today is simply that your ancestors and their burial grounds are sacred, and will remain so. In the larger scope of history, this is a very small thing. In the smaller scope of conscience, it may be the biggest thing we have ever done. (McKeown and Hutt, 2003: 153).

The secondary political motif behind NAGPRA was to return 'cultural patrimony' that was 'inalienable' at the time of removal and has ongoing tribal significance, as well as 'sacred objects' that are vital for present-day ceremonial and religious practices in Native communities across the US. These provisions ultimately aim at revitalising the cultural flourishing among 'America's first citizens'.

The key concept of NAGPRA is 'cultural affiliation'. It falls on the claimant to establish cultural affiliation which implies 'a relationship of shared group identity which can reasonably be traced historically or prehistorically' between a contemporary group and an identifiable earlier group. Cultural affiliation has to be established by the 'preponderance of different lines of evidence', such as geography, kinship, biology, archaeology, anthropology, linguistics, or oral tradition. More generally, NAGPRA serves as one of the most prominent current examples in the world of a bold and extreme form of legal positivism in the field of cultural property.

UTIMUT is not the name of a uniform and codified property regime, like NAGPRA, but designates the transfer of about 35,000 ethnographic and archaeological artefacts from the collections of the NMDK to the National Museum of Greenland (NKA), from 1982–2001. Literally, the term means 'return' in Greenlandic, but it has taken on a more comprehensive meaning in metropolitan institutions in Copenhagen referring to a 'successful model of shared stewardship'. I deploy the term to designate not only this specific Greenlandic transfer, but the emblematic model of and for the institution of cultural property in Denmark, at large. Formally, UTIMUT came into existence in 1983, when the Directors of the two national museums in Nuuk and Copenhagen signed a contractual agreement about a large scale cooperation comprising education, preservation, exhibition, documentation and transfer of material collections. The overall rationale for the subsequent material transfers was to enable the National Museum in Nuuk to manage its duties and responsibilities, prescribed by a new legislative framework for cultural heritage management adopted in 1979 in connection with the establishment of Home Rule in Greenland.

The crux of UTIMUT was to de-politicise the transfer process, by making it into a professional museum-to-museum cooperation. The institutional architecture of this idea took the form of a joint committee, akin to the NAGPRA Review Committee, consisting of three representatives appointed by Greenland and three by Denmark 'with an academic or museum professional background rather than a political one'.[12] This committee established a set of 'professional museum criteria' for UTIMUT, such as that both Greenland and Denmark should hold 'representative museums collections'; that collections 'naturally belonging together should not be separated'; and that Greenlandic 'wishes' for items of cultural patrimony should be respected, while Danish 'interests' in objects of significance for the history of collecting should be equally respected.

Based on the above criteria, about 100,000 objects remained in Copenhagen and 35,000 objects were transferred to Nuuk over a span of 15 years in nine distinct clusters each representing a 'culture' in the national imaginary of Greenland defined by territoriality (settlement patterns) and time (migration periods),

---

12   B. Grønnow and E.L. Jensen (2008). 'UTIMUT: Repatriation and Collaboration between Denmark and Greenland', in *UTIMUT: Past Heritage – Future Partnerships*, (ed.) M. Gabriel and J. Dahl, pp. 180–91. Copenhagen: IWIGIA/NKA.

established primarily by Danish ethno-historical research and arctic archaeology. Thus, in terms of materiality, 'the returned items and collections [UTIMUT] represent every archaeologically defined culture present in Greenland up to 1900, and thus cover the entire Greenlandic cultural history, with the exception of recent times'.[13] To mark the closure of the transfer process in 2001, an exhibition entitled UTIMUT was co-produced, which travelled from Copenhagen to Nuuk. Danish museum authorities have generally flagged UTIMUT as 'a model that, with appropriate modifications, could be used as an inspiration for repatriation projects in other parts of the world'[14] and emphasised its key components as 'dialogue', 'cooperation' and 'relationships of trust'. UNESCO has commended UTIMUT for the 'admirably creative way in which both parties rose above purely individual interests to ensure that a people's cultural identity would not be lost' and recommended it as a 'successful experiment [which] may well serve as a source of inspiration to a post-colonial international community'.[15]

If we were to sum up the main contrasts between NAGPRA and UTIMUT, I would contend that in the US, cultural property is built on law; in Denmark on contractual obligation. Thus, we may say that NAGPRA is a rights-based property regime; UTIMUT is based on duties and obligations. NAGPRA is a legal machine fuelled by evidence producing verdicts which have to be justified with recourse to principle and precedence; UTIMUT is an anti-politics machine fuelled by largely curatorial criteria producing decisions which have to be rationalised with recourse to ethical values. To sum up, NAGPRA gravitates towards legal formalism and involuntary generalised transactions; UTIMUT gravitates towards rule scepticism and voluntary particularised transactions.

Prior Possessions versus Patrimonial Partage

Now I will explore these formal features of the regimes in Washington, DC and Copenhagen respectively where we shall meet the foremost experts of each regime and listen to their own explications of NAGPRA and UTIMUT.

According to an offcial of NAGPRA this particular regime is a strand of Native American Law and Property Law. NAGPRA is Native American Law, because it requires the federal government to deal with Native American tribes on a government-to-government basis which the employee understands as a form of preferential treatment, based on the *parens patriae* doctrine (parent of the nation). The *parens patriae* doctrine was applied to children throughout the seventeenth and eighteenth centuries and has since developed into a doctrine

---

13   Ibid. 185

14   Ibid. 190

15   M. Bouchenaki (2004). 'Preface', in *UTIMUT – RETURN: The Return of more than 35.000 Cultural Objects to Greenland.* (ed.) P. Pentz, pp. 7–8. Copenhagen: The National Museum of Denmark; Greenland National Museum and Archives; UNESCO.

concerning the absolute rights and obligations of the sovereign state to limit civil rights violations caused by unjustified government interference. The basic tenet of this doctrine is that in public policy, the state is justified in intervening against the neglect of its natural parent or caretaker. Thus, the modern state can legitimately intervene as the natural parent of any child in need of protection, because its rights have been violated. The line of thinking here is that since the colonial state neglected to uphold and protect the property interests of incapacitated Native American individuals, because their hands were tied behind their backs, the postcolonial state acts to restore these property rights and re-*patriate* the objects alienated without their control or consent. Thus, the modern state acts in the best interest of the tribes, which are the single most important concern for the State.

During my encounters with the employee, she elaborated that NAGPRA is property law, because it protects the property rights of items under NAGPRA for Native American tribes. She further argued that NAGPRA simply acknowledges and reinstates the common law property rights of Native people for human remains, funerary objects, sacred objects, and objects of cultural patrimony – that is, the object categories which NAGPRA covers. The employee explained that under common law, human remains and funerary objects could not be owned and descendants had an infinite authority of disposition. She further elaborated that sacred items could be owned individually or by a group and were used for ceremonies by traditional adherents. Finally, cultural patrimony was something so central to the being of a group that it defines the group. In other words, cultural patrimony is inalienable, she said. According to NAGPRA, the employee explained, a museum can never own any of these objects, only have right of possession. The tribe holds the inalienable original ownership, she contended.

Throughout our meetings, the official emphasised that NAGPRA is first and foremost about property both in a retrospective and prospective sense. According to the official, section seven of the law addresses existing collections: the way these objects were obtained in the first place was flawed. Section three of the law is prospective and addresses new finds, basically saying that we will no longer use the flawed way of appropriation. The official said that both sections of the law were about determining ownership in a new way, which is based on an old common law principle. Finally, the official challenged the anthropologist stating that up until now, nobody has accepted my challenge to find me one word in NAGPRA, which is not common property law. Will you? Finally, the Manager explained that NAGPRA was human rights law in so far as it gave Native people their civil rights back, which they already had and always will have, but which have not been acknowledged up until NAGPRA was adopted. Thus, according to the employee: NAGPRA is a type of codification, which responds to the question of how we treat non- Native Americans; the point being that we should treat Native Americans just the same way as any other group. My interviews at the Solicitor's Office, Division of Indian Affairs, confirmed the conception of property in NAGPRA. Along the lines of the NAGPRA official, the employee in the solicitor's office to NAGPRA claimed that this regime gave a disenfranchised group property rights on an equal footing with more mainstream society. The employee saw NAGPRA as a piece of restorative or reparative legislation based on sixteenth-century common law property doctrines.

In my hunt for the doctrines of NAGPRA, three strands of legal thinking pregnant with doctrines emerged during my interviews with the experts of the regime in Washington, DC: Native American Law; Common Law and Human Rights Law. It appeared to me that the NAGPRA employee, throughout the interview, constantly shifted between two fundamental doctrinal knowledge practices (parens patriae/Native American law and prior possessions/common law), which came together in the assertion that the Native American was both sovereign and conquered. From Native American law they drew the doctrine of *parens patria* implicating that the weakest should prevail. From Common Law they pulled the doctrine of personal property and prior possessions implicating equality under the law. The basic precept of NAGPRA seemed that you cannot treat cultural objects any differently from personal property.

According to these elite insider interpretations, NAGPRA came into being because Native American people had their personal property taken away from them at a time where they were incapacitated or when 'their hands were tied behind their backs, as the NAGPRA employee coined it. According to them, the federal government would never have allowed skeletal remains to be taken from churchyards or religious relics to be taken from the Catholic Church. But archaeologists got away with taking remains and relics from Native American gravesites. So what NAGPRA does is to give a disenfranchised group property rights on an equal footing with more mainstream society. In that sense, I would argue that NAGPRA is a piece of restorative or reparative legislation based on sixteenth-century common law property doctrines enabling claimants to get their prior possessions back.

To conclude the hunt for doctrines undergirding NAGPRA, we may say that the Act responds to the question of how to govern a conquered people. NAGPRA's answer is to give the conquered common law to recover personal property as prior possessions, although construing the law as Native American Law, where the weaker prevails. Thus, my argument is that NAGPRA is sustained by two underpinning doctrines drawn from Native American Law and Common Law, which work in a switchback configuration. The result is remedial law subscribing to restorative justice underpinned by two Canons of Construction. Thus, in a doctrinal sense NAGPRA is a form of righteousness to the conquered enabling them to recover prior possessions as personal property in the name of American Common Law.

Patrimonial Partage

I shall now describe what UTIMUT (1984–2001) entails and argue how this model is forged by a doctrine I call *patrimonial partage*, because it involves the division of an existing material collection in the metropolis, between a subaltern museum and a metropolitan museum, according to a set of museological criteria, which are defined by the metropolis.

In 1983 the Directors of the National Museum of Greenland and the National Museum of Denmark signed an agreement on cooperation. The rationale was to enable the new National Museum in Nuuk to conduct research, stage exhibitions and manage its duties and responsibilities under a new regulation on museums and protected sites and monuments in Greenland. A bi-museum committee was set up to establish the criteria for the division of the Greenlandic collection in Copenhagen, comprising more than 130,000 objects.[16] This process was de-politicised by making it essential that the repatriation and the cooperation as a whole should be carried out according to professional museum criteria that were discussed and defined by the committee itself. Seven guiding curatorial criteria formed the basis for the deliberations within this expert body:

1. After the division, representative museum collections from Greenland should be present in both Greenland and Denmark.
2. At both National Museums, the collections should be suitable for public outreach, research and educational purposes.
3. A favourable attitude should be taken towards wishes from Greenland for collections or individual items that are of special importance to the cultural identity of Greenland.
4. And likewise, wishes from Denmark to keep collections of special interest to Danish museum history should be respected.
5. Special consideration should be taken to keep single collections and complete find materials undivided.
6. Transferred items and collections should be accompanied by available contextual information.
7. All items should be registered in a database and transferred items should, if needed, be cleaned and preserved.[17]

On the basis of these criteria, from 1984 to 2001 about 35,000 items were selected and separated from the collections of the National Museum in Denmark and transferred to the National Museum in Greenland: 'The returned items and

---

16 Generally, the larger part of the 135,000 objects – regarded as the world's most comprehensive Arctic collection – originates from archaeological excavations and surveys, whereas ethnographic objects comprise a minor part.

17 See Grønnow and Jensen (2008). 'UTIMUT: Repatriation and collaboration between Denmark and Greenland'.

collections represent every archaeologically defined culture present in Greenland up to 1900, and thus cover the entire Greenlandic cultural history, with the exception of recent times' (Grønnow and Jensen, 2008: 180). So what we have is an expert construction of the cultural patrimony of Greenland, construed by Danish archaeological expertise, which produced a so-called representative material record of the 'entire Greenlandic cultural history' (op.cit.) to be transferred to the museum in Nuuk.

In an internal memo from 2002, serving as basis for the discussions about a more comprehensive and unified institutional policy, presented by the former Head of International Collections to the board of directors of the NMDK, the former Head asserted:

> There are no simple solutions to the question of return and no decision is 100 per cent right or wrong. The political, emotional, religious, and ethical issues surrounding a claim are extremely complex and each case has to be dealt with according to these issues. Ultimately, the responsibility for making decisions rests with the Director of the NMDK (with final approval and authorization from the Minister of Culture) and every single decision must be taken on the basis of the particulars of each case.[18]

Thus, from the perspective of the experts of the regime, things were dealt with on a case-by-case ad hoc basis.

However, UTIMUT did signal a more uniform approach, which was set out in a UNESCO publication marking the formal closure of UTIMUT. Here the former Head of the International Collections of the NMDK confirmed the non-codified approach to cultural property: 'When considering the return of objects in the collection, decisions are taken on a case-by-case basis. However, some general rules of ethics are normally followed (e.g. in regard to UNESCO and ICOM), thus requests for the return of human remains, for example, are normally granted'.[19] The former Head goes on to explain the nature of UTIMUT:

> Among the first steps taken to nurture continuous collaboration between the two countries with regard to the returns, a research centre (*SILA*) was established in 2000 at the National Museum of Denmark to concentrate on Greenland's culture, archaeology and history. We have continuous collaboration and mutual access to the now divided collections. In this sense the return of objects is to be understood as a mutual obligation of both the 'sender' as well as the 'recipient'

---

18 P. Pentz (2002). 'Papir om Nationalmuseets Politik', p. 5. Copenhagen. (unpublished; interim memo; my translation from the Danish. Quoted with permission from the National Museum of Denmark)

19 P. Pentz (2004). 'The Policy of Returning Cultural Objects: The Danish Perspective', in *UTIMUT-RETURN*. (ed.) P. Pentz, pp. 17–20. Gylling: UNESCO; NKA; NMDK. (p.18)

to pay respect to the history of the objects. Subsequently the situation might even occur that the 'recipient' provides the 'sender' with objects missing in the collections of the latter, in order to enable this institution to perform research and activities tied to the mutual history of the two parties![20]

Thus, the undergirding rationale of UTIMUT was based on a reciprocal obligation of exchange in the mutual interest of enhancing archaeological research.

In an interview, the former Head elaborated on the UTIMUT model: 'Denmark doesn't need laws, because laws produce losers and winners, whereas the UTIMUT model has produced an enduring partnership with two winners and no losers'.[21] The former Head explained that Denmark does not need a formal policy, since the Danish Law on Museums[22] makes such a document irrelevant. He explained that the primary obligation of the NMDK is to preserve material objects, since the Danish Museum Act prescribes that if an object enters a public museum, it cannot be alienated. The former Head told me furthermore that in practice the NMDK navigates between the Scylla of NAGPRA and the Charybdis of just ignoring any request and dismissing the claim without further notice. Elaborating on this predicament, the former Head said that the NAGPRA model meant 'unconditional surrender of the object' implying that the 'irrevocable loss of a research and educational potential and the pure dismissal of a claim equals the lack of respect for the victims of history, bordering on racism'.[23]

Thus, what we seem to have in Copenhagen is the antithesis of a codified framework; the antithesis of standardisation; the antithesis of law. More importantly, this non-codified approach skirts the question of property, which is at heart of NAGPRA. The Danish ideology of voluntarism, so to speak, implies that decision-making is distributed within semi-closed bodies of expertise. What is significant in this mode of reasoning is that the question of legitimacy in acquisitions is skirted, as is the notion of rightful ownership. I would argue that the internal logic of this mode of reasoning is the primacy of the materiality; that is, the continued museological preservation of the material in question overrides any other single criterion in the expertise matrix.

However, my caveat to this argument is that the doctrine of *patrimonial partage* was shaped in the shadow of law. It was proposed in 1961 and passed

---

20   Pentz (2004). 'The Policy of Returning Cultural Objects: The Danish Perspective', (p. 20).

21   Transcribed from the author's fieldnotes (December 2002).

22   Museumsloven nr. 1505 af 14. december 2006. In fact, **§ 30, section 2 of this Code does stipulate that** *Danefæ* is the cultural property of the State, but the law remains silent about foreign claims for cultural property, except that international conventions apply if Denmark has ratified these. In 2003, Denmark ratified UNESCO 1970 and in 2008, UNIDROIT 1995.

23   Internal memo from NMDK (Pentz, (2002). 'Papir om Nationalmuseets Politik', p. 5.). Quoted with permission.

in 1965, after having withstood a constitutional challenge in the Supreme Court that year. In April 1971 it effected the transfer of the Icelandic Saga Manuscripts *Flateyjarbók* and *Codex Regius* as 'priceless gifts' from Copenhagen to Reykjavik. This 'transfer' was governed by the discursive term 'Icelandic cultural property' (*islandsk kultureje*), which the 1961 law introduced to Danish judicial discourse as an empty rhetorical category left to be defined by scholarly expertise. The single most significant feature of this law is that the only time it speaks about ownership, it appears as a *partition principle* based on the concept of 'Icelandic cultural property'. In other words, the law remains silent about who actually owns the manuscripts. An expert committee composed of Danish and Icelandic philologists were left to define the empty discursive term 'Icelandic cultural property'. This committee of Danish and Icelandic philologists came up with a set of scholarly criteria for what could be said to count as 'Icelandic cultural property'. I would argue that this consensus model practised within semi-closed bodies of expertise later became the blueprint for UTIMUT.

Conclusion

According to some American museum professionals, European cultural property policy is conservative, irreligious and paternalistic in its care for 'big art' and museological preservation as an absolute, whereas their European colleagues often consider American repatriation policy as adversarial, rule fixated, litigious and without much respect for the educational and scientific value of an object. I hope to have made clear that such transatlantic stereotypes miss the fact that UTIMUT is primarily about mutuality, horizontal networks of cooperation, archaeological expertise, informal negotiations and consensus-building. On the contrary, NAGPRA is about principled argument, transparency and the preponderance of evidence, construed in a non-positivistic sense within what I would call pseudo-litigious institutions,[24] where expert judgement carries weight, albeit the constitution of expertise is more plural and contested than within UTIMUT, where it is always tied to curatorial criteria. At the level of systemic contrasts between the two regimes, we may say that rights-based cultural property regimes, such as NAGPRA, are laboratories of redistribution, which fabricate histories of evidential fact and construe commodity exchange, which unbind transactors. In contrast, debts-based cultural property regimes, such as UTIMUT, are laboratories of recognition, which fabricate memories of amnesia and construe gift exchange, that bind transactors in mutual obligations. The objective of transactors is to create and affirm relationships to foster mutual recognition. Thus, as I hope to have made clear, we not only have two different models of cultural property in NAGPRA and UTIMUT, we have what looks like two antipodes for the distribution and

---

24 I am here thinking of the NAGPRA Review Committee, which I followed throughout much of the United States, during my doctoral fieldwork.

allocation of cultural property. At conferences such as the one in Athens – which we visited in the opening section of this chapter – such models compete for global superiority and in the act redeem the colonial legacies of the nation-states which manufactured them.

Acknowledgements

For their financial support of my research on cultural property, I thank the Wenner-Gren Foundation for Anthropological Research. I would also like to offer special thanks to Helle Porsdam for inviting me to the final CULTIVATE conference at the Tate Modern in London, where a draft version of this chapter was presented. At this event, I received much inspiration, critique and encouragement from the participants in just the right proportion, which has greatly benefitted my contribution.

References

Appadurai, A. (ed.) (1986). *The Social Life of Things: Commodities in Cultural Perspective.* Cambridge: CUP.
Bouchenaki, M. (2004). 'Preface', in *UTIMUT – RETURN: The Return of More than 35.000 Cultural Objects to Greenland,* (ed.) P. Pentz. Copenhagen: The National Museum of Denmark; Greenland National Museum and Archives; UNESCO.
Grønnow, B. and Einar Lund Jensen (2008). 'UTIMUT: Repatriation and Collaboration between Denmark and Greenland', in *UTIMUT: Past Heritage – Future Partnerships,* (ed.) Jens Dahl and Mille Gabriel. Copenhagen: IWGIA.
Latour, B. (2005). *Reassembling the Social: An Introduction to Actor-Network-Theory.* New York: Oxford University Press.
Marcus, G.E. (ed.) (2000). *Para-Sites: A Casebook against Cynical Reason.* Chicago: University of Chicago Press.
McKeown, T.C. and S. Hutt (2003). 'In the Smaller Scope of Conscience: The Native American Graves Protection & Repatriation Act Twelve Years After'. *UCLA Journal of Environmental Law and Policy* 21:153–212.
Pentz, P. (2004). 'The Policy of Returning Cultural Objects: The Danish Perspective', in *UTIMUT-RETURN.* (ed.) P. Pentz. Gylling: UNESCO; NKA; NMDK.
———(2002). 'Papir om Nationalmuseets Politik', p.5. Copenhagen. (unpublished memo)

Chapter 2

Museums Revisited: The Position of the Museum in the New Governance of the Protection of Cultural Heritage and Cultural Diversity

Lucky Belder*

Introduction

We regard our museums as treasure houses of cultural manifestations and traditions that provide historical and cultural context to social relations and contribute to cultural diversity. In recent decades, the international community developed a framework of international law supporting the protection of museums as guardians of cultural heritage and cultural diversity.

The ICOM Statutes, adopted during the 21st General Conference in Vienna, Austria in 2007 present the following definition: 'A museum is a non-profit, permanent institution in the service of society and its development, open to the public, which acquires, conserves, researches, communicates and exhibits the tangible and intangible heritage of humanity and its environment for the purposes of education, study and enjoyment'.

At the 2012 ICOM/UNESCO Rio de Janeiro Meeting of 2012 it was recommended that more nation states ought to ratify existing international legal instruments addressing the protection and promotion of museums and their collections. To support these objectives it was advised to advocate the importance of museums as forums for cultural diversity.[1] At the same time it was recommended that it was necessary to work on international cooperation mechanisms for the protection and promotion of museums and collections. This points to an increasing tendency in international law where the realisation of policy objectives is being

---

*   Lucky Belder LLM MA PhD, is assistant professor at the University of Utrecht, the CIER Centre of Intellectual Property Law and the Renforce Centre of Regulation and Enforcement in Europe. This contribution is in part based on the report of the research project Cultivate! Cultural heritage institutions, copyright and cultural diversity in the European Union and Indonesia, (L.Belder, ed.), published by Delex publishers, Amsterdam, 2014.

1   Expert Meeting on the protection and promotion of museums, Rio de Janeiro, Brazil, 11–14 July, http://unesdoc.unesco.org/images/0021/002169/216952E.pdf.

achieved by soft law and new governance tools. While these instruments always have a basis in treaty law, the realisation of policy objectives depends on a variety of collaborative platforms in which governmental institutions as well as civil parties participate. In our global network society, this indicates that the position of museums is being revisited. This also signifies that museums should perhaps reconsider their position within this new playing field of objectives and interests. This contribution aims to provide, first, a short overview of the existing international legal framework in UNESCO cultural heritage conventions and the Convention on the Protection and Promotion of the Diversity of Cultural Expressions. In Europe, the 2005 Council of Europe Faro Convention presented general principles on the value of cultural heritage to society. The European Union, having only had subsidiary powers for the protection of cultural heritage and the shaping cultural policies for Member States, nevertheless recognised the importance of mainstreaming the protection of cultural diversity in all its policies in the TFEU. This demonstrates that these instruments give a legal basis for new governance tools in which museums are expected to participate as responsible actors. The subsidiary nature of the EU policies on cultural diversity has resulted in alternative tools to obtain policy objectives and the use of soft law instruments. This means that museums are not only the objects of top-down legislation, but are increasingly expected to participate in and contribute to networks that are part of new governance policies.

UNESCO Cultural Heritage Conventions

Introduction

The main source of international law on the protection of cultural heritage is UNESCO, the UN specialised agency of international law for the protection of cultural heritage. The most important Conventions concerning the protection of cultural heritage were the 1970 Convention on the Means of Prohibiting and Preventing the Illicit Import, Export and Transfer of Ownership of Cultural Property, the 1982 World Heritage Convention, the 2003 Convention on the Safeguarding of Intangible Cultural Heritage and the 2005 Convention on the Protection and Promotion of the Diversity of Cultural expressions.

The 1970 Convention on Illicit Trade in Cultural Property

The 1970 Convention concerned the protection of cultural objects against the 'dangers of theft, clandestine excavation and illicit export of cultural property'.[2] To this end cultural institutions such as museums as well as libraries and archives are to ensure that their collections are kept in accordance with universally

---

2   Preamble to the 1970 Convention.

recognised moral principles.[3] Article 2 of the Convention states that 'international co-operation constitutes one of the most efficient means of protecting each country's cultural property against all the dangers resulting therefrom' and that 'States Parties are to oppose such practices with the means at their disposal, and particularly by removing their causes, putting a stop to current practices, and by helping making the necessary reparations'.[4]

The cultural property relevant to the 1970 Convention is outlined in Article 1 of the Convention. States Parties are to designate which objects they consider to be of importance for archaeology, prehistory, literature, art or science within specific categories such as rare collections (a), antiquities more than a 100 years old (e), objects of ethnological interest (f) and property of artistic interest (g).[5]

States Parties are to establish the necessary measures to prevent museums and similar institutions within their territories from acquiring cultural property,

---

3   Ibid.

4   To date the convention counts 190 states parties, see http://whc.unesco.org/en/statesparties/

5   Article 1: 'For the purposes of this Convention, the term "cultural property" means property which, on religious or secular grounds, is specifically designated by each State as being of importance for archaeology, prehistory, history, literature, art or science and which belongs to the following categories:

(a) Rare collections and specimens of fauna, flora, minerals and anatomy, and objects of palaeontological interest;

(b) property relating to history, including the history of science and technology and military and social history, to the life of national leaders, thinkers, scientists and artist and to events of national importance;

(c) products of archaeological excavations (including regular and clandestine) or of archaeological discoveries;

(d) elements of artistic or historical monuments or archaeological sites which have been dismembered;

(e) antiquities more than one hundred years old, such as inscriptions, coins and engraved seals;

(f) objects of ethnological interest;

(g) property of artistic interest, such as:

(i) pictures, paintings and drawings produced entirely by hand on any support and in any material (excluding industrial designs and manufactured articles decorated by hand);

(ii) original works of statuary art and sculpture in any material;

(iii) original engravings, prints and lithographs;

(iv) original artistic assemblages and montages in any material;

(h) rare manuscripts and incunabula, old books, documents and publications of special interest (historical, artistic, scientific, literary, etc.) singly or in collections;

(i) postage, revenue and similar stamps, singly or in collections;

(j) archives, including sound, photographic and cinematographic archives;

(k) articles of furniture more than one hundred years old and old musical instruments'.

This categorization has proven to be standard setting, as it has been used in the following UNIDROIT Convention, and was also guiding in the EU Directive and Regulation.

and also to prohibit the import of cultural property stolen from a cultural heritage institution in another State Party, provided that such property is documented as part of the inventory of this institution.[6] This means also, that the documentation of these cultural objects should include references to the historic context of the collection, the provenance of collection items, as well as references to the original cultural community and the historic context of the individual collection.

Article 5 stipulates that States Parties are to establish and update a list of important public and private cultural property whose export would constitute an 'appreciable impoverishment of the national cultural heritage'.[7] Furthermore, under Article 5(c) national states are to promote the development or the establishment of scientific and technical institutes (museums, libraries, archives, laboratories, and workshops…) to ensure the preservation of cultural property. This also relates to the obligations regarding the obligation of States Parties to provide for the educational means to contribute to the awareness of the value of cultural property.[8]

The 1972 World Heritage Convention

The 1972 World Heritage Convention was initiated after a number of serious threats to well-known heritage monuments, starting with the flooding of the Abu Simbel Temples in Egypt due to the building of the Aswan Dam in Egypt in 1960.[9] The international response to this threat resulted in the UNESCO raising of funds and the organisation of expertise to dismantle the temples and move them to higher ground. This was followed by massive international support for restoration projects after the flooding of Venice in 1966. The success of these initiatives signalled a rising consensus on the need for international cooperation in case of serious threats to monuments of international importance.

The main objective of the 1972 Convention was the protection of monumental cultural heritage. The aim was to establish an international network to monitor the preservation of designated monuments in national states, and to support collaborative projects, research and education. Chapters I and II of the Convention regard general obligations of states parties, both national and international. Article 4 sees a duty to identify, protect, conserve, present, and transmit to future generations the cultural heritage situated on a State Party's territory. Article 5 sets policy objectives for national states to 'endeavor, in so far as possible, and as appropriate for each country to develop and support heritage studies and research, and to establish institutions to realise these objectives'. These objectives may be regarded as contributing to the raising of awareness on the importance of the safekeeping of the monuments that are considered to be part of the cultural heritage.

---

6   Article 7(a) and (b).
7   Article 5(b).
8   Article 10(b).
9   As of 19 September 2012 this Convention counts 190 States Parties. See http://whc. unesco.org/en/statesparties/.

On an international level, the Convention contains policy objectives with regard to international cooperation, which imply a shared responsibility towards national heritage as part of the world heritage.[10]

The 2003 Safeguarding of Intangible Cultural Heritage Convention

The 2003 Safeguarding of Intangible Cultural Heritage Convention builds on the work in the World Heritage Convention. The conceptual framework of the World Heritage Convention was based on a concept of cultural heritage which could rely on the Classic-Christian tradition of monumental building. Non-Western cultures, on their part, either have far fewer monumental remnants from the past, or these monuments have lost their significance to their contemporary cultural communities or national governments. Intangible cultural heritage as such has no physical presence, although manifestations thereof may take on a physical form. The definition in Article 2 of the Intangible Cultural Heritage Convention clarifies this aspect of intangibility by referring to

> ... the practices, representations, expressions, knowledge, skills – as well as the instruments, objects, artefacts and cultural spaces associated therewith – that communities, groups and, in some cases, individuals recognize as part of their cultural heritage. This intangible cultural heritage, transmitted from generation to generation, constantly recreated by communities and groups in response to their environment, their interaction with nature and their history, and provides them with a sense of identity and continuity, thus promoting respect for cultural diversity and human creativity.

The Intangible Cultural Heritage Convention operates on the central criterion of Representative Value, highlighting the social and cultural context of manifestations of intangible cultural heritage and its role in the community.[11] This is further emphasised by the procedure for the nomination of elements of intangible cultural heritage for the Convention's List, which requires that a nomination must follow 'the widest possible participation of the community, group or, if applicable, individuals concerned and with their free, prior and informed consent'.[12] States Parties to the Convention are under obligation to develop national policies on the identification and the drawing up of inventories in Articles 11 and 12. Moreover they are to ensure the development and promotion of intangible cultural heritage by – among other things – fostering scientific, technical and artistic studies (Article 13(c)), as well as fostering the creation of institutions for the transmission of intangible heritage through forums and spaces (Article 13(d) under i); and the

---

10   Article 6 World Heritage Convention.

11   Intangible Cultural Heritage Convention, Article 16.

12   Intangible Cultural Heritage Convention, Operational Directives 2008, Criteria for Inscription, R.4.

establishment of documentation institutions and facilitating access (Article 13(d) under iii).

The 2005 UNESCO Convention on the Diversity of Cultural Expressions

The focus on cultural diversity was translated in the 2005 Convention into the objective of protecting the diversity of cultural expressions and the support of cultural industries with the purpose of securing a diversity of cultural goods and services. Cultural expressions are thereby repositioned in an economic context: providing the services of conservation and access and generating spin-off economic transactions in local economies.

Article 1 states the objectives of this Convention to be the protection and promotion of the diversity of cultural expressions by creating the conditions for cultures and their expressions to flourish and to interact freely. The market of cultural expressions is to be supported by policies aimed at the safeguarding of cultural identity and intercultural relations. The scope of the Convention is global with specific attention to the needs of emerging economies and developing countries. One important objective is therefore the strengthening of international cooperation to enhance the capacities of developing countries. These objectives are guided by principles enumerated in Article 2 such as the principle of respect for human rights and fundamental freedoms, the principle of sovereignty; the principle of international solidarity, the principle of complementarity of economic and cultural aspects of development and the need to support sustainable development; and the principles of equitable access, openness and balance.

In particular in Article 6(e), the Convention regards the support of public and private museums in the context of the development and promotion of the free exchange and circulation of ideas, cultural expressions, and cultural goods and services. Articles 8, 9 and 10 relate to Cultural heritage institutions as centres of knowledge and research, information sharing and education. Article 12 refers to international cooperation, the reinforcement of partnerships and the promotion of the use of new technologies. In this context, the digitisation of heritage collections is regarded as an important instrument in generating new business models targeting local as well as global markets.

Guidelines for the International Treaties on the Protection of Cultural Heritage

The operationalisation of these cultural conventions depends on their implementation in the national jurisdictions in the states parties. This process is supported by Convention Committees which consist of a rotating representation of the countries involved. The work on the objectives of the cultural heritage conventions is further supported by operational guidelines and, in the case of the Intangible Cultural Heritage Convention, by operational directives. These guidelines are regularly revised and updated and contain further rules on the implementation of all the aspects that are relevant in this operationalisation. As such they are part of the soft law on the protection of cultural heritage which has been defined as those 'rules of conduct that are laid down in instruments which have not been attributed legally binding force as such, but nevertheless may have certain indirect-legal effects, and that are aimed at and may produce practical effect'.[13]

So if the provisions in the conventions lay down the general rules, the guidelines and directives outline the meaning of these provisions for the work of cultural heritage institutions. As such therefore, they are an important indication of the developments of the rules of conduct within the conventions and an indication of developments in thinking on the governance of cultural heritage conventions in general.

The most recent version of the Operational Guidelines for the World Heritage Convention dates from 2013, the last of more than 15 revisions since 1977.[14] Since the revision of 2005, it is stated that these guidelines address not only the States Parties, the Committee and the Advisory Bodies, but also the 'site managers, stakeholders and partners in the protection of World Heritage properties'.[15] This provision is indicative of the development that has taken place over the last decades: the move from a top-down approach, towards a more horizontal, networking approach, in which stakeholders and partners are brought in to develop and uphold governance of the objectives and policies outlined in the conventions. This means that also museums are given more responsibility in the realisation of these objectives and policies. As such, they serve as centres of education and research, but also as meeting places and platforms for cultural activities.

The Operational Directives of the Intangible Cultural Heritage Convention encourages states parties to establish functional cooperation between communities, groups and individuals and experts, centres of expertise and research institutes that are to participate in regional networks to develop joint approaches on the intangible cultural heritage.[16]

The 2005 Convention on the diversity of cultural expressions emphasised the importance of the role and participation of civil society including non-governmental organisations, non-profit organisations, professionals in the culture sector and associated sectors and groups that support the work of artists and cultural communities.[17]

---

13 Linda Senden (2004). *Soft Law in European Community Law*. Oxford: Hart Publishing, pp.111–12.

14 Available at http://whc.unesco.org/en/guidelines/, last visited 1 May 2014.

15 Operational Guidelines World Heritage Convention 2005/2008/2013, par. 3 (e).

16 Operational Directives Intangible Cultural Heritage Convention, 2008, paragraphs 76–86.

17 Operational Guidelines on Article 11 of the Convention on the Protection and Promotion of Cultural Diversity, par. 3.

The Convention recognises the importance of civil society and its potential to act as innovator and change agent in the implementation of the Convention.[18] Of interest, also, is the further emphasis on the partnerships aimed at the cooperation between developing countries and public and private sectors and non-profit organisations, to support capacity building; giving voice to cultural communities; and the development of innovative partnerships.[19] These partnerships are to build on existing and potential structures and networks with and among the public sector and civil society, including non-governmental organisations, non-profit organisations, and the private sector.[20]

The Protection of Cultural Heritage in Europe

Introduction

The two main agents for the protection of cultural heritage in Europe are the Council of Europe and the European Union. The 2005 Faro Convention on the Value of Cultural Heritage for Society aims to establish 'a unifying principle' to provide a framework for the various heritage policies of the Council of Europe by highlighting the importance of the protection of the common European cultural heritage in the context of globalisation.[21] At the same time, this cultural heritage concept is presented as an umbrella concept for a diversity of cultural expressions and the communities involved.

In 2003, the EU became officially involved in the UNESCO negotiations on the Convention on the Protection and Promotion of the Diversity of Cultural Expressions.[22] This was an important step, as it was indicative of the growing awareness of the importance of the culture/trade nexus, as well as the recognition of the scope of EU competence on cultural policies, both on an internal community level, as well as an external foreign policy level. Representing 'Unity in Diversity' thus, it was the first time in UNESCO history that a group of Member States such as the EU negotiated alongside the Member States on trade-related aspects of the Convention.

---

18 Ibid. par.6.

19 Operational Guidelines on Article 15 of the Convention, par. 3.

20 Ibid. par. 6.3.

21 COE Explanatory Report to the Council of Europe Framework Convention (CETS no. 199), p. 2. In particular the European Cultural Convention (1954), the Convention for the Protection of the Architectural Heritage of Europe (1985), the European Convention on the Protection of the Archaeological Heritage (1992, revised) and the European Landscape Convention (2000).

22 The European Community ratified the UNESCO Convention on the protection and promotion of the diversity of cultural expressions, on 18 December 2006.

The following short introduction of the concept of valorisation of cultural heritage as presented by the Faro Convention and the EU Treaty culture provisions provides the context for the introduction of new governance methods such as the Open Method of Coordination by the European Union and how museums are positioned to be included in this new governance strategy.

The Valorisation of Cultural Heritage in the 2005 Council of Europe Faro Convention on the Value of Cultural Heritage for Society

The French-speaking states introduced the concept of the *valorisation* of cultural heritage which is directed at questions of why, and for whose benefit, we should protect cultural heritage. The Convention is dedicated to the safeguarding of access to cultural heritage on the one hand, and the recognition of the potential of cultural heritage in economic progress on the other. To this end, a new definition seeks to cover a more comprehensive concept of cultural heritage, and to include the discussion on cultural rights and the rights of indigenous peoples while avoiding any quality judgement or proprietary claim. Article 2 of the Faro Convention defines cultural heritage as: ' ... a group of resources inherited from the past which people identify, independently of ownership, as a reflection and expression of their constantly evolving values, beliefs, knowledge and traditions. It includes all aspects of the environment resulting from the interaction between people and places through time'.

The same article provides for the definition of a *heritage community*, consisting of people ' ... who value specific aspects of cultural heritage which they wish, within the framework of public action, to sustain and transmit to future generations'.

This definition in the Convention of the *heritage community* emphasises the element of choice by which an individual can be part of various communities at the same time. The explanatory memorandum refers to 'a heritage community as a "variable geometry" without reference to ethnicity or rigid communities'.[23] In the light of the specific references to human rights and cultural rights in the Convention's preamble and Article 1, the subtext of this definition is that ultimately the individual, in the context of his self-chosen community, is central in the protection of cultural heritage. It is also significant that in this perspective, cultural heritage is no longer linked to nation states, but relates to horizontal community networks that may operate independently of nationalistic interests.

The Convention explains the intrinsic meaning of cultural heritage as a cultural resource in a globalising world, providing a sense of place and identity. Cultural heritage is regarded as a resource of sustainable development by supporting other cultural, ecological, economic and social policies. A third important aspect is the recognition of the potential of cultural heritage to contribute to social cohesion

---

23 This explicit reference to heritage communities also bears the imprint of the discussion on imagined communities in the work of Benedikt Anderson (1991). *Imagined Communities: Reflections on the Origin and Spread of Nationalism.* London: Verso.

and social identity, including the contribution to dialogue and debate in regional conflicts.[24] As a result, cultural heritage is positioned explicitly in the context of a human rights and, in particular, a cultural rights discourse.

The main obligations in the Convention are stipulated in Articles 4, 5 and 6. Article 4 commits Parties to recognise that everyone, alone or collectively, has a right to benefit from cultural heritage and to contribute to its enrichment and to respect the cultural heritage of others. These rights may only be restricted when necessary in a democratic society. This formula clearly refers to the European Convention of Human Rights. In particular Article 10 on the freedom of expression contains the same dual objective of both the active and the passive right to obtain and impart information. Article 5 on cultural heritage laws and policies is formulated as an obligation 'to undertake' and actively pursue a cultural heritage policy, in law, as well as in practice, and more in particular in 'integrated strategies'.

EU Cultural Policy on Cultural Diversity

EU protection of cultural diversity may be seen to rely on two narratives. One is based on the inherent strength of cultural diversity, while the other is based on the inherent vulnerability of cultural diversity. At the core of the European project there has always been a narrative based on the strength of cultural diversity, the belief in the added value of the dynamics between a diversity of entities. The protection of cultural diversity in this perspective is not only a demonstration of respect for the wealth of cultural heritage, it is also essential to the safeguarding of cultural diversity to support future cultural life. Thereby it can be argued that the exchange of a diversity of cultural expressions is fundamental to the omnipresent rationale of the European Project: the pursuit of the 'open society' characterised by access to open markets, free movement and democratic transparency.[25]

The 'protection of the weak' narrative may be recognised in the dual approach in the Convention to trade in the creative industries in general and the aspect of trade between the industrialised States Parties and the developing world. This was represented by a set of obligations that would ensure that Member States were to allow for favourable measures with regard to trade in cultural goods and services with developing countries.[26]

---

24   This objective was articulated as a result of the agenda set by the COE Declaration on Intercultural Dialogue and Conflict Prevention (The Opatija Declaration) of 2003; G. Dolff-Bonekämper (2008). 'The philosophical, political and pragmatical roots of the Convention', in D. Thérond (ed.), *Heritage and Beyond*. Strasbourg: COE Publishing, p.21.

25   See also Karl Popper (1945). *The Open Society and its Enemies*. London: Routledge.

26   See L. Bellucci and R. Soprano, 'The WTO System and the implementation of the UNESCO Convention: two case studies', in Germann, *Cultural Diversity Report*, pp.159–64.

The Treaty on European Union proclaims in its Article 3 that it shall respect its rich cultural and linguistic diversity, and shall ensure that Europe's cultural heritage is safeguarded and enhanced. This commitment is further elaborated upon in the Lisbon Treaty Chapter on Culture, which specifically states that: 'The Community shall contribute to the flowering of the cultures of the Member States, while respecting their national and regional diversity and at the same time bringing the common cultural heritage to the fore'.[27] This provision is furthermore supported by the Charter of Fundamental Rights of the European Union, stating in Article 22 that cultural, religious and linguistic diversity is to be respected. This is to be observed as a fundamental right in all situations that fall under the competencies of the European Union.[28]

The message of this provision, which has been part of the EU *acquis* since the 1992 Treaty of Maastricht establishing the European Union, is that the Community of Member States is not to ignore national and regional diversity.[29] On the contrary, it is to ensure that the Community affirms its principle of subsidiarity as to its power to develop cultural policies. At the same time, the Community makes the important statement that there is a common cultural heritage for all the Member States. This demonstrates an underlying consensus on the need to acknowledge the 'unity in the diversity' of Member States.

Admittedly, in its early stages, the European project was primarily focused on economic integration and the creation of a common market supported by increasing political integration. It took until the Treaty of Maastricht (1992) to include the provision on Culture in Article 167 TFEU.[30] Paragraph 167.2 TFEU confirms that EU actions are only to support and supplement the actions of Member States in the 'i. improvement of the knowledge and dissemination of the culture and history of the European peoples; ii. conservation and safeguarding of cultural heritage of European significance; iii. non-commercial cultural exchanges; and iv. artistic and literary creation, including in the audiovisual sector'. The aspiration to 'contribute to'; 'support' and 'supplement' underscores the subsidiary character of the Culture provision, as an answer to objections against interference with national cultural identity. But at the same time, the cultural mainstreaming clause in Article 167 Paragraph 4 posits that all Community acts and actions are to take 'cultural aspects

---

27   TFEU, Article 167(1).

28   EU Charter of Fundamental Rights, Article 51(1), and its explanations; CJEU, C-617/10, Åkerberg and CJEU, C-399/11, Melloni.

29   Introduced as Article 128 in the Treaty of Maastricht, together with then Article 92 paragraph 3d allowing for State Aid pertaining to culture and heritage conservation. Renumbered in the Treaty of Nice as Article 151 TEC and Article 87 TEC. In the Treaty of Lisbon these provisions are inserted as Article 167 TFEU and Article 107 TFEU.

30   Treaty of Maastricht, Article 128, renumbered into TEU, Article 151, renumbered into TFEU, Article 167.

into account in its actions under other provisions of this Treaty, in particular in order to respect and to promote the diversity of its cultures'.[31]

Thus, the Culture provision serves to contribute to a European identity, or as it was phrased in 1993:

> We are Europeans, and are proud of it. What is happening is that we are realizing our identity. In asserting our position in the world, we assert the richness of our culture, which is diverse and deep, a rich mosaic rather than an artificial 'ism'. The European Union has deep, diverse, and powerful roots. We are many in one: In uno plures, and we want to keep and nurture our diverse cultures that together make us the envied focus of culture, civilization.[32]

New Governance of Cultural Heritage and Cultural Diversity in the EU

Under Article 6 (c) of the TFEU, the Union may support, coordinate or supplement the actions of the Member States in cultural policies. However, the subsidiary nature of EU competence on culture makes it difficult to come to the effective realisation of these policy objectives. At the same time there is an increasing need for participatory and parliamentary democracy that provides real solutions to common social and economic problems.[33] The rise of new governance instruments may be regarded as a practical solution for the challenges that are the result of the increasing complexity of society in which the traditional constitutional model produces insufficient results. The Open Method of Coordination (OMC), an umbrella concept that was introduced in the Lisbon Strategy, is a new governance method, in which a network of actors, including representatives of civil society, are involved in a process of decision making, evaluation, benchmarking and peer review.[34] It was presented as a way of encouraging cooperation and the exchange of best practices, which would lead to agreement on common targets and guidelines for Member States, thereby relying on regular monitoring of progress to meet these targets.[35] In governance theory, this method is characterised as providing a forum for participation and powersharing, multi-level integration, diversity and decentralisation, flexibility and revisability, experimentation and

---

31   E. Psygochiopoulou (2008). *The Integration of Cultural Considerations in EU Law and Policies.* Leiden: Brill/Nijhoff, p. 337–46.

32   W. de Clercq (1993). *Reflection on Information and Communication Policy of the European Community,* Brussels: Commission of the European Communities, p.33.

33   G. De Burca (2003). 'The Constitutional Challenge of New Governance in the European Union', *European Law Review* 28, pp. 814–39, p. 815.

34   Communication from the Commission, Action plan 'Simplifying and improving the regulatory environment', COM (2002) 278 final, 5 June 2002, p. 7.

35   European Commission, 'European governance: a white paper', COM (2001) 428 final, 25 July,pp. 19–20.

knowledge-creation, in conformity with the distinct EU and national competences on particular policy fields.[36]

After the successful introduction of this method in other policy fields such as employment and environmental policies, it was introduced in the 2007–2013 Culture programme including – among other things – the Media programme, European Heritage Days and the Europeana website hosting a digital database of the collections of all public cultural heritage institutions.[37] The culture programme was built on three interrelated sets of objectives: (i) the promotion of cultural diversity and intercultural dialogue; (ii) the promotion of culture as a catalyst for creativity; and (iii) the promotion of culture as a vital element in the Union's international relations.

It was expected that the OMC would lead to closer engagement in dialogue between EU institutions and professional cultural organisations, cultural institutions, non-governmental organisations, networks and foundations to support the development of new EU policies and actions, as well as dialogue among themselves.

After the review of the first Work Plan covering the period 2008–2010, a number of adjustments were made leading to a more integrated guiding framework and better defined objectives. The 2013 Report on the OMC in cultural policies concluded that the field of cultural policy has a distinct identity, which is characterised by a high degree of subsidiarity, general absence of EU legislation and a diverse and fragmented sector in Europe. The Culture OMC therefore was seen to provide positive benefits, because it gives valuable opportunities for high quality exchanges and mutual learning activities around issues of common interest.[38] This conclusion is in line with the analyses of the effects of OMC projects in other policy fields, which recognised in particular the learning effect and thereby the shaping of policy discourse and policy networks.[39]

Concurrent with the OMC, the EU initiated three Structured Dialogue Platforms, providing a framework on exchanges with civil society actors on policy development on 'Access to Culture'; the Platform on 'Cultural and Creative Industries' and the Platform on 'Intercultural Europe'.

---

36 J. Scott and D. Trubek (2002). 'Mind the Gap: Law and new approaches to Governance in the EU', *European Law Journal* 7, p. 1.

Merli Tamtik (2012). 'Rethinking the Open Method of Coordination: Mutual Learning Initiatives Shaping the European Research Enterprise', *Review of European and Russian Affairs* 7: 2, 2012, p.4.

37 Communication 'On a European agenda for culture in a globalising world', COM (2007) 242 final. Brussels 10.5.2007, p.8.

38 N. McDonald, N. Mozuraityte, L. Veart and S. Frost. *Evaluation of the Open Method of Coordination and the Structural Dialogue as the Agenda for Culture's implementing tools at European Union Level*, Final Report for the EC DG Education and Culture, Ecorys UK Ltd. 2013, ii., and Finding 26.

39 Tamtik (2012), p. 3.

What this means is that the EU practice of new governance methods like the OMC, by working around the competence issue, and in line with the demand for subsidiary action and the mainstreaming of cultural action under Article 167 TFEU and Article 6 TFEU, may be expected to lead to a far more active role for cultural heritage institutions. As such they become participants in the process of achieving learning effects, and thereby the shaping of policy discourse and networks which these OMC projects are recognised to lead to.

Conclusion

New Tasks for Museums

The global legal framework on the protection of cultural heritage seeks to support museums because they are considered to be important to society at large. The guidelines of the UNESCO treaties indicate that museums need to demonstrate their overall relevance to the public and at the same time take into account the active involvement of the communities that are closely connected to the cultural heritage at stake. The documentation and the presentation of elements of intangible heritage are to bear witness to their social and cultural context and with the interests and the demands of the relevant communities in mind. On the other hand, the cultural heritage institutions are expected to reach out to the public and find ways to present their collections which demonstrate their relevance to the public interest.

Article 167 TFEU and Article 3 TFEU provide the basis for new governance instruments in line with the subsidiary powers of the EU in the field of cultural policies. The instrument of OMC gives a direct opportunity to cultural heritage institutions to give input in cultural policies on the EU level. This means that museums are to engage and participate in these policy dialogues and contribute to the policy networks and the legal framework of the protection of cultural heritage.

The future for museums, as flagships of the past, lies in their active involvement in the shaping of policy objectives that will support the protection of cultural heritage and cultural diversity. It will also support their position in this policy field. Museums thereby need to be aware of their position as agents in the local, regional, national and international framework of cultural policy objectives.

References

Anderson, B. (1991). *Imagined Communities: Reflections on the Origin and Spread of Nationalism*. London: Verso.

Belder, L. (ed.) (2014). *Cultivate! Cultural Heritage Institutions, Copyright and Cultural Diversity in the European Union and Indonesia*. Amsterdam: Delex publishers.

Bellucci, L. and R. Soprano. 'The WTO System and the Implementation of the UNESCO Convention: Two Case Studies', in C. Germann (ed.), *Implementing the UNESCO Convention of 2005 in the European Union*, available at http://www.europarl.europa.eu/studies.

Commission of the European Union (W. de Clercq) (1993). Reflection on Information and Communication Policy of the European Community. Brussels.

Commission of the European Union, Communication, Action Plan (2002). 'Simplifying and improving the regulatory environment', COM (2002) 278 final.

Commission of the European Union, Communication (2001). 'European governance: a white paper', COM (2001) 428 final.

Commission of the European Union, Communication (2007). 'On a European agenda for culture in a globalising world', COM (2007) 242 final.

De Burca, G. (2003). The Constitutional Challenge of New Governance in the European Union, *European Law Review* 28.

Dolff-Bonekämper, G. (2008). 'The Philosophical, Political and Pragmatical Roots of the Convention', in D. Thérond (ed.), *Heritage and Beyond*. Strasbourg: COE Publishing.

McDonald, N., N. Mozuraityte, L. Veart and S. Frost (2013). *Evaluation of the Open Method of Coordination and the Structural Dialogue as the Agenda for Culture's implementing tools at European Union Level*. Final Report for the EC DG Education and Culture, Ecorys UK Ltd.

Popper, K. (1945). *The Open Society and its Enemies*. London: Routledge.

Scott, J. and D. Trubek (2002). 'Mind the Gap: Law and New Approaches to Governance in the EU', *European Law Journal* 7.

Senden, L. (2004). *Soft Law in European Community Law*. Oxford: Hart Publishing.

Psygochiopoulou, E. (2008). *The Integration of Cultural Considerations in EU Law and Policies*. Leiden: Nijhoff/Brill.

Tamtik, M. (2012). 'Rethinking the Open Method of Coordination: Mutual Learning Initiatives Shaping the European Research Enterprise', *Review of European and Russian Affairs* 7: 2.

Chapter 3

Libraries, Creativity and Copyright

Darryl Mead

Fred Saunderson

This chapter explores the question 'What is and what ought to be the relationship between cultural heritage institutions, creativity and copyright?' Analysis is in two parts. In the first part we discuss the state of the current relationship between these three. In the second part we move on to elucidate what the relationship should – or could – be.

We write from practical experience at the National Library of Scotland (NLS). NLS is the largest library in Scotland, embodying 325 years of heritage. Between us we have the perspective of one who runs NLS as a library and one who specialises in intellectual property management for the Library. Additionally, we bring broader views gained through work in most types of cultural institutions, including archives, museums, galleries, universities and archaeology.

Cultural Heritage, Creativity and Copyright: The State of the Relationship

The Role of Institutions

Cultural heritage institutions are privileged to exist with the primary (if not sole) purpose of collecting, maintaining and affording access to society's cultural material. These organisations have for centuries been in prime position to support both the strength of collective memory and the cumulative diversity of creativity. It is this foundational role of cultural heritage institutions in the expansion and development of creativity that is of particular interest here. This role for the sector is only set to increase in significance as technologies enable ever greater content access and connectivity between peoples. The cultural heritage sector is, uniquely, positioned within this expanding ecosystem to facilitate access to the existing corpus of knowledge. In other words, cultural heritage institutions hold and provide access to that which has gone before.

Libraries

Libraries have come over time to fill a particular remit within what can today been seen as the broader range of cultural heritage institutions. With a focus on the printed and recorded word, libraries have over centuries collected a vast proportion of humanity's written output. Such collecting has formed incredible resources. However, as explored in more detail below, the remit of the library is by no means limited to the written word. Image, audio, cartographic material, databases and other forms of recorded content are very much at home in today's library collections. The library itself, as well as hosting an almost unbounded range of content, can arise in almost any guise. Perhaps the most readily obvious forms of library are those that exist on the local level (public libraries), those that exist within educational bodies (e.g. university libraries) and those that record and maintain national collections – national libraries.

A collecting privilege that is often, although not exclusively, unique to national libraries is the right of legal deposit. In the United Kingdom, this right is presently afforded by terms laid out in the Legal Deposit Libraries Act 2003. The Act begins by stating the fundamental logic of legal deposit: 'A person who publishes in the United Kingdom a work to which this Act applies must at his own expense deliver a copy of it to an address specified (generally or in a particular case) by any deposit library entitled to delivery under this section'.[1]

As a particularly complex country, the UK in fact operates not one but several deposit libraries with entitlement under this Act. Five domestic libraries – the British Library, the National Library of Wales (Llyfrgell Genedlaethol Cymru), the National Library of Scotland (Leabharlann Nàiseanta na h-Alba), the Bodleian Library, Oxford and the University Library, Cambridge – as well as the Library of Trinity College, Dublin in the Republic of Ireland are entitled to legal deposit of UK publications. Not only, therefore, does the UK's legal deposit framework cross between national and university libraries, it also crosses international borders. While the UK's legal deposit establishment has helped to ensure that institutions around the British Isles have collected printed output with some consistency for over three centuries, the scope of this framework has also been gradually expanded over this period. UK legal deposit libraries have been collecting recorded sound and visual material (photographs, film, and related content), in addition to print, for over a century. In 2013 the scope of the Act was widened further to include works produced in non-print format (for example, web content).

This facility for mandated collection means that deposit libraries have accumulated collections significantly more expansive than those held by other types of cultural heritage institution. Taking the Scottish cultural sector as a contained example within the greater UK ecosystem, the National Galleries of Scotland have a permanent collection of just over 96,000 major art works[2] (and a complete collection of around half a million items, when content such as photographs and documents are included), while the National Museum of Scotland houses around three million items. By contrast, the National Library of Scotland holds in excess of 24 million physical items in its collection, equivalent to some two and a half

---

1   http://www.legislation.gov.uk/ukpga/2003/28 1(1)
2   http://www.nationalgalleries.org/collection/online-collection/

billion pages of content. The National Library's legal deposit entitlement plays no small part in this collection disparity.

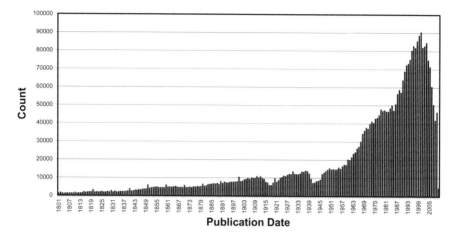

Figure 3.1   National Library of Scotland collections by publication date

In both the operating model of the library and the collecting framework of legal deposit privilege there is inherent non-discrimination. Library collections hold fact and fiction, acclaimed literary masterpieces and routine technical manuals. Likewise, libraries have content access at the core of their purpose and function. The National Library of Scotland is incorporated under the National Library of Scotland Act 2012, a piece of legislation which clearly spells out the institution's obligations to the nation. Inter alia, the National Library exists with the mandate to 'make collections accessible to the public', exhibit and interpret its collections, promote collaboration, encourage education and research, and contribute to the development of 'Scotland's national culture'.[3] The library operating model, more broadly, is most frequently access to content free at the point of use. In the case of legal deposit libraries, this means access to millions of unique and varied items. Centuries of collecting, whether within or outwith legal deposit legislation, means that libraries such as the National Library have built up an accessible, open repository of past creative processes that is available for current use and secured for future application.

Because legal deposit libraries are able to collect with such breadth and depth, they provide collections that are representative as well as large. However, legal deposit library collections also benefit from being filled with raw data material and interpreted content. The institutions designated under legal deposit legislation have changed and morphed over time, but the fact remains that libraries in the UK, in one guise or another, have been entitled for centuries to ensure deposit and

3   http://www.legislation.gov.uk/asp/2012/3/enacted section 2

retention of a copy of any work printed in the country. As impressive as the scale and diversity of the National Library of Scotland's collection is, as a secondary legal deposit library within the UK's uniquely complex system, the collection is in fact only about one-quarter the size of the country's largest library collection: that of the British Library.

Unlike the National Library of Scotland or any of the four other legal deposit libraries, the British Library is the location where publishers are obliged to deliver their content – the National Library of Scotland and the others, while entitled to claim a copy, must specifically *request* that copy. This structure means that the British legal deposit framework encourages both comprehensive collection (British Library) and the development of distinct national or specialist collections (the five other libraries). This means that, when the National Library of Wales focuses on collecting Welsh publications and the National Library of Scotland ensures collection of Scottish publications, these libraries in fact hold countless items that are likely not to be found in any other (legal deposit) library.

Non-Print Legal Deposit

While library collecting approaches developed significantly over time, particularly in the twentieth century as new mediums of content became common (such as film and sound), the core of legal deposit legislation changed little. The Legal Deposit Libraries (Non-print Works) Regulations 2013, which supplement the 2003 Act, granted the framework one of its most fundamental expansions. The 2013 Regulations themselves are in fact fairly straightforward, and almost entirely mirror the process laid out in the 2003 Act for deposit of printed material. Crucially, the non-print regulations are *not* solely a web-collecting mandate, although evidently that is a huge and vital entitlement within them.

The 2013 Regulations allow the six legal deposit libraries to mandate timely delivery into their collections of works published in non-print format, in addition to 'traditional' print deposits. Such non-print works can be online material or offline material (for example, works encoded on a CD or similar data storage device). It is worth bearing in mind, however, that the 2013 Regulations exclude published material consisting only of sound recording, film recording or a combination of the two. This can be seen as fairly analogous to printed material deposit legislation, which does not include audio or moving image material. Indeed – in many respects – the 2013 Regulations are as liberal and conservative as existing legal deposit was previously: the British Library remains the site of ultimate collection, where works must be deposited, while the remaining five libraries may request material that they wish to be deposited in their own collections. All of this means that the 2013 Regulations allow UK legal deposit libraries to collect a far greater bulk of published material than was previously permissible, while continuing to enable distinct collecting strategies to be pursued at the different libraries.

Since taking effect on 6 April 2013, the 2013 Regulations have enabled deposit libraries to much more comprehensively collect from what is increasingly the dominant publishing platform: the World Wide Web. The regulations ensure that the designated libraries may collect websites that are published under a UK domain (for example, .co.uk, .ac.uk, .london, .cymru, and so on) as well as any website made available to the public by a person where 'any of that person's activities relating to the creation or the publication of the work take place within the United Kingdom'.[4] In some respects this is an even more expansive collection mandate than that afforded to print works and takes into account the increasingly (if not already entrenched) transnational nature of the Web. Additionally, as mentioned, deposit libraries are entitled under the 2013 Regulation to collect non-web-based sources of non-print publication, including e-books, electronic journals, and digital mapping.

Creativity

If any body holds and offers access to a comprehensive collection of society's recorded knowledge (printed, electronic; old, new; artistic, technical; raw, interpreted), it is likely to be a legal deposit library. In patent terms, these institutions hold as close as possible to the complete prior art. Therefore, these collections are naturally a tremendous resource for creativity.

Using Content: Adding value

Ultimately, collections in libraries exist as the basis for future creativity. Creative work[5] is built upon preceding work. You don't reinvent the wheel. Instead, you take the power of the wheel to the next level and invent the axle and the cog. Fundamentally, creativity emerges from a coming together of existing material and novel insight: a combination of pre-existing knowledge and new ideas. As the bodies that hold the prior art, libraries are central to this cycle of creativity.

As discussed, in content terms legal deposit libraries provide unbiased access, based on unbiased collecting. Libraries are a source both of rich, interpreted material and raw, unexplored data. A library deposit can hold a well-known literary novel and an author's extensive drafts and notes in one location: in other words, the outputs and the data. Library collections, particularly of the deposit libraries, are often centuries old. Deposit libraries, at the same time, maintain collections of highly contemporary material. In this way, libraries bring the state of the art from three centuries prior directly alongside today's state of the art. As a source for material therefore, library collections are broad and deep, processed and raw, old and new.

---

4   http://www.legislation.gov.uk/ukdsi/2013/9780111533703 18(b)

5   Taken in the broadest sense, and therefore including not only 'literary' works such as stories, songs and illustrations, but also inventions, formulae, standards, processes and other forms of work produced by application of the human mind.

Naturally, the sheer scale of deposit library collections go far beyond the level of content ingest that any human can hope to obtain in a lifetime. The National Library of Scotland holds approximately four and half million monograph printed books. A good reader might hope to pore through four thousand of these in a lifetime. It would take a thousand lifetimes to read NLS's entire monograph collection.Furthermore, printed monographs account for only a fraction of the NLS collection of 24 million items. Designate another thousand lifetimes for reading magazines, a further hundred for flicking over maps, and tens of thousands for scouring over what will become the largest collection of all: the Web.

Were creativity to hinge upon each individual comprehensively familiarising themselves with the complete prior art, humanity would face an impossible uphill battle that no library could address. Fortunately, this is not the case. Creativity hinges instead upon individuals coming across, finding or knowing about the right prior content at the right time. People do not need to read every book and watch every film in order to generate new ideas and develop fresh creative outputs. However, people do need access to as close to the full range of existing material as possible, since different works will prove valuable to different people at different times. This is exactly how deposit libraries act as a central resource for the creative process.

Because humanity cannot digest everything it has made previously, there need to be mechanisms for collecting, organising, storing, interpreting and promoting the prior art: teasing out the valuable material relative to particular interests, needs, uses and desires. This is a role for the library. Libraries do not simply shuffle their physical collection in and out. Instead, libraries undertake and fulfil a range of roles that serve more holistically to connect disparate sources of knowledge. An individual accessing the NLS is not, in this respect, even 'limited' to the millions of items housed in the Library in Edinburgh. The National Library is connected to ten thousand libraries around the world, through the WorldCat union catalogue of global collections. The British Library in London makes more than 1.6 million of its items available externally every year through inter-lending. On top of it all, NLS was entitled to collect in excess of one billion URLs during the first year that non-print legal deposit legislation was in force in the UK. All of these collections, whether in one location or linked together from numerous sites, represent a phenomenal resource for the combining of prior art and new ideas. That is, for creativity.

Capturing the Process: Future Value

As well as providing a contemporary resource to stimulate and nurture creativity, libraries serve as a particularly robust recorder of the creative process. This ability comes back to the library's general position of being non-discriminatory in terms of the types and styles of content that it collects. Deposit libraries and research libraries in particular serve to bolster the value of their collections by gathering and maintaining valuable manuscripts, papers, diagrams, documents and other materials that creators generate in the process of their work (for example, by collecting the working papers as well as the finished novel, the working diagrams as well as the finished artwork). When institutions such as NLS gather these materials they add to the existing breadth and depth of their collections with a further layer of value, gained through the uniqueness of these materials. An institution that holds, maintains and provides access to finished items and working/process materials represents a remarkably valuable resource for future insight, and thus for creativity. This collecting allows the actual creative process, in so far as is possible, to be captured, recorded and preserved for future generations. Creativity can learn both from the existing raw materials – the prior art – and the methods and processes previously applied. Libraries collect and provide access to both.

Creativity and Copyright: The Overlap

As described, collections held by the National Library of Scotland and similar libraries are almost limitless in terms of their variety. Equally, while these institutions hold huge quantities of material, there is no realistic possibility that individuals will use all or even most of this content in creative processes. Part of a library's role, therefore, is to provide interpretation and curated access, so that potential value may be best realised. This is where external restrictions placed upon libraries begin to become apparent. Libraries face various constraints on their operations and their ability to fulfil their primary objectives. However, restrictions on library budgets or on staff numbers are limited in their effect when compared to the restrictions that copyright legislation places upon the ability of NLS and similar bodies to step up fully to the task of adding creative value through ideal use of their collections for the generation of creativity.

The reality of this restriction becomes apparent when consideration is given not just to the potential and long-term significance of libraries to the creative process, as discussed above, but also to the real and day-to-day significance of libraries to this process. In other words, it is particularly important to consider the more particular demand for content that is placed on libraries, to consider which items library users are seeking to generate the most creativity with most often.

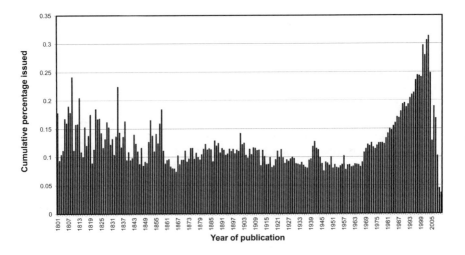

Figure 3.2   Cumulative percentage of NLS material issued

We take here the empirical example of the National Library. Up until about 1860 NLS holdings were fairly limited in number, but the books were used quite intensively. In the century from 1860 to 1960 levels of use were fairly flat, averaging about 1.5 per cent of the book stock per year. For works published before 1800, cumulative circulation from NLS remains in the tens per year. Publications from 1801 onwards see circulation jump into the low hundreds per year, and post-1900 publications have circulated in the high hundreds and low one thousands per year. Materials published in the 1960s, 70s and 80s have circulated from NLS in the two to five thousands per year, while items published in the 1990s have seen circulation jump into the tens of thousands per year of publication. Circulation of 2003 publications stand (as of 2010) at around 26,000, a considerable increase that should be considered alongside the concurrent growth in the Library's collection size over the period 1800 to 2003 (see Figure 3.2). By far, the highest demand levels are consistently for modern publications in the decade following publication, which is not surprising. A theme consistent throughout the history of the Library is that, while the full range of the collection is always valued and used in moderation, in terms of 'traditional' published materials, contemporary works are consistently the most valued and most pertinent items for users. It is both this 'high demand' content as well as the 'long tail' of valuable, but much less in-demand content (which should be seen to include unpublished materials), where copyright constricts the ability of libraries to meet creativity demands.

Copyright

As has been explored above, the cultural heritage sector, and in particular libraries, is strongly placed to facilitate, encourage and enrich both collective memory and contemporary (and future) creativity. The richness of collections built up and maintained over centuries means that there exists through library collections the potential for those with access – the population – to generate far richer and more informed creative content. Libraries offer an extremely low barrier of entry, while the collections amassed by them offer anyone interested an almost limitless range of raw data and informed knowledge. Naturally, libraries face constant pressures and restrictions, whether in the form of budget constraints or insufficient computer infrastructure. However, these are not the factors that truly inhibit the ability of libraries ultimately to ensure their collections are encouraging creativity to the greatest extent possible. It is copyright, or more specifically the way copyright is implemented, that truly places restriction on libraries and on creativity.

The Point of Copyright

Copyright is an essential protection. With a long history, generally cited as beginning in its present form with the Great Britain's Statute of Anne in 1710, copyright at its basic level affords a monopoly to content creators (known, irrespective of the type of work, as authors). Since 1710, the norm has become to afford monopoly rights to authors and attach to that protection a predetermined time limit. This is known as copyright duration. In 1886 the agreement that still forms the basis of modern copyright law around the world was laid down in the form of the Berne Convention. This agreement remains central to the copyright structure in the UK today.

Copyright, it should be noted, is one of several rights (including patents, trademarks and design rights) that are collectively known as intellectual property rights. Protections of creations of the mind, intellectual property rights are essential because, as with any property right, they confer ownership and afford protection of that ownership. Copyright, in particular, acts to limit what others are permitted to do with the intellectual content created by an author. The framework acts to restrict to the author certain rights regarding the exploitation of their outputs. This process allows authors to be able better to secure benefits from their work, and thus encourages the generation of new work in the first place, by assuaging fear that content will simply be appropriated by stronger agents (the basis of any property entitlement). Copyright protection does not *ensure* a work will benefit an author (copyright makes, like libraries or legal deposit legislation, no discrimination on the basis of quality), but it does ensure that from a legal perspective a rights owner maintains certain rights over a work, and that these rights last for a certain, limited period of time.

Copyright in the UK is governed by the Copyright, Designs and Patents Act 1988 (CDPA). This legislation, in line with the terms of the Berne framework, sets the copyright duration that authors can expect to benefit from. To obtain this protection authors need not register – copyright is a naturally arising right in the UK – but they must undertake to ensure work that they create is eligible for protection. Fundamentally, a work must be recorded, as copyright cannot protect ideas that exist only in the mind. A work must also to a clear extent be novel. It does not need to be novel in this sense of literary merit, but it must not be a like for like replication of a different work (for example, a simple facsimile copy).

While copyright serves foremost to protect an author's right, as with any form of property, copyright is a transferable entitlement. This means that authors may sell their rights, waive their rights, or otherwise transfer their rights. And, like other forms of property, copyright can be inherited, passed down, bequeathed, and so on. All of this means that, while copyright at base level affords monopoly to an author, in reality there are countless situations where the owner of copyright – the party with the monopoly right – is not the author. Therefore, it is important to distinguish between an author and a rights owner. An author may be a rights owner, but equally an author may no longer be a rights owner. A fairly common example of the latter is the publication of a commercial book. When an author writes their work and delivers it to a publisher, the agreement drawn up with the publisher will (in most cases) involve the assignation (or licensing) of the author's naturally arising copyright in the work to the publisher (likewise, a work authored in the course of employment will by default be the property of the employer, rather than the individual author). In this scenario, the rights transfer is a commercial necessity for the publisher and a trade-off for the author: the publisher gains intellectual rights (and the monopoly that comes with those rights) and the author gains a powerful channel for dissemination of their work along with (in most cases) a negotiated proportion of the return made from the publisher's exploitation of the work (a royalty).

Using Copyright Material

As the name implies, copyright restricts the copying of works. By extension, copyright also restricts the publication of works, the making available of works, the performance of works, the modification or adaptation of works, and so on. At face value, such restrictions appear almost total and seem to offer little chance for the use of material. The good news is that these restrictions are not ultimate.

There are certain exceptions to the basic law of copyright in the UK. One such exception allows the copying and use of parts of a work for the purposes of criticism or review, another allows the copying and use of parts of a work for the reporting of current affairs (although this does not apply in the case of stand-alone photographs), while a third exception allows copying and use of parts of a work for personal study or non-commercial research. Together these three exceptions are known in the UK as 'fair-dealing' exceptions: the legal copying (and, by extension, use) of a copyright work without the need for specific permission from the copyright owner.[6] These exceptions are outlined in the CDPA and allow uses of copyright work that is deemed to be fair within the specific situations described above. In other words, these uses are seen as uses that will not infringe upon the true protection that a rights owner retains (in other words, they will not, in principle, impinge upon the right of the author to control copying and make income from the work[7]).

Libraries in the UK benefit from further copyright exceptions, on top of the fair-dealing exceptions afforded by the CDPA more broadly to the populace. Libraries, crucially, may facilitate the exploitation of these fair-dealing exceptions by others, by providing copies of works to users, with the proviso that the user requires the copy for one of the above three 'fair-dealing' purposes. Furthermore, under exceptions laid out in the CDPA, including clauses added or amended as recently as June 2014, libraries (and in some cases certain other cultural or non-profit bodies) are permitted to copy works for supply to other libraries, copy works for the purposes of preservation, copy works for use by persons with a disability and copy works for the purposes of enabling computational analysis (in other words, copying a work into a machine-readable format to enable text and data mining). Most of these library exceptions were introduced or significantly amended in June 2014 (the result of recommendations for change made in the UK's 2011 Hargreaves Review of Intellectual Property) and as a result what libraries may legally do to facilitate the use of their copyright-protected collections has been very recently expanded. However, it is vital to note that there are still significant limitations facing libraries and creativity, many of which serve to benefit no one and have the very real potential to be remedied.

Copyright Restrictions on Libraries and Creativity

While it is clear that many aspects of the fundamentals of copyright are essential (for example, ensuring authors can create content with protection), there are two key complications within copyright law that serve significantly to constrain libraries and limit creativity. First is the vast range of potential, and often untraceable, owners of any particular copyright. Second is the duration of the monopoly protection period and the effect this has in particular on unpublished and non-commercial materials.

---

6   UK copyright exceptions are set to be expanded from October 2014 with the introduction of wider quotation and parody allowances. At the time of writing, in July 2014, the legislation for this expansion had been approved by Parliament.

7   It should be noted that this relates to economic rights in particular. Copyright law also confers certain moral rights – the right of attribution and protection against derogatory treatment of a work – which, unlike economic rights (such as the right to licence copying and raise fees), cannot be transferred, although they may be waived. While moral rights are significant, this chapter addresses economic rights in particular, as moral rights prove vastly less (if at all in any major sense) restrictive to the function of libraries or the development of creativity.

Ownership Certain works, such as a work published in a commercial book, may have clear copyright ownership (bearing in mind that rights ownership is often distinct from authorship). With a published book, there is likely to have been an agreement between the publisher and the author(s), which will specify which party or parties will own intellectual property rights in the finished product. Likewise, an intellectual work, such as a drawing, that an individual produces and then makes available, say through sale, will in general have clear rights ownership vested in the author. However, in two ways in particular, ownership becomes rapidly and hugely complicated for cultural heritage institutions like the National Library of Scotland.

While rights ownership might be apparent in the period shortly after a work is created, this clarity can fade with time. In particular, in the period after an author dies it can become increasingly difficult for NLS and other libraries to establish the identity of the rights owner(s). Because copyright may be bought, sold, transferred, bequeathed, and so on, it is frequently, if not always, passed on to owners who are not the author. This may happen transparently and directly, as in the case of an author and a publisher during the pre-publication process, or this may happen in an utterly opaque or even confused manner.

Because *any* intellectual creation (that is, recorded in some manner) automatically obtains copyright protection in the UK, there is a huge corpus of works that the National Library holds that possess copyright protection and in which this was almost certainly never a consideration of any party involved in the creation of said works. A photographer may be diligent to look after the rights in their photographs, and may be clear who (or what body) will own the rights after her/his death. This diligence is understandable, as the photographer clearly desires to maintain control over their creativity and provide protection to her/his livelihood. Likewise, such diligence proves useful to institutions like NLS, by making it evident where permission for use should be sought. However, that same photographer may, understandably, give no copyright ownership consideration to her/his notes, napkin doodles or half-finished speech begun writing but never actually delivered. All of this material retains copyright protection, placing very significant – and in all likelihood unintended and unneeded – restrictions on bodies like NLS. If and when the ownership in these works becomes unclear, the works would become effectively unusable for institutions like NLS. If the National Library held these items and subsequently hoped, or a user hoped, say 50 years after the photographer's death, to make use of them, without being able to trace the current rights owner it would be, in effect, not possible to use the content. In this manner, potentially valuable resources are restricted from the populace (despite being held by public bodies, for society) in situations where perhaps no agent, including the creator, ever desired this to be so.

Works such as these are known as orphan works and pose a major blockage to libraries and creativity. Even copyright ownership itself, as it is vested in almost any item and can be passed between parties at any stage of its existence, poses major challenges to libraries.

Copyright duration Copyright protection, in most cases, lasts for seven decades after the death of the author. A major hindrance to libraries like the National Library

in and of itself, as noted above, this is only a compound problem when consideration is also given to the increasing likelihood over time that the rights holder's identity will only become more vague and harder to establish. Furthermore, this 'life plus seventy' duration is not the only copyright duration in the UK. Works published by the government or the monarch (those protected by Crown copyright) have separate periods of protection, as do works that have not been published (whether Crown copyright or not), as do musical works that have been recorded, and so on. Copyright duration, therefore, is both extensive and hugely complex. Both of these factors act as major constraints on the ability of libraries to use and promote use of content, some of which has been in existence in an entirely non-commercial, non-personal manner for decades.

As illustrated in Figure 3.3, of the approximately four and a half million monographs in the NLS collection, the significant majority are in (right of the 70 year arrow) or are likely to be in (left of the 70 year arrow)copyright. Furthermore, as illustrated in Figure 3.4, the majority of items issued by NLS between 2004 and 2010 fall within the core duration periods. This means, unsurprisingly, that a large bulk of the content that users are interested in – the content that will help them most to be creative and generate new content for society – is content that is protected by copyright. Many of these works may be well beyond any period of commercial exploitation that they may have had. In many cases such a period will never have existed, yet the work remains locked into copyright restriction, that, due to the confluence of factors here outlined, is in many cases likely to be difficult to use beyond the confines of CDPA exceptions as authors die, rights are passed on or, perhaps worse, simply forgotten.

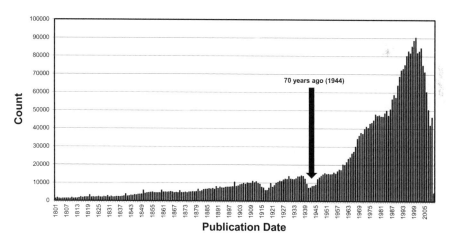

Figure 3.3   NLS Monograph collection copyright duration

Copyrighting Creativity

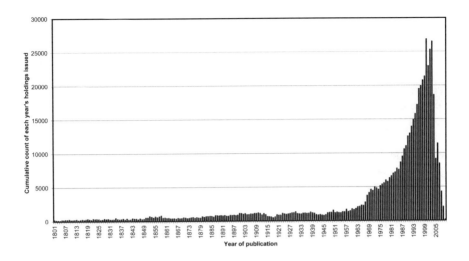

Figure 3.4   Cumulative issuing of NLS items 2004–2010

Using Copyright Exceptions in the Library: Two Questions to Answer
When we consider the impacts of copyright law, both in terms of restrictions and in terms of exceptions, it becomes clear that if one wishes to use a piece of in-copyright material from a library, such as the National Library of Scotland, there are two successive questions that can be posed in order to establish the form of access that might be possible: 'What is the material?' and 'What do you want to do with the material?'. 'Use' in this situation means to make use of material in a manner which is restricted by copyright law to the copyright owner as a monopoly right. Such actions, inter alia, include copying, publishing, etc. as discussed above.

What is the material? This first question takes the vital step of establishing, in so far as is possible (recall the orphan works issue), whether the material to be used is protected by copyright or not. Assuming the material is protected by copyright, or is deemed likely to be protected by copyright, the nature of the material will have a secondary impact on the next steps taken. Different classes of work (written word, photographs, music, and so on), all of which are held by NLS, attract different terms of protection. In fact, there are often many levels of detail about the material that may need to be considered. Let us say, therefore, that the material you're interested in is a collection of 30 poems. The poems were written by one author, who had them published 70 years ago. The author died 15 years after publication. The work, therefore, is protected by copyright (as the author died 55 years ago) and is published printed word (a literary work in the terminology used by the CDPA).

What do you want to do with the material? The first question focused on the nature of the material. This follow-up question focuses on the use and the user. Just as the details of the work itself (and the amount of this detail you are able to obtain) make a huge difference to copyright status, so too do the intentions for use. It is safe to assume that the use involves copying, since effectively any use of a literary work – in copyright terms – involves copying (this can be said for other classes of work, although the intellectual rights to protect broadcast, publication, communication to the public, and so on are also of consideration, particularly for sound and moving image works). It is safe to assume that the intended use does not involve manipulation of the original encoding of the item, but rather the use of a copy of the work. The reasons for copying, rather than the act itself, are the real deciding factors here. Specifically, the salient point is whether the reason for copying falls within the terms of fair dealing. Assuming intended use fits within the limitations of fair dealing, a library will likely be able to supply a copy of *part* of a copyright work. In the case of our example, if the intended use of the poetry was for personal, non-commercial research, the National Library would be able to supply a copy. The exception under which this copy would be supplied limits the amount that can provide to 'a reasonable' proportion of the entire work.[8] With our example of a book of 30 published poems, all by one poet, this is relatively straightforward: a library could likely supply a copy of one poem for private research. This, of course, only provides limited use of a work – for greater use permission in most cases would need to be sought, and as discussed above locating an owner and establishing what level of protection exists in a work serve only to add layers of complexity to the process outlined here.

The published poetry anthology example is a straightforward one. While a vital allowance to the cultural sector, library copyright exceptions (and fair-dealing exceptions in general) remain highly complex and restrictive, particularly with regard to the amount and quality of creativity that libraries are able to foster with their collections of in-copyright content. It should not go without note that highly successful copyright regimes, namely in the United States, have enabled much more nuanced and adaptive exception frameworks.[9]

Cultural Heritage, Creativity and Copyright: What the Relationship Should – and Could – Be

Copyright, creativity and cultural heritage institutions absolutely have scope to work together. Each derives value from and benefits the others. However, it is clear that copyright has not in the UK reached a stage at which it best helps libraries – and by extension library users – explore content fully. The barriers, whether in practice or in legislation, to smooth access to material are high, complex and frequently

---

8   The Copyright and Rights in Performances (Research, Education, Libraries and Archives) Regulations 2014, http://www.legislation.gov.uk/uksi/2014/1372/contents/made

9   In the United States, fair dealing is replaced by a less-prescriptive 'fair use' principle. Unlike the UK framework, fair use is not limited to specific purposes, but rather is concerned simply with the 'fairness' of a use of a work without specific rights owner permission.

lack essential nuance. In other words, the copyright structure continues to restrict the creativity that cultural heritage institutions have the potential to incubate and encourage. In this section of the chapter we examine two particular areas where there is very real scope for the relationship to move closer to the optimum. Fundamentally, libraries, creativity and copyright can work more closely together and generate positive outcomes for the defenders and proponents of each.

At a base level, the relationship between libraries, creativity and copyright needs to be closer and clearer. The layers of complexity – where ownership in a work's rights lie, what institutions may do with a work, how long a work is protected and so on – between what are often seen as opposing objectives of rights owners, libraries, and content users can be reduced. In terms of real and attainable methods for improving this relationship, this section focuses on the two blockers to creativity that were discussed above: ownership and duration.

Ownership

In many cases, the owner of copyright in a work is either not the creator of that work or is not identifiable. In the worst situations, the rights owner is neither the author nor identifiable. These situations do not benefit content creators, libraries or creativity. There is clear scope here to reduce the complexity that hinders creative development and tie copyright protection more closely to the actual creation of a work. While the fundamentals of property should not be dispensed with, there is scope for reducing the degree to which copyright protection can shift so significantly away from creators. Were protection tied more closely to authors – if copyright served much more exclusively to protect individuals who make a work – there would be a real reduction in the complex layers of copyright ownership that frequently forestall the ability of libraries like the National Library of Scotland to enable creative use of collection material, whether for limited fair dealing or for more complex application.

Even more concretely, legislative change is beginning to address the orphan works aspect of copyright ownership in the UK and in Europe. Two new regulations, that at the time of writing are on the cusp of coming into effect in the UK, will allow public cultural heritage institutions such as NLS to digitise their orphan works collections. These two separate pieces of legislation take distinct approaches, but both evolve from the recognition that the largely untapped potential of Europe's orphan works, and the ongoing inability of content holders to promote use of their material, does little if anything to benefit society. The fruition of these laws indicates a recognition that there is a way for orphan works to be used in such a manner that is not detrimental to rights owners, or at least highly minimises any risk of unintended negative consequences for authors.

The first piece of legislation is a UK specific law, which has in many respects the wider remit of the two. The process outlined by this legislation will allow persons with access to an orphan work to make use of that work, based on satisfaction of a number of steps and conditions. A 'diligent search' for potential rights holders will need to be undertaken and an application made to use the work from an authorising body. Assuming that the search fails to identify an owner and the authorising body grants a licence to use the work, the interested party will need to pay a licence fee, a sum that the authorising body will hold for a set period of time on the premise that if a rights owner should emerge they can be provided with due compensation for the use of their intellectual property. This domestic process is applicable to libraries, but may be undertaken by any body or individual.

Conversely, the second new law is much more narrowly targeted. The EU Orphan Works Directive (2012/28/EU) applies specifically to certain cultural heritage institutions, including legal deposit libraries. This regime is aimed at enabling these organisations to digitise and make orphan works available online. As with the UK domestic process, a diligent search must be undertaken for any rights owner. However, unlike the UK licensing scheme, the EU process requires only that details of the search are registered on a central database and does not require the payment of a holding licence fee to an authorising body (in this manner, the EU scheme is less of a traditional licensing framework than the UK regime). Assuming an owner is not identified in the search process, cultural heritage bodies may then digitise and provide public access to a work.

These are two welcome developments, and are clearly indicative of the need to add much greater flexibility and realism to the copyright framework for the modern era. However, the degree to which either of these processes will prove valuable to libraries and to creativity remains to be seen. There is well placed scepticism that the diligent search demands (as well as the licence fee, in the case of the domestic process) outlined by both schemes will make them impractical for institutions to use with any true impact. It seems likely that the domestic UK licensing scheme may prove useful to individuals seeking to use a small number of items. It also seems likely that the two schemes will benefit libraries and related institutions when they prepare specific exhibitions, projects and other such small-scale endeavours. However, it will likely be fundamentally unrealistic for libraries like the National Library to use either of these processes for any meaningful mass-digitisation or mass provision of access to orphan works. There are simply too many works that would need to be diligently checked under these schemes, a demand on time and resources that could not be met. If the works cannot be checked as demanded by the legislation, libraries will have little choice but to continue to restrict use of these items, or access to the content by means that society increasingly (and rightly) has come to expect (namely, remote access following digitisation). It remains the case that more flexible, more realistic schemes will be needed in future to allow libraries truly to open up access to orphan works en masse.

Duration

While not making specific recommendations on the matter, as copyright term was beyond its scope, the Hargreaves Review of Intellectual Property nevertheless highlights the genuine concern that should be attached to increasingly long copyright duration.[10] The report cautions against extension of copyright protection in sound recordings in Europe, and calls upon the economic concerns that long protection periods raise. But, as the report also points out, economic concerns should not be the only consideration. From a public interest and creativity perspective, there are similar reasons to encourage, at times, more restricted copyright terms.

While there are at the time of writing no plans on the UK legislative agenda to revisit copyright duration, unlike plans to tackle some of the problems around ownership, there is still cause to make argument here for more restrained terms. As we have explored, while the purpose of copyright is to protect the interests of authors, it is hard to see how present terms that extend decades after death do this with best effect, particularly when those rights so frequently are not vested in authors from the start. Naturally, there is a need to protect authors and to provide assurance to heirs, especially when works are made towards the end of a creator's life. In spite of this, a blanket scheme of protection for 70 years after death does very little to encourage the growth of creativity based on library-held prior art collections, and it is questionable in how many instances this period does any real service to authors or their descendants in comparison to the sheer number of works that the system captures. This system simply fails to account for the countless items that need not be in protection – whether because an author never intended them to be restricted, the works hold no commercial value or the items have become orphans over time.

A Closer Relationship
Throughout this chapter we have compared the collection corpus in legal deposit libraries to the 'prior art' in patent terms. It is worth in this concluding section drawing again upon that analogy. In terms of offerings of opportunity and protection, patents and copyright act similarly. Each functions to protect a particular creative output of a human or a collective of humans. Likewise, each provides a monopoly right of exploitation to a rights owner, for a limited time period, with the aim of ensuring that the market can reward creativity. Thus, an incentive for new creativity is ensured. At this level the aims of both systems are clear and entirely correct. However, based on the concerns discussed above, it appears that there is scope for the copyright framework to learn from the patent system. This is not an advocation that copyright should function like patents – we are not calling for a strict application process for copyright protection or a requirement upon copyright works to represent a fresh and technologically novel addition to the foregoing corpus. However, there is a degree of closeness and clarity in the patent framework that copyright can learn from.

The patent system protects invention, while simultaneously exposing the state of the art developed in an invention to others. This means that others can build upon the prior art. In other words, patents protect monopoly exploitation rights and concurrently promote creativity and development of new ideas based

---

10   Hargreaves, p. 19. http://www.ipo.gov.uk/ipreview-finalreport.pdf

on what has come before. Naturally, such a framework would be much harder to obtain in the copyright field – the nature of copyrightable work is inherently different from patentable material, and intrinsically more nebulous and fluid. Such a framework would, whatever the changes made, look very different in the copyright system. However, particularly in terms of the two concerns highlighted in this chapter – copyright ownership and copyright duration – the model of the patent system's clarity can lend lessons for copyright's future relationship with libraries and creativity.

For creativity to thrive, society should provide access to the prior art. Society has, over centuries, built up phenomenal prior art resources, notably in the guise of legal deposit libraries. These are often maintained at public expense. Society has also developed an essential system of protections for safeguarding creativity and encouraging continuation of novel thinking and development of the state of the art. If conceived of in this manner, it is clear that libraries (holders of prior art), creativity (generation of the ongoing state of the art) and copyright (protection of the developing state of the art) are interconnected and mutually beneficial. The problem is that the final of these three, copyright, has become skewed too far towards protecting the prior art and shifted too far away from promoting development of the contemporary state of the art. This comes precisely in an era when technological advances are enabling greater, faster and more dynamic creative development on a much larger scale. Libraries have become caught in the middle: determined to incubate creativity and committed to safeguarding the state of the art – including the rights vested therein. When one push factor is too strong, it is inevitable the other will struggle. This is what libraries, including the National Library of Scotland, experience with an imbalance in copyright law. Promotion of creativity by libraries (for example, exploiting the vast potential of non-economically viable content or content of unclear intellectual ownership) thus becomes increasingly challenging at a time when the potential for creativity, that could increasingly derive real value from such content, is greatly expanding.

The patent system, as elaborated, protects inventions and concurrently encourages development upon those inventions (through publication of detailed diagrams and descriptions of inventions). In this manner the system has clarity and is self-encouraging. The copyright framework is considerably less clear and less self-encouraging. Copyright in the UK allows intellectual ownership to stray away from authors with incredible speed and worrying opacity. Copyright also asserts long terms of protection, in blanket terms. Taken individually, in a not-insignificant number of situations, each of these factors serves to reduce the degree to which copyright functions with the sort of clarity and mutual improvement found in the patent system. Taken together, these factors compound one another and tip the balance of the framework too far away from the promotion of creativity. The steps now being taken in Europe and the UK, as outlined above, are in the right direction. Recognition of the pressing need to improve use of orphan works is a welcome move, indicative of the growing understanding that a rebalance towards creativity promotion is both required and desirable. However, the improvements soon to be implemented will not go far enough for NLS, similar institutions or creativity. Likewise, there is yet to be a strong effort to address the considerable duration of protection that copyright confers on all works. In both of these respects there is clearly work still to be done in the UK in terms of developing a clearer copyright system that more sustainably brings together existing creative work, caretakers of the record of that work and future creative material.

Conclusion

We find the relationship between libraries, creativity and copyright to be strong, but less than ideal. Libraries, content creators and copyright owners do not fundamentally operate at odds. Each of these three players – who may often be the same actors – wants to encourage creativity and the benefits that come with advances to the state of the art. Because this relationship in practical terms is close and because fundamental interests are aligned, there is real potential for a more harmonised and effective relationship.

In the recent experience of the cultural heritage sector, and in particular legal deposit libraries such as the National Library of Scotland, this hinges upon a rebalancing of copyright more in favour of creativity promotion. There is, as expressed by contemporary developments in orphan works legislation, growing recognition of the need for these changes, and an understanding that change is viable. Legislation in favour of promoting the value locked in orphan work material is welcome, but there remains considerable scope in terms of ensuring that cultural heritage institutions can truly make use of these developments for the advancement of creativity. In this respect, there is scope to go much further. There is also scope to allow for more realistic, perhaps shorter, terms of copyright protection on a more nuanced basis without detriment to those authors who do wish to exert a genuine and beneficial period of intellectual command over their work.

Copyright protection remains vital and should be encouraged and protected, but the experience of libraries in attempting to make use of their prior art collections of content – resources that should be, with ease, the first point of reference for creatives – demonstrates and highlights that copyright remains skewed towards ownership protection. This skew is to a degree that libraries remain in the unhelpful position of protecting ownership in works that may never have been intended to be protected by their creators and works that have no clear owner (and may be very old). This neither promotes creativity nor protects or serves rights owners or authors. With a copyright framework that, akin to the patent system, is clearer and more flexible, there is scope for a rebalance in this relationship towards a more centralised position in which authors themselves are protected by monopoly rights in their works, libraries are empowered to use and provide genuine access to a much greater extent of their collections and creativity is better able to exploit modern technologies and means of creative development through application of the prior art. This is what the relationship between libraries, creativity and copyright should – and could – be.

References

The European Parliament and the Council of the European Union (2012). 'Directive 2012/28/EU of the European Parliament and of the Council of 25 October 2012 on Certain Permitted Uses of Orphan Works'. *Official Journal of the European Union* 27 October 2012. http://eur-lex.europa.eu/LexUriServ/LexUriServ.do?uri=OJ:L:2012:299:0005:0012:EN:PDF

Hargreaves, Ian (2011). *Digital Opportunity: A Review of Intellectual Property and Growth*. Intellectual Property Office. May 2011. http://www.ipo.gov.uk/ipreview-finalreport.pdf.

Intellectual Property Office. *Government Response to the Technical Consultation on Orphan Works*. Intellectual Property Office. https://www.gov.uk/government/uploads/system/uploads/attachment_data/file/315078/Orphan_Works_Government_Response.pdf.

National Galleries of Scotland. 'Online Collection'. National Galleries of Scotland. https://www.nationalgalleries.org/collection/online-collection/

United Kingdom Government. *Copyright, Designs and Patents Act 1988*. http://www.legislation.gov.uk/ukpga/1988/48/contents

United Kingdom Government (2014). *The Copyright and Rights in Performances (Research, Education, Libraries and Archives) Regulations 2014*. http://www.legislation.gov.uk/uksi/2014/1372/contents/made

United Kingdom Government (2003). *Legal Deposit Libraries Act 2003*. http://www.legislation.gov.uk/ukpga/2003/28

United Kingdom Government (2013). *Legal Deposit Libraries (Non-Print Works) Regulations 2013*. http://www.legislation.gov.uk/ukdsi/2013/9780111533703

United Kingdom Government (2012). *National Library of Scotland Act 2012*. http://www.legislation.gov.uk/asp/2012/3/enacted

World Intellectual Property Organisation. *Berne Convention for the Protection of Literary and Artistic Works*. World Intellectual Property Office. http://www.wipo.int/treaties/en/text.jsp?file_id=283698

Chapter 4

Libraries in the Post-Scarcity Era

Balázs Bodó

Introduction

In the digital era where, thanks to the ubiquity of electronic copies, the book is no longer a scarce resource, libraries find themselves in an extremely competitive environment. Several different actors are now in the position to provide low cost access to knowledge. One of these competitors is the shadow library – piratical text collections which amassed electronic copies of millions of copyrighted works and provide access to them usually free of charge to anyone around the globe. While such shadow libraries are far from being universal, they are able to offer certain services better, to more people and under more favourable terms than most public or research libraries. This contribution offers insights into the development and the inner workings of one of the biggest scientific shadow libraries on the internet in order to understand what kind of library people create for themselves if they have the means and if they don't have to abide by the legal, bureaucratic and economic constraints that libraries usually face. I argue that one of the many possible futures of the library is hidden in the shadows, and those who think of the future of libraries can learn a lot from book pirates of the twenty-first century about how users and readers expect texts in electronic form to be stored, organised and circulated.

The library is society's last non-commercial meeting place which the majority of the population uses. (Committee on the Public Libraries in the Knowledge Society, 2010)

With books ready to be shared, meticulously cataloged, everyone is a librarian. When everyone is librarian, library is everywhere. (Marcell Mars, www. memoryoftheworld.org)

I have spent the last few months in various libraries visiting – a library. I spent countless hours in the modest or grandiose buildings of the Harvard Libraries, the Boston and Cambridge Public Library systems, various branches of the Openbare Bibliotheek in Amsterdam, the libraries of the University of Amsterdam, with a computer in front of me, on which another library was running, a library which is perfectly virtual, which has no monumental buildings, no multi-million euro budget, no miles of stacks, no hundreds of staff, but which has, despite lacking everything that apparently makes a library, millions of literary works and millions of scientific books, all digitised, all available at the click of the mouse for everyone on earth without any charge, library or university membership. As I was sitting in these physical spaces where the past seemed to define the present, I was wondering where I should look to find the library of the future: down to my screen or up around me.

The library on my screen was Aleph, one of the biggest of the countless piratical text collections on the internet. It has more than a million scientific works and another million literary works to offer, all free to download, without any charge or fee, for anyone on the net. I've spent months among its virtual stacks, combing through the catalogue, talking to the librarians who maintain the collection, and watching the library patrons as they used the collection. I kept going back to Aleph both as a user and as a researcher. As a user, Aleph offered me books that the local libraries around me didn't, in formats that were more convenient than print. As a researcher, I was interested in the origins of Aleph, its modus operandi, its future, and I was curious where the journey to which it has taken the book-readers, authors, publishers and libraries would end.

In this chapter I will introduce some of the findings of a two-year research project conducted on Aleph. In the project. I reconstructed the pirate library's genesis in order to understand the forces that called it to life and shaped its development. I looked at its catalogue to understand what it has to offer and how that piratical supply of books is related to the legal supply of books through libraries and online distributors. I also acquired data on its usage, so I was able to reconstruct some aspects of piratical demand. After a short introduction, in the first part of this chapter I will outline some of the main findings, and in the second part will situate the findings in the wider context of the future of libraries.

Book Pirates and Shadow Librarians

Book piracy has a fascinating history, tightly woven into the history of the printing press (Judge, 1934), into the history of censorship (Wittmann, 2004), into the history of copyright (Bently, Davis and Ginsburg, 2010; Bodó, 2011a) and into the history of European civilisation (Johns, 2010). Book piracy, in the twenty-first or in the mid-seventeenth century is an activity that has deep cultural significance, because ultimately it is a story about how knowledge is circulated beyond and often against the structures of political and economic power (Bodó, 2011b), and thus it is a story about the changes this unofficial circulation of knowledge brings.

There are many different types of book pirates. Some just aim for easy money, others pursue highly ideological goals, but they are invariably powerful harbingers of change. The emergence of black markets, whether they be of culture, drugs or arms is always a symptom, a warning sign of a friction between supply and demand. Increased activity in the grey and black zones of legality marks the emergence of a demand which legal suppliers are unwilling or unable to serve

(Bodó, 2011a). That friction, more often than not, leads to change. Earlier waves of book piracy foretold fundamental economic, political, societal or technological shifts (Bodó, 2011b): changes in how the book publishing trade was organised (Judge, 1934; Pollard, 1916, 1920); the emergence of the new, bourgeois reading class (Patterson, 1968; Solly, 1885); the decline of pre-publication censorship (Rose, 1993); the advent of the Reformation and of the Enlightenment (Darnton, 1982, 2003), or the rapid modernisation of more than one nation (Khan and Sokoloff, 2001; Khan, 2004; Yu, 2000).

The latest wave of piracy has coincided with the digital revolution which, in itself, profoundly upset the economics of cultural production and distribution (Landes and Posner, 2003). However technology is not the primary cause of the emergence of cultural black markets like Aleph. The proliferation of computers and the internet just revealed a more fundamental issue which has to do with the uneven distribution of the access to knowledge around the globe.

Sometimes book pirates do more than just forecast and react to changes that are independent of them. Under certain conditions, they themselves can be powerful agents of change (Bodó, 2011b). Their agency rests on their ability to challenge the status quo and resist cooptation or subjugation. In that effect, digital pirates seem to be quite resilient (Giblin, 2011; Patry, 2009). They have the technological upper hand and so far they have been able to outsmart any copyright enforcement effort (Bodó, 2015). As long as it is not completely possible to eradicate file sharing technologies, and as long as there is a substantial difference between what is legally available and what is in demand, cultural black markets will be here to compete with and outcompete the established and recognised cultural intermediaries. Under this constant existential threat, business models and institutions are forced to adapt, evolve or die.

After the music and audiovisual industries, now the book industry has to address the issue of piracy. Piratical book distribution services are now in direct competition with the bookshop on the corner, the used-book stall on the pavement, they compete with the Amazons of this world and, like it or not, they compete with libraries. There is, however, a significant difference between the book and the music industries. The reluctance of music rights holders to listen to the demands of their customers caused little damage beyond the markets of recorded music. Music rights holders controlled their own fates and those who wanted to experiment with alternative forms of distribution had the limited chance to do so. But while the rapid proliferation of book black markets may signal that the book industry suffers from similar problems as the music industry suffered a decade ago, the actions of book publishers, the policies they pursue have impact beyond the market of books and directly affect the domain of libraries.

The fate of libraries is tied to the fate of book markets in more than one way. One connection is structural: libraries emerged to remedy the scarcity in books. This is true both for the pre-print era and in the Gutenberg galaxy. In the era of widespread literacy and highly developed book markets, libraries offer access to books under terms publishers and booksellers cannot or would not. Libraries, to a large extent, are defined to complement the structure of the book trade. The other connection is legal. The core activities of the library (namely lending, copying) are governed by the same copyright laws that govern authors and publishers. Libraries are one of the users in the copyright system, and their existence depends on the limitations of and exceptions to the exclusive rights of the rights holders. The space that has been carved out of copyright to enable the existence of libraries has been intensely contested in the era of postmodern copyright (Samuelson, 2002) and digital technologies. This heavy legal and structural interdependence with the market means that libraries have only a limited control over their own fate in the digital domain.

Book pirates compete with some of the core services of libraries. And as is usually the case with innovation that has no economic or legal constraints, pirate libraries offer, at least for the moment, significantly better services than most of the libraries. Pirate libraries offer far more electronic books, with far fewer restrictions and constraints, to far more people, far cheaper than anyone else in the library domain. Libraries are thus directly affected by pirate libraries, and because of their structural interdependence with book markets, they also have to adjust to how the commercial intermediaries react to book piracy. Under such conditions libraries cannot simply \ rely on their legacy for their survival. Book piracy must be taken seriously, not just as a threat, but also as an opportunity to learn how shadow libraries operate and interact with their users. Pirate libraries are the products of readers (and sometimes authors), academics and laypeople, all sharing a deep passion for the book, operating in a zone where there is little to no obstacle to the development of the 'ideal' library. As such, pirate libraries can teach important lessons on what is expected of a library, how book consumption habits evolve, and how knowledge flows around the globe.

Pirate Libraries in the Digital Age

The collection of texts in digital formats was one of the first activities that computers enabled: the text file is the native medium of the computer, it is small, thus it is easy to store and copy. It is also very easy to create, and as so many projects have since proved, there are more than enough volunteers who are willing to type whole books into the machine. No wonder that electronic libraries and digital text repositories were among the first 'mainstream' application of computers. Combing through large stacks of matrix-printer printouts of sci-fi classics downloaded from gopher servers is a shared experience of anyone who had access to computers and the internet before it was known as the World Wide Web.

Computers thus added fresh momentum to the efforts of realising the age-old dream of the universal library (Battles, 2004). Digital technologies offered a breakthrough in many of the issues that previously posed serious obstacles to text collection: storage, search, preservation, access all became cheaper and easier than ever before. On the other hand, a number of key issues remained unresolved: digitisation was a slow and cumbersome process, while the screen proved to be too inconvenient, and the printer too costly an interface between the text file and the reader. Ultimately it were not these issues that put a break to the proliferation of digital libraries. Rather, it was the realisation that there are legal limits to the digitisation, storage and distribution of copyrighted works on the digital networks. That realisation soon rendered many text collections in the emerging digital library scene inaccessible.

Legal considerations did not destroy this chaotic, emergent digital librarianship and the collections the ad-hoc, accidental and professional librarians put together. The text collections were far too valuable to simply delete them from the servers. Instead, what happened to most of these collections was that they retreated from the public view, back into the access-controlled shadows of darknets. Yesterday's gophers and anonymous ftp servers turned into closed, membership only ftp servers, local shared libraries residing on the intranets of various academic, business institutions and private archives stored on local hard drives. The early digital libraries turned into book piracy sites and into the kernels of today's shadow libraries.

Libraries and other major actors, who decided to start large scale digitisation programmes soon found out that if they wanted to avoid costly lawsuits, then they had to limit their activities to work in the public domain. While the public domain is riddled with mind-bogglingly complex and unresolved legal issues, at least it is still significantly less complicated to deal with than copyrighted and orphan works. Legally more innovative (or as some would say, adventurous) companies, such as Google and Microsoft, who thought they had sufficient resources to sort out the legal issues, soon had to abandon their programmes or put them on hold until the legal issues were sorted out.

There were, however, a large group of disenfranchised readers, library patrons, authors and users who decided to ignore the legal problems and set out to build the best library that could possibly be built using digital technologies. Despite the increased awareness of rights holders to the issue of digital book piracy, more and more communities around text collections started to defy the legal constraints and to operate and use more or less public piratical shadow libraries.

Aleph[1]

Aleph[2] is a meta-library, and currently one of the biggest online piratical text collections on the internet. The project started on a Russian bulletin board

---

1   I have conducted extensive research on the origins of Aleph, on its catalogue and its users. The detailed findings, at the time of writing this contribution are being prepared for publication. The following section is a brief summary of those findings and is based upon two forthcoming book chapters on Aleph in a report, edited by Joe Karaganis, on the role of shadow libraries in the higher education systems of multiple countries.

2   Aleph is a pseudonym chosen to protect the identity of the shadow library in question.

devoted to piracy in around 2008 as an effort to integrate various free-floating text collections that circulated online, on optical media, on various public and private ftp servers and on hard drives. Its aim was to consolidate these separate text collections, many of which were created in various Russian academic institutions, into a single, unified catalogue, standardise the technical aspects, add and correct missing or incorrect metadata, and offer the resulting catalogue, computer code and the collection of files as an open infrastructure.

From Russia with Love

It is by no means a coincidence that Aleph was born in Russia. In post-Soviet Russia the unique constellation of several different factors created hospitable conditions for the digital librarianship movement that ultimately led to the development of Aleph. A rich literary legacy, the communist heritage, the pace with which various copying technologies penetrated the market, the shortcomings of the legal environment and the informal norms that stood in for the non-existent digital copyrights all contributed to the emergence of the biggest piratical library in the history of mankind.

Russia cherishes a rich literary tradition, which suffered and endured extreme economic hardships and political censorship during the Soviet period (Ermolaev, 1997; Friedberg, Watanabe, and Nakamoto, 1984; Stelmakh, 2001). The political transformation in the early 1990s liberated authors, publishers, librarians and readers from much of the political oppression, but it did not solve the economic issues that stood in the way of a healthy literary market. Disposable income was low, state subsidies were limited, the dire economic situation created uncertainty in the book market. The previous decades, however, have taught authors and readers how to overcome political and economic obstacles to access to books. During the Soviet times authors, editors and readers operated clandestine samizdat distribution networks, while informal book black markets, operating in semi-private spheres, made uncensored but hard-to-come-by books accessible (Stelmakh, 2001). This survivalist attitude and the skills that came with it became handy in the post-Soviet turmoil, and were directly transferable to the then emerging digital technologies.

Russia is not the only country with a significant informal media economy of books, but in most other places it was the photocopy machine that emerged to serve such grey/black book markets. In pre-1990 Russia and in other Eastern European countries the access to this technology was limited, and when photocopiers finally became available, computers were close behind them in terms of accessibility. The result of the parallel introduction of the photocopier and the computer was that the photocopy technology did not have time to lock in the informal market of texts. In many countries where the photocopy machine preceded the computer by decades, copy shops still capture the bulk of the informal production and distribution of textbooks and other learning material. In the Soviet-bloc PCs offered a less costly and more adaptive technology to copy and distribute texts.

Russian academic and research institutions were the first to have access to computers. They also had to deal with the frustrating lack of access to up-to-date and affordable western works to be used in education and research (Abramitzky and Sin, 2014). This may explain why the first batch of shadow libraries started in a number of academic/research institutions such as the Department of Mechanics and Mathematics (MexMat) at Moscow State University. The first digital librarians in Russia were mathematicians, computer scientists and physicists, working in those institutions.

As PCs and internet access slowly penetrated Russian society, an extremely lively digital librarianship movement emerged, mostly fuelled by enthusiastic readers, book fans and often authors, who spared no effort to make their favourite books available on FIDOnet, a popular BBS system in Russia. One of the central figures in these tumultuous years, when typed-in books appeared online by the thousands, was Maxim Moshkov, a computer scientist, alumnus of the MexMat, and an avid collector of literary works. His digital library, lib.ru was at first mostly a private collection of literary texts, but soon evolved into the number one text repository which everyone used to depose the latest digital copy on a newly digitised book (Мошков, 1999). Eventually the library grew so big that it had to be broken up. Today it only hosts the Russian literary classics. User generated texts, fan fiction and amateur production was spun off into the aptly named samizdat. lib.ru collection, low brow popular fiction, astrology and cheap romance found its way into separate collections, and so did the collection of academic/scientific books, which started an independent life under the name of Kolkhoz. Kolkhoz, which borrowed its name from the commons-based agricultural cooperative of the early Soviet era, was both a collection of scientific texts, and a community of amateur librarians, who curated, managed and expanded the collection.

Moshkov and his library introduced several important norms into the bottom-up, decentralised, often anarchic digital library movement that swept through the Russian internet in the late 1990s and early 2000s. First, lib.ru provided the technological blueprint for any future digital library. But more importantly, Moshkov's way of handling the texts, his way of responding to the claims, requests, questions, complaints of authors and publishers paved the way to the development of copynorms (Schultz, 2007) that continue to define the Russian digital library scene up to today. Moshkov was instrumental in the creation of an enabling environment for the digital librarianship while respecting the claims of authors, during times when the formal copyright framework and the enforcement environment were both unable and unwilling to protect works of authorship (Elst, 2005; Sezneva, 2012).

Guerilla Open Access

Around the time of the late 2000s when Aleph started to merge the Kolkhoz collection with other, free-floating text collections, two other notable events took place. In 2008 Aaron Swartz penned his Guerilla Open Access Manifesto (Swartz,

2008), in which he called for the liberation and sharing of scientific knowledge. Swartz forcefully argued that scientific knowledge, the production of which is mostly funded by the public and by the voluntary labour of academics, cannot be locked up behind corporate paywalls set up by publishers. He framed the unauthorised copying and transfer of scientific works from closed access text repositories to public archives as a moral act, and by doing so, he created an ideological framework which was more radical and promised to be more effective than either the creative commons (Lessig, 2004) or the open access (Suber, 2013) movements that tried to address the access to knowledge issues in a more copyright friendly manner. During interviews, the administrators of Aleph used the very same arguments to justify the raison d'être of their piratical library. While it seems that Aleph is the practical realisation of Swartz's ideas, it is hard to tell which served as an inspiration for the other.

It was also at around the same time when another piratical library, gigapedia/ library.nu started its operation, focusing mostly on making English language freely available scientific works (Liang, 2012). Until its legal troubles and subsequent shutdown in 2012, gigapedia/library.nu was the biggest English language piratical scientific library on the internet, amassing several hundred thousand books, including high-quality proofs ready to print and low resolution scans possibly prepared by a student or a lecturer. During 2012 the mostly Russian-language and natural sciences focused Aleph absorbed the English language, social sciences rich gigapedia/library.nu, and with the subsequent shutdown of gigapedia/library.nu Aleph became the centre of the scientific shadow library ecosystem and community.

Aleph by Numbers

By adding pre-existing text collections to its catalogue Aleph was able to grow at an astonishing rate. Aleph has added, on average, 17,500 books to its collection each month since 2009, and as a result, in April 2014 it had more than 1.15 million documents. Nearly two thirds of the collection is in English, one fifth of the documents is in Russian, while German works amount to the third largest group with 8.5 per cent of the collection. The rest of the major European languages, like French or Spanish have less than 15,000 works each in the collection.

More than 50 thousand publishers have works in the library, but most of the collection is published by mainstream Western academic publishers. Springer published more than 12 per cent of the works in the collection, followed by the Cambridge University Press, Wiley, Routledge and Oxford University Press, each having more than 9,000 works in the collection.

Most of the collection is relatively recent, more than 70 per cent of the collection being published in 1990 or after. Despite the recentness of the collection, the electronic availability of the titles in the collection is limited. While around 80 per cent of the books that had an ISBN registered in the catalogue[3] were available in print either as a new copy or a second hand one, only about one third of the titles were available in e-book formats. The mean price of the titles still in print was 62 USD according to the data gathered from Amazon.com.

The number of works accessed through Aleph is as impressive as its catalogue. In the three months between March and June, 2012, on average 24,000 documents were downloaded every day from one of its half-a-dozen mirrors.[4] This means that the number of documents downloaded daily from Aleph is probably in the 50,000 to 100,000 range. The library users come from more than 150 different countries. The biggest users in terms of volume were the Russian Federation, Indonesia, USA, India, Iran, Egypt, China, Germany and the UK. Meanwhile, many of the highest per-capita users are Central and Eastern European countries.

What Aleph Is and What it is Not

Aleph is an example of the library in the post-scarcity age. It is founded on the idea that books should no longer be a scarce resource. Aleph set out to remove both sources of scarcity: the natural source of scarcity in physical copies is overcome through distributed digitisation; the artificial source of scarcity created by copyright protection is overcome through infringement. The liberation from both constraints is necessary to create a truly scarcity free environment and to release the potential of the library in the post-scarcity age.

Aleph is also an ongoing demonstration of the fact that under the condition of non-scarcity, the library can be a decentralised, distributed, commons-based institution, created and maintained through peer production (Benkler, 2006). Aleph's message is clear: users left to their own devices can produce a library by themselves for themselves. In fact, users are the library. And when everyone has the means to digitise, collect, catalogue and share his/her own library, then the library suddenly is everywhere. Small individual and institutional collections are aggregated into Aleph, which, in turn, is constantly fragmented into smaller, local, individual collections as users download works from the collection. The library is breathing (Battles, 2004) books in and out, but for the first time, this circulation of books is not a zero sum game, but a cumulative one: with every cycle the collection grows.

On the other hand Aleph may have lots of books on offer, but it is clear that it is neither universal in its scope, nor does it fulfil all the critical functions of a library. Most importantly Aleph is disembedded from the local contexts and communities

---

3   Market availability data is only available for that 40 per cent of books in the Aleph catalogue that had an ISBN on file. The titles without a valid ISBN tend to be older, Russian language titles, in general with low expected print and e-book availability.

4   Download data is based on the logs provided by one of the shadow library services which offers the books in Aleph's catalogue as well as other works also free and without any restraints or limitations.

that usually define the focus of the library. While it relies on the availability of local digital collections for its growth, it has no means to play an active role in its own development. The guardians of Aleph can prevent books from entering the collection, but they cannot pay, ask or force anyone to provide a title if it is missing. Aleph is reliant on the weak copy-protection technologies of official e-text repositories and the goodwill of individual document submitters when it comes to the expansion of the collection. This means that the Aleph collection is both fragmented and biased, and it lacks the necessary safeguards to ensure that it stays either current or relevant.

Aleph, with all its strengths and weaknesses carries an important lesson for the discussions on the future of libraries. In the next section I'll try to situate these lessons in the wider context of the library in the post-scarcity age.

The Future of the Library

There is hardly a week without a blog post, a conference, a workshop or an academic paper discussing the future of libraries. While existing libraries are buzzing with activity, librarians are well aware that they need to redefine themselves and their institutions, as the book collections around which libraries were organised slowly go the way the catalogue has gone: into the digital realm. It would be impossible to give a faithful summary of all the discussions on the future of libraries in such a short contribution. There are, however, a few threads, to which the story of Aleph may contribute.

Competition

It is very rare to find the two words, libraries and competition, in the same sentence. No wonder: libraries enjoyed a near perfect monopoly in their field of activity. Though there may have been many different local initiatives that provided free access to books, as a specialised institution to do so, the library was unmatched and unchallenged. This monopoly position has been lost in a remarkably short period of time due to the internet and the rapid innovations in the legal e-book distribution markets. Textbooks can be rented, e-books can be lent, a number of new start-ups and major sellers offer flat rate access to huge collections. Expertise that helps navigate the domains of knowledge is abundant, there are multiple authoritative sources of information and meta-information online. The search box of the library catalogue is only one, and not even the most usable, of all the different search boxes one can type a query into.[5] Meanwhile, there are plenty of

---

5   ArXiv, SSRN, RePEc, PubMed Central, Google Scholar, Google Books, Amazon, Mendeley, Citavi, ResearchGate, Goodreads, LibraryThing, Wikipedia, Yahoo Answers, Khan Academy, specialised Twitter and other social media accounts are just a few of the available discovery services.

physical spaces which offer good coffee, an electrical socket, comfortable chairs and low levels of noise to meet, read and study, from local cafes via hacker- and makerspaces, to co-working offices. Many library competitors have access to resources (human, financial, technological and legal) way beyond the possibilities of even the richest libraries. In addition, publishers control the copyrights in digital copies which, absent of well fortified statutory limitations and exceptions, prevent libraries keeping up with the changes in user habits and with the competing commercial services.

Libraries definitely feel the pressure: '*Libraries' offers of materials ... compete with many other offers that aim to attract the attention of the public. ... It is no longer enough just to make a good collection available to the public*'. (Committee on the Public Libraries in the Knowledge Society, 2010) As a response, libraries have developed different strategies to cope with this challenge. The common thread in the various strategy documents is that they try to redefine the library as a node in the vast network of institutions that provide knowledge, enable learning, facilitate cooperation and initiate dialogues. Some of the strategic plans redefine the library space as an '*independent medium to be developed*' (Committee on the Public Libraries in the Knowledge Society, 2010), and advise libraries to transform themselves into culture and community centres which establish partnerships with citizens, communities and with other public and private institutions. Some librarians propose even more radical ways of keeping the library relevant by, for example, advocating more opening hours without staff and hosting more user-governed activities.

In the research library sphere, the Commission on the Future of the Library, a task force set up by the University of California Berkeley defined the values the university research library will add in the digital age as '*1) Human expertise; 2) Enabling infrastructure; and 3) Preservation and dissemination of knowledge for future generations*' (Commission on the Future of the Library, 2013). This approach is one of the more conservative ones, still relying on the hope that libraries can offer something unique that no one else is able to provide. Others, working at the Association of Research Libraries are more like their public library counterparts, defining the future role of the research libraries as a '*convener of "conversations" for knowledge construction, an inspiring host; a boundless symposium; an incubator; a 3rd space both physically and virtually; a scaffold for independence of mind; and a sanctuary for freedom of expression, a global entrepreneurial engine*' (Pendleton-Jullian et al., 2014), in other words, as another important, but in no way unique node in the wider network of institutions that create and distribute knowledge.

Despite the differences in priorities, all these recommendations carry the same basic message: the unique position of libraries in the centre of a book-based knowledge economy, on the top of the paper-bound knowledge hierarchy is about to be lost. As libraries are losing their monopoly of giving low cost, low restriction access to books which are scarce by nature, they are losing their privileged and powerful position as the guardians of and guides to the knowledge stored in the stacks. If they want to survive, they need to find their role and position in a network of institutions, where everyone else is engaged in activities that overlap with the historic functions of the library. Just like the books themselves, the power that came from the privileged access to books is in part dispersed among the countless nodes in the knowledge and learning networks, and in part is being captured by those who control the digital rights to digitise and distribute books in the digital era.

Libraries are trying to redefine themselves as providers of ancillary services is because the lack of digital lending rights prevents them from competing on their own traditional home turf – in giving free access to knowledge. The traditional legal limitations and exceptions to copyright that enabled libraries to fulfil their role in the analogue world do not apply in the digital realm. In the European Union, the Infosoc Directive (Directive 2001/29/EC on the harmonisation of certain aspects of copyright and related rights in the information society, 2001) allows for libraries to create digital copies for preservation, indexing and similar purposes and allows for the display of digital copies on their premises for research and personal study (Triaille et al., 2013). While in theory these rights provide for the core library services in the digital domain, their practical usefulness is rather limited, as off-premises e-lending of copyrighted works is in most cases[6] only possible through individual license agreements with publishers.

Under such circumstances libraries complain that they cannot fulfil their public interest mission in the digital era. What libraries are allowed to do under current limitations and exceptions is seen as inadequate for what is expected of them. But doing more requires them securing the appropriate e-lending licenses from rights holders. In many cases, however, libraries simply cannot license digitally for e-lending. In those cases when licensing is possible, they see transaction costs as prohibitively high; they feel that their bargaining positions vis-à-vis rights holders is unbalanced; they do not see that the license terms are adapted to libraries' policies, and they fear that the licenses provide publishers with excessive and undue influence over libraries (Report on the responses to the Public Consultation on the Review of the EU Copyright Rules, 2013).

What is more, libraries face substantial legal uncertainties even where there are reasonably well-defined digital library exceptions. In the EU, questions such as whether the analogue lending rights of libraries extend to e-books, whether an exhaustion of the distribution right is necessary to enjoy the lending exception, and whether licensing an e-book would exhaust the distribution right are under consideration by the Court of Justice of the European Union in a Dutch case (Rosati, 2014b). And while in another case (Case C-117/13 *Technische Universität*

---

6 The notable exception being orphan works which are presumed to be still copyrighted, but without an identifiable rights owner. In the EU, the Directive 2012/28/EU on certain permitted uses of orphan works in theory eases access to such works, but in practice its practical impact is limited by the many constraints among its provisions. Lacking any orphan works legislation and with the Google Book Settlement still in limbo, the US is even farther from making orphan works generally accessible to the public.

Darmstadt v Eugen Ulmer KG) the CJEU reaffirmed the rights of European libraries to digitise books in their collection if that is necessary to give access to them in digital formats on their premises, it also created new uncertainties by stating that libraries may not digitise their entire collections (Rosati, 2014a).

US libraries face a similar situation, both in terms of the narrowly defined exceptions in which libraries can operate, and the huge uncertainty regarding the limits of fair use in the digital library context. US rights holders challenged both Google's (*Authors Guild v Google*) and the libraries (*Authors Guild v HathiTrust*) rights to digitise copyrighted works. While there seems to be a consensus of courts that the mass digitisation conducted by these institutions was fair use (Diaz, 2013; Rosati, 2014c; Samuelson, 2014), the accessibility of the scanned works is still heavily limited, subject to licenses from publishers, the existence of print copies at the library and the institutional membership held by prospective readers. While in the highly competitive US e-book market many commercial intermediaries offer e-lending licenses to e-book catalogues of various sizes, these arrangements also carry the danger of a commercial lock-in of the access to digital works, and render libraries dependent upon the services of commercial providers who may or may not be the best defenders of public interest (OECD, 2012).

Shadow libraries like Aleph are called into existence by the vacuum that was left behind by the collapse of libraries in the digital sphere and by the inability of the commercial arrangements to provide adequate substitute services. Shadow libraries are pooling distributed resources and expertise over the internet, and use the lack of legal or technological barriers to innovation in the informal sphere to fill the void left behind by libraries.

What Can Aleph Teach us About the Future of Libraries?

The story of Aleph offers two closely interrelated considerations for the debate on the future of libraries: a legal and an organisational one. Aleph operates beyond the limits of legality, as almost all of its activities are copyright infringing, including the unauthorised digitisation of books, the unauthorised mass downloads from e-text repositories, the unauthorised acts of uploading books to the archive, the unauthorised distribution of books, and, in most countries, the unauthorised act of users' downloading books from the archive. In the debates around copyright infringement, illegality is usually interpreted as a necessary condition to access works for free. While this is undoubtedly true, the fact that Aleph provides no-cost access to books seems to be less important than the fact that it provides an access to them in the first place.

Aleph is a clear indicator of the volume of the demand for current books in digital formats in developed and in developing countries. The legal digital availability, or rather, unavailability of its catalogue also demonstrates the limits of the current commercial and library-based arrangements that aim to provide low cost access to books over the internet. As mentioned earlier, Aleph's catalogue is mostly of recent books, meaning that 80 per cent of the titles with a valid ISBN are still in print and available as a new or used print copy through commercial retailers. It is also clear, is that around 66 per cent of these books are yet to be made available in electronic format. While publishers, in theory have a strong incentive to make their most recent titles available as e-books, they lag behind in doing so.

This might explain why one third of all the e-book downloads in Aleph are from highly developed Western countries, and two third of these downloads are of books without a Kindle version. Having access to print copies either through libraries or through commercial retailers is simply not enough anymore. Developing countries are a slightly different case. There, compared to developed countries, twice as many of the downloads (17 per cent compared to 8 per cent in developed countries) are of titles that aren't available in print at all. Not having access to books in print seems to be a more pressing problem for developing countries than not having access to electronic copies. Aleph thus fulfils at least two distinct types of demand: in developed countries it provides access to missing electronic versions, in developing countries it provides access to missing print copies.

The ability to fulfil an otherwise unfulfilled demand is not the only function of illegality. Copyright infringement in the case of Aleph has a much more important role: it enables the peer production of the library. Aleph is an open source library. This means that every resource it uses and every resource it creates is freely accessible to anyone for use without any further restrictions. This includes the server code, the database, the catalogue and the collection. The open source nature of Aleph rests on the ideological claim that the scientific knowledge produced by humanity, mostly through public funds, should be open for anyone to access without any restrictions. Everything else in and around Aleph stems from this claim, as they replicate the open access logic in all other aspects of Aleph's operation. Aleph uses the peer produced Open Library to fetch book metadata, it uses the BitTorrent and ED2K P2P networks to store and make books accessible, it uses Linux and MySQL to run its code, and it allows its users to upload books and edit book metadata. As a consequence of its open source nature, anyone can contribute to the project, and everyone can enjoy its benefits.

It is hard to quantify the impact of this piratical open access library on education, science and research in various local contexts where Aleph is the prime source of otherwise inaccessible books. But it is relatively easy to measure the consequences of openness at the level of Aleph, the library. The Aleph collection was created mostly by those individuals and communities who decided to digitise books by themselves for their own use. While any single individual is only capable of digitising a few books at the maximum, the small contributions quickly add up. To digitise the 1.15 million documents in the Aleph collection would require an investment of several hundred million Euros, and a substantial subsequent investment in storage, collection management and access provision (Poole, 2010). Compared to these figures the costs associated with running Aleph are infinitesimal, as it survives on the volunteer labour of a few individuals, and annual donations in the total value of a few thousand dollars. The hundreds of thousands who use Aleph on a more or less regular basis have an immense amount of resources, and by disregarding the copyright laws Aleph is able to tap into those resources and use them for the development of the library. The value of these resources and of the peer produced library is the difference between the actual costs associated with Aleph, and the investment that would be required to create something remotely similar.

The decentralised, collaborative mass digitisation and making available of current, thus most relevant, scientific works is only possible through massive copyright infringement at the moment. It is debatable whether the copyrighted corpus of scientific works should be completely open, and whether the blatant disregard of copyright through which Aleph achieved this openness is the right path towards a more openly accessible body of scientific knowledge. It is also yet to be measured what effects shadow libraries may have on the commercial intermediaries and on the health of scientific publishing and science in general. But Aleph, in any case, is a case study in the potential benefits of open sourcing the library.

Conclusion

If we take Aleph as an expression of what users around the globe want from a library, then the answer is that there is a strong need for a universally accessible collection of current, relevant (scientific) books in restriction-free electronic formats. Can we expect any single library to provide anything even remotely similar in the foreseeable future? Does such a service have a place in the future of libraries? It is as hard to imagine the future library with such a service as without.

While the legal and financial obstacles to the creation of a scientific library with as universal a reach as Aleph may be difficult to overcome, other aspects of it may be more easily replicable. The way Aleph operates demonstrates the amount of material and non-material resources users are willing to contribute to build a library that responds to their needs and expectations. If libraries plan to only 'host' user-governed activities, it means that the library is still imagined to be a separate entity from its users. Aleph teaches us that this separation can be overcome and users can constitute a library. But for that, they need opportunities to participate in the production of the library: they need the right to digitise books and copy digital books to and from the library, they need the opportunity to participate in the cataloguing and collection building process, they need the opportunity to curate and programme the collection. In other words, users need the opportunity to be librarians in the library if they wish to do consequently, and so libraries need to be able to provide access not just to the collection but to their core functions as well. The walls that separate librarians from library patrons, private and public collections, insiders and outsiders can all prevent the peer production of the library, and through that, prevent the future that is the closest to what library users think of as ideal.

References

Abramitzky, R. and Sin, I. (2014). *Book Translations as Idea Flows: The Effects of the Collapse of Communism on the Diffusion of Knowledge* (No. w20023). http://papers.ssrn.com/abstract=2421123

Battles, M. (2004). *Library: An Unquiet History.* WW Norton & Company.

Benkler, Y. (2006). *The Wealth of Networks : How Social Production Transforms Markets and Freedom.* New Haven: Yale University Press.

Bently, L., Davis, J. and Ginsburg, J.C. (eds) (2010). *Copyright and Piracy. An Interdisciplinary Critique.* Cambridge University Press.

Bodó, B. (2011a). *A szerzői jog kalózai.* Budapest: Typotex.

Bodó, B. (2011b). 'Coda: A Short History of Book Piracy', in J. Karaganis (ed.), *Media Piracy in Emerging Economies.* New York: Social Science Research Council.

Bodó, B. (2015). 'Piracy vs Privacy – the Analysis of Piratebrowser', *IJOC* 9, 21.

Commission on the Future of the Library (2013). Report of the Commission on the Future of the UC Berkeley Library. Berkeley: UC Berkeley.

Committee on the Public Libraries in the Knowledge Society (2010). *The Public Libraries in the Knowledge Society.* Copenhagen: Kulturstyrelsen.

Darnton, R. (1982). *The Literary Underground of the Old Regime.* Cambridge, Mass: Harvard University Press.

Darnton, R. (2003). 'The Science of Piracy: A Crucial Ingredient in Eighteenth-Century Publishing', *Studies on Voltaire and the Eighteenth Century* 12, 3–29.

Diaz, A.S. (2013). 'Fair Use & Mass Digitization: The Future of Copy-Dependent Technologies after Authors Guild v. Hathitrust', *Berkeley Technology Law Journal* 23.

Directive 2001/29/EC on the Harmonisation of Certain Aspects of Copyright and Related Rights in the Information Society. (2001). *Official Journal L* 167, 10–19.

Elst, M. (2005). *Copyright, Freedom of Speech, and Cultural Policy in the Russian Federation.* Leiden/Boston: Martinus Nijhoff.

Ermolaev, H. (1997). *Censorship in Soviet Literature: 1917–1991.* Rowman and Littlefield.

Friedberg, M., Watanabe, M. and Nakamoto, N. (1984). 'The Soviet Book Market: Supply and Demand', *Acta Slavica Iaponica* 2, 177–92.

Giblin, R. (2011). *Code Wars: 10 Years of P2P Software Litigation.* Cheltenham, UK ; Northampton, MA: Edward Elgar Publishing.

Johns, A. (2010). *Piracy: The Intellectual Property Wars from Gutenberg to Gates.* University Of Chicago Press.

Judge, C.B. (1934). *Elizabethan Book-Pirates.* Cambridge: Harvard University Press.

Khan, B.Z. (2004). *Does Copyright Piracy Pay? The Effects of U.S. International Copyright Laws on the Market for Books, 1790–1920.* Cambridge, MA: National Bureau Of Economic Research.

Khan, B.Z. and Sokoloff, K.L. (2001). 'The Early Development of Intellectual Property Institutions in the United States', *Journal of Economic Perspectives* 15(3), 233–46.

Landes, W.M., and Posner, R.A. (2003). *The Economic Structure of Intellectual Property Law*. Cambridge, Mass.: Harvard University Press.

Lessig, L. (2004). *Free Culture : How Big Media Uses Technology and the Law to Lock Down Culture and Control Creativity*. New York: Penguin Press.

Liang, L. (2012). Shadow Libraries. *e-flux*. http://www.e-flux.com/journal/shadow-libraries/

OECD (2012). 'E-books: Developments and Policy Considerations'. OECD Digital Economy Papers, 208.

Patry, W.F. (2009). *Moral Panics and the Copyright Wars*. New York: Oxford University Press.

Patterson, L.R. (1968). *Copyright in Historical Perspective* (p. vii, 264 p.). Nashville: Vanderbilt University Press.

Pendleton-Jullian, A., Lougee, W.P., Wilkin, J. and Hilton, J. (2014). Strategic Thinking and Design – Research Library in 2033 – Vision and System of Action – Part One. Colombus, OH: Association of Research Libraries. http://www.arl.org/about/arl-strategic-thinking-and-design/arl-membership-refines-strategic-thinking-and-design-at-spring-2014-meeting

Pollard, A.W. (1916). 'The Regulation of the Book Trade in the Sixteenth Century', *Library, s3-VII* 25, 18–43.

Pollard, A.W. (1920). *Shakespeare's Fight with the Pirates and the Problems of the Transmission of his Text*. Cambridge, UK: The University Press.

Poole, N. (2010). The Cost of Digitising Europe's Cultural Heritage – A Report for the Comité des Sages of the European Commission. http://nickpoole.org.uk/wp-content/uploads/2011/12/digiti_report.pdf

Report on the responses to the Public Consultation on the Review of the EU Copyright Rules. (2013). European Commission, Directorate General for Internal Market and Services.

Rosati, E. (2014a). 'Copyright Exceptions and User Rights in Case C-117/13 Ulmer: A Couple of Observations', *IPKat*. http://ipkitten.blogspot.co.uk/2014/09/copyright-exceptions-and-user-rights-in.html

Rosati, E. (2014b). 'Dutch Court Refers Questions to CJEU on E-lending and Digital Exhaustion, and Another Dutch Reference on Digital Resale may be just about to Follow', *IPKat*. http://ipkitten.blogspot.co.uk/2014/09/dutch-court-refers-questions-to-cjeu-on.html

Rosati, E. (2014c). 'Google Books' Library Project is Fair Use', *Journal of Intellectual Property Law & Practice* 9: 2, 104–6.

Rose, M. (1993). *Authors and Owners : The Invention of Copyright*. Cambridge, Mass: Harvard University Press.

Samuelson, P. (2002). 'Copyright and Freedom of Expression in Historical Perspective', *J. Intell. Prop. L.* 10, 319.

Samuelson, P. (2014). 'Mass Digitization as Fair Use', *Communications of the ACM* 57: 3, 20–22.

Schultz, M.F. (2007). 'Copynorms: Copyright Law and Social Norms', *Intellectual Property And Information Wealth v01* 1, 201.

Sezneva, O. (2012). 'The Pirates of Nevskii Prospekt: Intellectual Property, Piracy and Institutional Diffusion in Russia', *Poetics* 40: 2, 150–66.

Solly, E. (1885). 'Henry Hills, the Pirate Printer', *Antiquary* xi, 151–4.

Stelmakh, V.D. (2001). 'Reading in the Context of Censorship in the Soviet Union', *Libraries & Culture* 36: 1, 143–51.

Suber, P. (2013). *Open Access* (Vol. 1). Cambridge, MA: The MIT Press. doi:10.1109/ ACCESS.2012.2226094

Swartz, A. (2008). Guerilla Open Access Manifesto. https://archive.org/stream/ GuerillaOpenAccessManifesto/Goamjuly2008_djvu.txt

Triaille, J.-P., Dusollier, S., Depreeuw, S., Hubin, J.-B., Coppens, F. and Francquen, A. de (2013). Study on the Application of Directive 2001/29/EC on Copyright and Related Rights in the Information Society (the 'Infosoc Directive'). European Union.

Wittmann, R. (2004). 'Highwaymen or Heroes of Enlightenment? Viennese and South German Pirates and the German Market', Paper presented at the History of Books and Intellectual History conference. Princeton University.

Yu, P.K. (2000). 'From Pirates to Partners: Protecting Intellectual Property in China in the Twenty-First Century', *American University Law* 50. http:// papers.ssrn.com/sol3/papers.cfm?abstract_id=245548

Мошков, М. (1999). 'Что вы все о копирайте. Лучше бы книжку почитали (Библиотеке копирайт не враг)', *Компьютерры* 300.

PART II
The Arts, Literature, Design and Copyright

Chapter 5

Arts Festivals as Cultural Heritage in a Copyright Saturated World

Fiona Macmillan

Cultural Heritage In and Out of International Law

While the concept of cultural heritage is arguably as old as recorded history,[1] it first became a recognised concept in international law at the time of the Vienna Treaty of 1815, which was imposed by the British victors after the conclusion of the Napoleonic wars. This treaty reflected the rise of a discourse that linked people, territory and cultural objects.[2] Such a discourse necessarily prompts questions about whom cultural heritage belongs to and, thus, carries with it debates about how history relates to, or is translated into, present day identity.[3] This invests the concept with a highly contingent political nature, which is reflected in the trajectory of modern international law governing this question. When, after the first and second world wars, the newly remade international legal order turned again to this question, it initially expressed the object of its concern as being 'cultural property'.[4] The return to the use of the expression 'cultural heritage' in international law instruments[5] and its widespread appearance in cultural and political discourse has not, however, produced any clear definition of this concept. One effect of this is that, while rights in relation to cultural heritage/property are

---

1   See, e.g., M.M. Miles (2008). *Art as Plunder: The Ancient Origins of Debate About Cultural Property*. New York: Cambridge University Press.

2   A.F. Vrdoljak (2008). *International Law, Museums and the Return of Cultural Objects*. Cambridge: Cambridge University Press, 13, citing W.G. Grewe (2000). *The Epochs of International Law* (trans and rev M Byers), Berlin, xviii.

3   See, e.g., T. Flessas (2003). 'Cultural Property Defined, and Redefined as Nietzschean Aphorism', *Cardozo Law Review* 24, 1067–97; R. Handler (1991). 'Who Owns the Past? History, Cultural Property and the Logic of Possessive Individualism', in B. Williams (ed.), *The Politics of Culture*. Washington: Smithsonian Institution Press.

4   UNESCO Convention on the Protection of Cultural Property in the Event of Armed Conflict (Hague Convention), 1954; UNESCO Convention on the Means of Prohibiting and Preventing the Illicit, Import, Export and Transfer of Ownership of Cultural Property 1970.

5   UNESCO Convention Concerning the Protection of the World Cultural and Natural Heritage 1972; UNESCO Convention on the Protection of the Underwater Cultural Heritage 2001; UNESCO Convention for the Safeguarding of Intangible Cultural Heritage 2003.

weakly protected in law, the concept of cultural heritage is a rhetorical moving feast that enjoys potency in cultural and political discourse.[6]

Attempts to define cultural heritage have a tendency to focus on an open-ended account of the objects of protection rather than the concept itself. Thus, for example, in the recent European Union *Heritage Plus* funding call, the first footnote observes that:

> Cultural heritage exists in tangible, intangible and digital forms. Tangible heritage includes artefacts (for example, objects, paintings, archaeological finds etc.), buildings, structures, landscapes, cities, and towns including industrial, underwater and archaeological sites. It includes their location, relationship to the natural environment and the materials from which all these are made, from prehistoric rock to cutting edge plastics and electronic products. Intangible heritage includes the practices, representations, expressions, memories, knowledge and skills that communities, groups and individuals construct, use and transmit from generation to generation. Digital heritage includes texts, databases, still and moving images, audio, graphics, software and web pages. Some of this digital heritage is created from the scanning or converting of physical objects that already exist and some is created digitally, or 'born digital'.[7]

Since it is seems reasonably clear that not every instantiation of the contents of this list would be regarded as cultural heritage, there is a need for some overarching concept of cultural heritage that provides some basis for distinguishing between, for example, buildings and structures that constitute cultural heritage and those that do not. Strangely, such an overarching concept is difficult to pin down. Perhaps this is because we all think we know what we are talking about when we talk about cultural heritage. In order to give scope to our general sense that we know what we are talking about, this chapter proposes to use an overarching concept of cultural heritage as being those things (moveable and immoveable, tangible and intangible) that a community or people considers worth handing on to the future.[8]

The task of reconciling this concept with legal notions of cultural heritage derived from international law instruments needs to be undertaken with an eye on the fact that there is an obvious political element in identifying what is considered to be worth handing on to the future[9] and this carries with it a degree of malleability and slipperiness. The sources of the legal concept of cultural heritage are the

---

6   F. Macmillan (2013). 'The Protection of Cultural Heritage: Common Heritage of Humankind, National Cultural "Patrimony" or Private Property?' *Northern Ireland Legal Quarterly* 64, 351–64.

7   *Cultural Heritage: A Challenge for Europe* (JPI Cultural Heritage and Global Change – Heritage Plus Call, 2014).

8   See J. Blake (2000). 'On Defining the Cultural Heritage', *International and Comparative Law Quarterly* 49, 61–85, at 68–9.

9   Blake, ibid., at 68.

various international law instruments that have been generated under the auspices of UNESCO, where the politically determined, malleable and slippery concept of cultural heritage has gradually emerged from the earlier concern with cultural property. In this century, the UNESCO regime's concern with tangible cultural heritage has given way to an increased focus on the intangible aspects of cultural heritage. In the festival context, where the cultural heritage aspects appear to be largely intangible, the two Conventions of particular importance are the Convention for the Safeguarding of Intangible Cultural Heritage and the Convention for the Protection and Promotion of the Diversity of Cultural Expressions.

According to Article 2.1 of the former Convention, 'intangible cultural heritage' means:

> ... the practices, representations, expressions, knowledge, skills – as well as the instruments, objects, artefacts and cultural spaces associated therewith – that communities, groups and, in some cases, individuals recognise as part of their cultural heritage. This intangible cultural heritage, transmitted from generation to generation, is constantly recreated by communities and groups in response to their environment, their interaction with nature and their history, and provides them with a sense of identity and continuity, thus promoting respect for cultural diversity and human creativity.

Article 2.2 provides:

> The 'intangible cultural heritage', as defined in paragraph 1 above, is manifested inter alia in the following domains:
>
> (a) oral traditions and expressions, including language as the vehicle of the intangible cultural heritage;
> (b) performing arts;
> (c) social practices, rituals and festive events;
> (d) knowledge and practices concerning nature and the universe;
> (e) traditional craftsmanship.

In the context of this definition there seems to be ample scope for an argument that arts festivals, or at least some arts festivals, fall within the concept of intangible cultural heritage. This is particularly the case given the strong identification that many (if not the overwhelming majority) of arts festivals have with a particular place.

The Cultural Diversity Convention employs the concept of cultural heritage in order to define the idea of cultural diversity with which it is concerned. Article 4.1 provides:

'Cultural diversity' refers to the manifold ways in which the cultures of groups
and societies find expression. These expressions are passed on within and among
groups and societies. Cultural diversity is made manifest not only through the
varied ways in which the cultural heritage of humanity is expressed, augmented
and transmitted through the variety of cultural expressions, but also through
diverse modes of artistic creation, production, dissemination, distribution and
enjoyment, whatever the means and technologies used.

According to Article 4.3, '"cultural expressions" are those expressions that result
from the creativity of individuals, groups and societies, and that have cultural
content', while Article 4.2 tells us that '"cultural content" refers to the symbolic
meaning, artistic dimension and cultural values that originate from or express
cultural identities'. There is, of course, some circularity in these definitions.[10]
Nevertheless, it seems reasonable to suggest that arts festivals may act as a
means of expressing, preserving and promoting cultural diversity. This is perhaps
particularly so when festivals operate as a means of reinforcing a particular
traditional culture or community identity, although it would not seem to be limited
to this case.

Arts Festivals as Cultural Heritage

Arts festivals are a pervasive, and flourishing, part of modern life. There is some
unsurprising evidence that the economic crisis has had a constraining effect on the
arts festival sector, but overall it appears to have withstood the worst effects of this
crisis. One of the reasons for this may be the wide range of interests and functions
served by arts festivals, many of which are clearly identifiable with the concept
of cultural heritage described in the preceding section. In order to understand
more precisely the cultural heritage functions served by arts festivals, and then to
analyse their relationship with the private property relations imposed by copyright,
it is necessary to put some flesh and bones on the concept of the arts festival. The
following discussion first focuses on what is meant by the term 'festival' and then
moves on to a more detailed assessment of the effects of the qualifier 'arts'. As this
discussion reveals, attempts to define the arts festival expose both its fundamental
relationship with cultural heritage and the extent to which that relationship is
permeated by the copyright system.

　　In the literature the concept of the 'festival' tends to be defined compositely in
both positive and negative terms. In other words, it is defined by both what it is and
what it is not. On the positive side of this coin, the overriding and perhaps most
general characterisation of the festival is that it is, in some sense, a suspension in

---

　　10　See F. Macmillan (2008). 'The UNESCO Convention as a New Incentive to Protect
Cultural Diversity', in H. Schneider and P. van den Bossche (eds), *Protection of Cultural
Diversity from a European and International Perspective*. Mortsel: Intersentia, 163–92.

time and space, during which life – or business – does not carry on as normal.[11] Developing this idea of the festival as a period of suspension, the festival has also been described by commentators as: a space of openness, de-territorialisation and exchange;[12] part of the 'public sphere';[13] a site of democratic debate and transnational identifications;[14] an 'interpretation of cosmopolitan community';[15] and, in the words of Jean Cocteau, an 'apolitical no-man's land'.[16] As all of these characterisations suggest, the idea of the festival is closely tied in to the notion of being in a particular community, or being together, in a distinct place in time and space. In his description of the Cannes Film Festival, Cocteau also described the festival as 'a microcosm of how the world would be if people could have direct contacts and speak the same language'.[17] Thus, Sassatelli citing Durkheim's work on festivals,[18] describes them as an 'intensification of the collective being' and, in Durkheim's words, a 'collective effervescence'.[19] Along similar lines, Vrettos conceives of festivals as a manifestation of the human need to gather, socialise and exchange ideas.[20] Developing this line of thought, O'Grady and Kill argue that in an age of digital and social media with its consequent personal isolation, the festival presents the chance to be with other people, and thus represents an opportunity for '[s]ociability, participation, togetherness and excitement'.[21]

---

11   See (amongst many possible citations for this proposition), e.g., A. Falassi (1987). 'Festival: Definition and Morphology', in A. Falassi (ed.), *Time Out of Time: Essays on the Festival*. Albuquerque: University of New Mexico Press, 1–10.

12   S. Nordmann (2009). 'A History of Cultural Festivals in Europe', in J. Segal and L. Giorgi (eds), *European Arts Festivals from a Historical Perspective*. EURO-FESTIVAL Project: European Arts Festivals and Public Culture, Deliverable 2.1, WP2 Main Report, July 2009; http://www.euro-festival.org/publications.html, 19–29, at 28.

13   L. Giorgi (2009). 'Between Tradition, Vision and Imagination: Literature(s) in Search of a Festival', in Segal and Giorgi (eds), n 12 *supra*, 30–52; M. Sassatelli (2008). 'Public Culture, Cosmopolitanism and Festivals', in M. Sassatelli (ed.), *European Public Culture & Aesthetic Cosmopolitanism*. EURO-FESTIVAL Project: European Arts Festivals and Public Culture, Deliverable 1.1, WP1 Main Report, October 2008; http://www.euro-festival.org/publications.html, 15–40.

14   Sassatelli, n 13 *supra*.

15   Sassatelli, n 13 *supra*, at 25.

16   Jean Cocteau quoted in J. Segal and C. Blumauer (2009). 'Cannes: A French International Festival', in Segal and Giorgi (eds), n 12 *supra*, 53–82, at 53.

17   Jean Cocteau quoted in Segal and Blumauer, n 16 *supra*, at 53.

18   E. Durkheim [1912](1954). *The Elementary Forms of Religious Life*. Glencoe: Free Press.

19   Sassatelli, n 13 *supra*, at 18–19.

20   A. Vrettos (2009). 'About the economic impacts studies of arts festivals', *Economia della cultura* 3, 341–50.

21   A. O'Grady and R. Kill (2011a). 'Exploring Festival Performance as a State of Encounter'. Unpublished paper, May 2011; (on file with author), at 2.

Building on the idea of the festivals as distinct[22] and sociable places in time and space, are conceptions of festivals that refer to their value as social, cultural, economic or political institutions and, thus, as expressing values associated with such institutions.[23] O'Grady and Kill write about the festival as a cultural artefact,[24] while Guerzoni refers to them as a way of filling 'il vuoto pneumatico della cultura televisiva'.[25] Values such as the promotion of cultural diversity,[26] internationalisation[27] or alternative social identities[28] frequently form part and parcel of the festival concept. Festivals may also be understood as a form of asserting identity 'in the face of a feeling of cultural dislocation brought about by rapid structural change, social mobility and globalisation processes'.[29] Other types of cultural values pave the way for understanding the festival as a type of socio-economic institution. For instance, festivals may play a role in legitimating new artistic forms or new genres within existing artistic forms.[30] At the same time, they function to commodify those new forms or genres.[31] Importantly, they may also offer an alternative avenue for distribution,[32] particularly in highly commodified

---

22   Albeit semi-permeable (Sassatelli, n 13 *supra*, at 22) and paradoxical (A. O'Grady and R. Kill (2011b). 'Environments for Encounter and the Processes of Organizing for Interactivity and Performative Participation within the Festival Space', Conference on *Visuals and Performativity: Researching Beyond Text*, Segovia, Spain, May 2011 (copy on file with author), at 3).

23   See also K. Turan (2002). *Sundance to Sarajevo: Film Festivals and the World They Made*. Los Angeles: University of California Press, who writes about three classes of festivals: *Festivals with Business Agendas*; *Festivals with Geopolitical Agendas*; and *Festivals with Aesthetic Agendas*.

24   O'Grady and Kill, n 21 *supra*, at 20.

25   'the pneumatic vacuum of television culture' (my translation), G. Guerzoni (2009) 'L'impatto economico dei festival: un'annosa prospettiva di ricerca', *Economia della cultura* 19.

26   J. Segal, 'Film Festivals', in Sassatelli (ed.), n 13 *supra*, 111–17, at 115 and 117.

27   L. Giorgi, 'Literature Festivals: Literature (Festivals) as a Subject of Sociological Inquiry in Search of Cosmopolitanism', in Sassatelli (ed), n 13 *supra*, 95–110, at 107; L. Mazdon (2006). 'The Cannes Film Festival as Transnational Space', *Post Script* 25:2, 19–30.

28   M. Santoro, J. Chalcraft and P. Magaudda, 'Music Festivals: An Interdisciplinary Literature Review', in Sassatelli (ed.), n 13 *supra*, 77–93, at 83.

29   D. Picard and M. Robinson (2006). *Festivals, Tourism and Social Change: Remaking Worlds*. Clevedon: Channel View Publications, at 2, quoted in Sassatelli, n 13 *supra*, at 26.

30   Santoro, Chalcraft and Magaudda, n 28 *supra*, at 82.

31   Santoro, Chalcraft and Magaudda, n 28 *supra*, at 83, where it is argued that this observation applies, in particular, to music festivals.

32   See Turan, n 23 *supra*, at 8.

cultural industries like the film industry, where one effect of commodification has been to suppress independent production and diversity.[33]

Festivals can be distinguished from the regular programming of concerts, theatre, film and so on that occur in concert halls, auditoriums, theatres, cinemas and other such venues on the basis that: first, these are not generally a single cultural event containing a series of connected events;[34] second, the concept of the arts festival seems to imply some degree of audience participation, which might be considered to be linked to the idea, asserted above, of the festival as a period of being in community in a physical sense;[35] third, and perhaps most significantly, regularly programmed arts events might be considered to be part of the ordinary course of life, precisely because they are regularly programmed in venues established for this purpose, and accordingly not occasions of suspension in time and space.

While some concept of what constitutes the 'arts' is clearly present in the foregoing discussion, a more detailed consideration of this question provides a clear link between the cultural heritage role of festivals and their operation within the copyright system. This is because one of the open questions pervading the relationship between copyright law and the 'arts' is that of constitution and authorisation. In other words: is it some generally accepted definition of what amounts to the 'arts' that constitutes and authorises the subject matter of copyright or, on the other hand, does copyright law constitute and authorise concepts of what are the 'arts'? In either case, it seems clear that there are recognised disciplines within the arts and, at the very least, copyright law has contributed to the compartmentalisation of these disciplines.

The historical association between the subject matter of copyright and the concept of the arts is somewhat ambiguous. There seems to be some general acceptance that copyright was born out of the device of printers' privileges, most probably originating in fifteenth-century Venice[36] and then subsequently adopted with local variations in a range of other European countries.[37] Under the Venetian system, which was designed to stimulate foreign trade rather than to engage in aesthetic debates about forms of creative output, the important distinction drawn between various possible forms of the arts was whether they were reproducible

---

33   See F. Macmillan (2002a). 'Copyright and Corporate Power', in R. Towse (ed), *Copyright and the Cultural Industries*. Edward Elgar Publishing, 99–118; and F. Macmillan (2002b). 'The Cruel ©: Copyright and Film', *European Intellectual Property Review* 483–92.

34   Falassi, n 11 *supra*, 2.

35   O'Grady and Kill, n 21 *supra* and n 22 *supra*.

36   See J. Stapleton (2002). *Art, Intellectual Property & the Knowledge Economy.* Doctoral Thesis, Goldsmiths College, University of London, http://www.jaimestapleton. net/download.html, ch 2.

37   See further E. Armstrong [1990](2002). *Before Copyright: The French Book Privilege System 1498–1526.* Cambridge: Cambridge University Press.

through the new(ish) technique of printing or not. Consequently, nothing in the law turned on the general distinction between, for example, written works and images. Considerations of local market stability and foreign trade value were paramount in obtaining a printing privilege.[38] In this sense, the origins of the intellectual property system lie in market regulation and not in a particular aesthetic theory. Nevertheless, there is some evidence that in framing their arguments for privileges the petitioners came to reflect the predominant discourse or paradigm of creativity, which was based on theories of rhetoric. The rhetorical paradigm of creativity, which continues to retain considerable purchase in some quarters, focused upon the labour or creativity of the artist in gathering together and arranging 'ideas' into a particular and distinctive end product.[39]

Despite the tortuous and twisting path from the Venetian system to the modern systems of copyright protection, this early history resonates through modern copyright protection of the 'arts' in a number of ways. In particular, the fact that creativity is protected under copyright law only where its product falls within one of the categories of 'copyright work' has various implications for the relationship between copyright and the creative arts, two of which might be usefully emphasised in the present context. First, to the extent that any concept holds the list of copyright protected works together, however loosely, it is one derived from the rhetorical discourse of the Renaissance period. In the hands of modern copyright law, this is reduced to a focus on the production of the discrete 'work' by a recognisable creator (or creators). Secondly, while copyright recognises that more than one of its protected subject matters can exist simultaneously in one creative work, there is no evidence that it applies to hybrid works that cross the boundaries between the different categories of protected works. In this way, copyright law, and its pervasive influence on the concept of the arts, tends to harden the divisions between different types of creative works.

Overall, it might be said that while, at certain points in its history, copyright law reacted to developments in the creative arts by drawing them into its scheme of protection,[40] it seems that this scheme of protection has now become relatively rigid. One of the results of this is that there is relatively little space for the copyright protection of innovation in form in the arts. Another important result is that it increasingly appears that copyright law defines, controls or affects the meaning of 'arts' in the broader social and cultural spheres. This very effect is evident in the

---

38   Stapleton, n 36 *supra*.

39   Between the Medieval and the Renaissance periods an important alteration had taken place in relation to the origins of the 'ideas', which resulted in an emphasis on the creator's contribution to the ensuing artistic work: Stapleton, n 36 *supra*, 70–71, citing E. Panofsky (1968). *Idea: A Concept in Art Theory* (trans J.J.S. Peake), London: Harper & Row, 35–40 and 51; and U. Eco (1986). *Art & Beauty in the Middle Ages*. London: Yale University Press.

40   L. Bently and B. Sherman (2009). *Intellectual Property Law*. Oxford and New York: Oxford University Press, 3rd edn, 33–4.

way in which many arts festivals brand themselves as being literary festivals, film festivals, music festivals, theatre festivals, dance festivals and so on.

Copyright and Arts Festivals

The role of copyright in defining what constitutes the arts, and the way in which this impacts on how we understand arts festivals, constitutes the foundation upon which copyright interests have saturated the arts festival environment. In fact, a great deal of what happens in the course of the arts festival as event seems to have copyright implications of one type or another. The following discussion seeks to illustrate this in relation to various types of arts festivals, including film festivals, music festivals and what are described, generically, as culture festivals.

As far as film festivals are concerned, the copyright interests in the films that are shown arise at the time of the making of the film and, depending on the jurisdiction, usually belong either solely to the producer or jointly to the producer and director. There are other creative contributions to films that are recognised by copyright law, such as the copyright in the screenplay and in the sound track, but almost invariably these copyright interests are acquired by the copyright owner of the film. At film festivals, the more interesting copyright questions are posed by the 'live' events, such as interviews, workshops and other public encounters with directors and actors, which, while being apparently supplementary to the main event of showing the films are, in reality, what makes the festival as event distinct from daily life. As with all live and unscripted events, there is a question about whether the event has satisfied the copyright requirement of fixation in a material form.[41] Slightly strangely (at least to anyone who is not a copyright lawyer), a recording of the event, whether it is authorised or unauthorised,[42] has the effect of achieving fixation in a material form and conferring copyright on the participants – usually, in the context of film festivals, in their words. Authorised recorders, such as the festival organisers, acquire, subject to the terms of the authorisation, a copyright in the recording that they have made.

Despite the high degree of commodification of the relevant cultural product that prevails in both the film and music industries,[43] the copyright aspects of music festivals are different to those of film festivals because music festivals are (usually, if not always) primarily concerned with live musical performances. This adds certain complications to the copyright picture, which means that it is necessary to consider a number of different situations in which music is performed at a festival. From a copyright point of view, the simplest of these situations is where the music performed is no longer protected by copyright, as is generally the case at early music festivals. Recordings of such music, the copyright in which resides in the

---

41 See, e.g., UK Copyright Designs and Patents Act 1988 (CDPA), s 3(2).
42 See, e.g., CDPA, s 3(3).
43 See n 33 *supra*.

producer of the recording, may be available to purchase at the festival. While this type of marketing is part of the festival environment it is not clear that it should be regarded as forming part of the network of copyright relations at the festival itself since it is based on creative relations occurring prior to the festival and has no necessary relationship with the creative relations taking place at the festival as event.

On the other hand, the copyright interests that are clearly implicated in the music festival environment relate to the performances occurring during the festival as event where the works performed are subject to copyright protection. Where the copyright in the music and, in the case of songs, the literary works comprised in the lyrics, belongs to the festival performers, as often might be the case in rock music festivals, then the copyright situation is relatively straightforward. The interesting questions in this situation relate to variations from the original copyright work made in the course of the festival performance, and to recordings of the performances. Variations in the course of the performance will be protected by copyright where they are reduced to material form. The obvious way of achieving such a reduction to material form is through recording, either authorised or unauthorised. As anyone who has ever spent any time on YouTube knows, the Internet is swamped by unauthorised recordings of performances, usually made on mobile phones. While making such recordings and disseminating them on the Internet is a breach of copyright (and, in some jurisdictions, may also be a breach of performers' rights),[44] they do have the advantage of reducing a live performance to material form and thus satisfying this requirement for establishing the subsistence of the copyright interest. As in relation to any other performance or public event, authorised recordings generate a copyright interest in the recording that belongs to its producer.

The final lot of copyright interests that might be relevant in a music festival are those copyright interests in music and lyrics, performed during the festival, which might belong to people other than the performers. The most obvious circumstance where this situation will occur is where the composers/lyricists and the performers are different people. This might be because the composer and/or lyricist never intended to be involved in the performance of the work, or because performers are covering the copyright work of another performer. The default position in both these cases is that the consent of the copyright owner must be sought in order to avoid infringement. However, it is worth noting that covers, which are a particular feature of rock/folk/blues music festivals, are capable of raising questions in what might be considered the grey zone of copyright. Straightforward covers of songs that differ little from their original versions are not particularly problematic from a copyright point of view, but covers that differ substantially from the original copyright work – for example, because they make minimal reference to the original lyrics or music, or because they use a different musical style or genre – raise questions about whether there has been sufficient substantial taking from the

---

original to constitute an infringement[45] and/or whether the use of the material might be justified under the fair use/fair dealing exception in jurisdictions where such defences exist.[46] Covers that incorporate enough of the original to make reference to it, but very little of the actual expression of the work, may not be infringing.[47] If such works are considered to be infringing they may also be saved by the fair use/fair dealing defences. Similarly, covers that employ a completely different musical style or genre may be considered to fall within the fair use/fair dealing defences in some jurisdictions.[48] Added to these complications are the fact that any new work, whether it is infringing or not, is potentially capable of creating a new copyright interest in the person performing it if it shows sufficient creativity or sufficient investment of skill and labour.[49] Another very grey zone relates to genres of music that depend on a tradition of re-working what has gone before. This applies, for example to jazz and blues music,[50] where the creative culture of re-working and riffing creates numerous questions relating to: who, if anyone, can be considered the owner of the original work, if one can be identified, or of any subsequent re-working; and whether, in the context of the usual traditions applying to this music, such activities can (or should) ever be considered infringing.

Many of these same issues arise in relation to what are here described as culture festivals, which are extremely diverse and might very well comprehend elements of film/video and music among their rich diet of cultural activities. These sorts of festivals also tend to encompass – variously – activities such as poetry and prose readings, dance, theatre, story-telling, circus acts, puppetry, busking, blogging, visual art installations, exhibitions of various sorts (photographic, comics, videoart, digital art), interviews and public discussions. Four copyright issues that are of particular importance to a number of these types of festivals are: first, the relationship of performances, or performative elements, to texts (if any); second, the question of subsistence of copyright in ephemeral performances; third, the impact of interactive works on questions of copyright ownership; and, fourth, the question of what constitutes a copyright work.

---

45 See, e.g., CDPA, s 16(3), which requires the taking of a 'substantial part' of the protected work in order to constitute an infringement.

46 These exceptions tend to be found in common law copyright jurisdictions, rather than in jurisdictions based on the civil law tradition of *droit d'auteur*. E.g., US Copyright Law 1976, s 10, which contains the fair use defence; and CDPA, s 30, which contains the relevant fair dealing defence.

47 See, e.g., Joy Music v Sunday Pictorial Newspapers [1960] 2 WLR 615; Williamson Music v Pearson Partnership [1987] FSR 97.

48 See, e.g., Campbell (2 Live Crew) v Acuff-Rose Music Inc, 114 S Ct 1164 (1994).

49 The question of the degree of input necessary to establish the preconditions for the creation of a copyright interest varies between jurisdictions. See, further, Bently and Sherman, n 40 *supra*, at 93–111.

50 See e.g., S. Vaidhynathan (2001). *Copyrights & Copywrongs: The Rise of Intellectual Property & How it Threatens Creativity*. New York, New York University Press.

The question of the relationship of performance to text, and the copyright issues that consequently arise with respect to ownership and infringement are not, in substance, different from those that arise in relation to performances of existing musical works. Where the performer is not the owner of the copyright interest in any text upon which a performance is based then there will be questions about whether there has been substantial taking from the text and, if so, whether fair use or fair dealing defences might apply. The law and its practitioners are generally better at understanding these questions in relation to text, where it is clear that the protected subject matter of copyright is the way in which the author of the text has expressed their ideas, and not the ideas themselves. Thus performances that make reference to a text, as a type of jumping-off point, rather than using the expression from the text itself are generally unproblematic in this respect. Further, it should be noted that a number of the types of performances that take place in the context of culture festivals involving texts are more likely than not to be performances by the author, who is likely to be the copyright owner.[51] For example, it is generally the case at poetry festivals that poets read their own work. Similarly, at literary festivals authors often read their own prose works. This is obviously, of course, often not the case in relation to theatrical texts unless they are texts written especially for the festival, as is frequently the case in relation to interactive theatrical pieces.[52]

Although the same principles apply in theory, the situation can be more complicated in relation to non-textual works. A good example of this, which often arises in the festival context, is dance, which is characterised by a generally problematic relation to copyright law. While dance is technically a protected work under copyright law in most jurisdictions,[53] what Yeoh has described as 'the ontological instability'[54] of dance means that questions of the relationship between the work of a choreographer[55] and a dance performance can be fraught with difficulties. The basic problem here is that the material form to which a protected dance work is reduced is frequently a form of notation.[56] In the copyright context, understanding the relationship between this notation and a performance is challenging. A dance work tends, even when performed with the involvement

---

51   See, e.g., CDPA, s 11(1), subject to the first owner not having transferred the copyright interest to another person.

52   See e.g., O'Grady and Kill, n 21 *supra*; and O'Grady and Kill, n 22 *supra*.

53   See, e.g., CDPA, s 3(1), which protects dance as a 'dramatic work'. Cf., e.g., the US Copyright Act 1976, which protects dance works as such; and the Canadian Copyright Amendment Act 1988, which protects 'any work of choreography, whether or not it has any storyline'.

54   See F. Yeoh (2012). *Copyright Does Not Adequately Accommodate the Artform of Dance*. PhD Thesis, Birkbeck, University of London, ch 1 and ff.

55   Who is considered to be the author, and therefore the first owner, of the copyright work: see, CDPA, ss 9 and 11.

56   For an excellent account of the various forms of dance notation, see Yeoh, n 54 *supra*, ch 2.

of the choreographer, to mutate with each performance, with the result that significant differences between the notation and the dance as performed are likely to develop over time. A dance work, of course, can also be recorded on film. While this might overcome some of the limitations of traditional notation in capturing particular movements of the dancers, it is also subject to the problem that a film of one performance is unable to capture evolutions of the work over time. All this means that the dance community has traditionally tended to operate, in a certain sense, outside the copyright regime and according to its own norms on questions of authorship and ownership of works.[57] However, these norms are increasingly likely to become entangled with copyright law.[58]

Different problems are posed by works that are ephemeral in the sense that they are not based on a text or are not otherwise reduced to what copyright law considers a material form. This problem might arise in relation to dance works that have not been recorded in some form. Other performances at culture festivals that might raise this type of issue are things like story-telling, circus acts, puppetry and busking. At first blush it might seem strange to include, for example, story-telling because it might be assumed that a text exists somewhere. However, the point of these festivals is (usually) that there is no strict relation between any text and the performance, rather the performances are interactive and 'free-form'. They are, by nature, unstable in the sense that one such performance or work by the performers or artists will not be the same as the next due to differences in the way that the public interacts with the basic structure of the work. Busking is also a classic example of the same style of performance, as are many interactive theatrical performances. Without, for example, a recording these ephemeral works cannot be protected by copyright.

If a recording exists, with the result that the work is reduced to material form and the basis for copyright protection in the work is established, there will often be questions about who is the author of an interactive work. According to copyright law, the author of a work is its generator or creator.[59] Given that copyright law does not seem to recognise the concept of an interactive work, it is probably not surprising that there is no general principle according to which the authorship of such works is conferred on the person who makes the arrangements, or invests the necessary resources, for its coming into being.[60] Under these circumstances, to resolve the question of who is the author, and thus first owner, of works that

---

57   Yeoh, n 54 *supra*.

58   See, e.g., the recent controversy concerning Beyoncé's alleged infringement of De Keersmaeker's *Rosas danstrosas* (1983): R. Sulcas (2011). 'Has Beyoncé stepped over the line?' *The Times*, 26 October 2011, at 11, and the discussion in Yeoh, n 54 *supra*, ch 5. See further, F. Yeoh (2013). 'The copyright implications of Beyoncé's "borrowings"', *Choreographic Practices* 4:1, 95–117.

59   See, e.g., CDPA, s 9(1).

60   Despite the fact that this idea arguably underlies the conferral of the status of author on producers of sound recordings, broadcasters, publishers and film producers

are interactively produced by performers and members of the public, it would seem necessary to fall back on copyright's concept of joint authorship. The UK legislation, for example, describes a work of joint authorship as being 'a work produced by the collaboration of two or more authors in which the contribution of each author is not distinct from that of the other author or authors'.[61] The room for manoeuvre around the question of whether contributions from the public would be regarded as distinct[62] does nothing to resolve the practical difficulties that could flow from the idea that members of the public were joint authors/ first owners of interactive works in circumstances in which the works were commercially exploited outside the festival environment. Inside the essentially participative environment of the festival, however, it is not clear that any particular problems would arise from this legal uncertainty. Questions of authorship also arise in relation to performances which are not typically text-based and involve a degree of interaction, sometimes improvised between the performers.[63] The classic example of this is circus and variety acts, in relation to which problems around the question of authorship are part of a larger issue concerned with the question of whether these types of performances are even copyright works.

The great diversity of what have been described here as culture festivals, tends to raise some questions about how much of what occurs in such festivals involves copyright works or other works protected by intellectual property rights. In most (if not all) jurisdictions there are limits on what can be considered a copyright work, even if there is a general lack of clarity at the relevant borders. Things like poetry and prose readings, dance and theatre present fewer problems in this respect. On the other hand, circus acts, general variety acts and puppetry give some pause for thought. There seems to be a lack of consensus on whether circus and general variety acts can be considered to be copyright works.[64] Similar doubts also exist with respect to the protection of things like busking and blogging, as such. With slight variations on the theme, all of these activities essentially raise questions

---

(see, e.g., CDPA, s 9(2)) as well on persons who make the arrangements necessary for the creation of computer-generated works (see, e.g., CDPA, 9(3)).

61   CDPA, s 10(1).

62   See Bently and Sherman, n 40 *supra*, at 125–7.

63   See R. Arnold (1999). 'Are Performers Authors?' *European Intellectual Property Review* 21, 464–9.

64   In the UK, e.g., there is a line of cases on the questions of protection and authorship of variety acts, which pre-dates the current legislation and which focuses on the question of whether they can be considered 'dramatic works': see Clark v Bishop, *The Law Times*, 17 February 1872; Fuller v The Blackpool Winter Gardens and Pavilion Company, Limited [1895] 2 QB 429; Karno v Pathé Frères, *The Law Times*, 26 September 1908 and 17 April 1909; Tate v Fullbrook [1908] 1 KB 821; Tate v Thomas [1921] 1 Ch 503. It seems that the lack of clarity on these questions persists under the current legislation: see Hadley v Kemp [1999] EMLR 589.

about what amounts to a 'dramatic work' in copyright law.[65] In addition to a lack of clarity around the word 'dramatic', it also seems likely that the use of 'work' in conjunction with it imports a concept of something that is able to be separately identified. Consequently, vaguely limited or indeterminate activities, which might be a characterisation applicable to things like story-telling, busking and blogging, always run the risk of not being considered a 'work'. This requirement of determinacy, which of course is an aspect of copyright's focus on product rather than process, also manifests itself with respect to visual art. Installations are, for this reason, at particular risk of falling outside the definition of works of visual art, as might be some types of digital art, particularly those that involve interactivity with the viewer.

However, it is important to note that the conclusion that copyright does not – or may not – exist, does not mean that there are not other relevant intellectual property rights to take into account. The consensus of opinion in the United Kingdom, for example, is that 'a performance of a variety act or any similar presentation'[66] gives rise to performers' rights irrespective of the existence of an underlying copyright work.[67] That is, in order to gain rights in the performance, it is not necessary for the performer to be performing a copyright work. (Obviously, performers performing copyright works – something that happens a lot at festivals, as the foregoing discussion illustrates – would also have performers' rights.) There may also be some types of performances or activities that take place at culture festivals that implicate other types of copyright works. For example, a puppetry festival, which involves the making of traditional puppets from around the world, may involve the production of copyright protected artistic works.

Re-reading Cultural Heritage as Property?

While it seems generally safe to assert that arts festivals have cultural heritage credentials, the more difficult problem is to try and understand exactly where they

---

65   CDPA, s 3(1), defines 'dramatic work' as including 'a work of dance and mime'. At the international level, the Berne Convention for the Protection of Literary and Artistic Works 1886 is not much more helpful. Its Art. 2(1) provides: 'The expression "literary and artistic works" shall include every production in the literary, scientific and artistic domain, whatever maybe the mode or form of its expression, such as books, pamphlets and other writings; lectures, addresses, sermons and other works of the same nature; dramatic or dramatico-musical works; choreographic works and entertainments in dumb show ...'.

66   CDPA, s 180(2)(d). It appears to be the case, particularly as a consequence of the Rome Convention for the Protection of Performers, Producers of Phonograms and Broadcasting Organisations 1961, Art 9, that circus acts fall within the definition of 'variety or any similar presentation'.

67   See the Whitford Committee *Report on the Reform of Copyright Law* (Cmnd 6732) and the UK Government (Department of Trade and Industry), *White Paper on Copyright* (Cmnd 9712), paragraph 14.5.

lie on an imaginary festival map and how they relate to the intellectual property rights that also seem to be an obvious part of the festival topography. Would cultural heritage be represented as the container or border on the basis that the festival, as event, is the vehicle of the cultural heritage? Such a representation might be based on the notion of the 'cultural space' provided by the festival within the meaning of Article 2.1 of the Convention on Intangible Cultural Heritage or on the reference to 'festive events' in Article 2.2(c). Or is the cultural heritage element of the festival more pervasive? Does it appear somewhere between the lines of what is already protected by copyright or other intellectual property interests? Or does it, in fact, overlap with what is already protected by intellectual property? Such a reading could easily be justified according to paragraphs (a) and (b) of Article 2.2 of the Convention on Intangible Cultural Heritage. Similarly, as already noted, many elements of festivals seem to offer expressions of the sort of cultural diversity with which the Convention on the Protection of Cultural Diversity is concerned. The most likely answer to all these questions is that the cultural heritage nature of festivals is evident in all these festival spaces. In other words, arts festivals are saturated by cultural heritage. It is also evidently the case that arts festivals are saturated with copyright interests, which means that some accommodation between cultural heritage and copyright needs to be reached. Bearing in mind that cultural heritage belongs to a community, while intellectual property rights are private, there are substantial difficulties, in theory and in practice, in arriving at such an accommodation. A failure, however, to find such an accommodation runs the risk of allowing private intellectual property rights to constrain the creative synergistic interactions that seem so essential to the festival as event.

One approach would be to regard the festival, and the activities that occur within its spatial and temporal boundaries as being a rupture in legal space that flows from its inherent nature as a rupture in space and time. Scholars have drawn on Turner's distinction[68] between 'liminal (obligatory, highly formalised) and liminoid (optional, free flowing) social events' to try and explain the space of the festival.[69] Lawrence, for example, conceives the festival as a state of 'ritual disorder'.[70] A similar notion of disorder in relation to festivals is also used by Abrahams, who however contrasts it with ritual:

> While ritual underscores the harmonies and continuities in the expressive resources of a culture, emphasizing the wholeness of the world's fabric, festivals work (at least at their inception) by apparently tearing the fabric to pieces, by displaying it upside-down, inside-out, wearing it as motley rags and

---

68   See, e.g., V. Turner (1974). 'Liminal to Liminoid, in Play, Flow and Ritual', *Rice University Studies* 60.

69   In the introductory notes to R.D. Abrahams (1987). 'An American Vocabulary of Celebrations', in Falassi (ed.), n 4 *supra*, 173–83, at 173.

70   D. Lawrence, 'Rules of Misrule: Notes on the Doo Dah Parade in Pasadena', in Falassi, n 11 *supra*, 123–36, at 134.

tatters … Festivals thus draw their own boundaries for the occasion and redraw the boundaries of the host community, ironically establishing themselves in areas that, in the everyday world, have their own boundaries … .[179] Openness, central to our experience of festival, is temporal as well as spatial.[71]

Festivals, on this argument, fit badly within the highly institutionalised and legally regulated world of private intellectual property law.[72] As Abrahams goes on to observe:

> Festivals are ultimately community affairs. Indeed, they provide *the* occasion whereby a community may call attention to itself and, perhaps more important in our time, its willingness to display itself openly. It is the ultimate public activity, given its need for preparation and coordination of effort, and its topsy-turvyness, in which many of the basic notions of community are put to test.[73]

What festivals thus represent is a public (in the sense of not being private), communal and bounded space of openness. This idea of the festival should be reflected in the law's treatment of the creative and synergistic reactions that occur within the rupture or suspension created by the festival space.

The problem here is how to pit the vague, poorly defined idea of cultural heritage against the strong private rights inherent in law's construction of intellectual property. One solution might lie in a carefully articulated and constructed idea of the public domain in intellectual space. Such a solution would require a legal architecture in this public domain, which is strong enough to pull material out of the domain of private rights and into the domain of community rights in order to defend particular values such as the communal interests in cultural heritage. As I have argued elsewhere, a substantial revision of how we think about the concept of the public domain, which has been greatly devalued in recent times, is required in order to achieve such a result. In particular, bearing in mind that the concept of the public domain has its roots in Roman law, it would be necessary to reinvigorate the public domain by giving full scope to the much more sophisticated version that existed under Roman law.[74] But, perhaps there is also another way of going

---

71   Abrahams, n 69 *supra*, at 178.

72   This argument might also be regarded as consistent with the observation of Lawrence, n 70 *supra*, that '[i]nstitutionalizing inherently unstable socio-cultural forms, such as ritual disorder [into which category he places festivals] and spontaneity, is theoretically as well as pragmatically problematic'.

73   Abrahams, n 69 *supra*, at 181.

74   See F. Macmillan (2010). 'Many Analogies, Some Metaphors, Little Imagination: The Public Domain in Intellectual Space', *Pòlemos* 2, 25–44; and F. Macmillan (2014). 'Arts Festivals: Property, Heritage or More?' in K. Bowrey and M. Handler (eds), *Law and Creativity in the Age of the Entertainment Franchise*. Cambridge: Cambridge University Press.

back to the future that would involve a temporally shorter diversion, and might also provide a way of giving cultural heritage rights greater strength in resisting the power of law's private property paradigm. This would involve a return to the concept of cultural property, abandoned by the UNESCO Conventions in the 1970s. Blake notes that the use of the expression was considered problematic on the basis that 'property' is a legal term of art implicating ownership rights over a particular subject matter.[75] Perhaps, however, that is exactly what is required here. While Blake's account explains the advantages of the use of 'heritage' rather than 'property' in terms of the width of its application, this change in language also obscures the dimensions of the systemic conflict between cultural property/ heritage and intellectual property. Writers who are specifically concerned with this conflict tend to face it head-on and use the expression cultural property, rather than cultural heritage.[76] Such a conceptual confrontation should be viewed in the light of the compelling arguments made for the theoretical importance and practical utility of the property paradigm in relation to the protection of community interests in what this chapter started off by describing as cultural heritage.[77] In the end, re-reading or re-conceptualising cultural heritage as property compels us to face up to the conflict, to decide when community property rights are more important than private property rights, and to put in place workable legal mechanisms to defend those rights. Considering the cultural property–intellectual property overlap in the context of arts festivals provides us with a focus for this task and an instance in which, exploiting the suspended nature of the festival as event, we might start moving towards a real level of legal protection for the legally invisible communities to whom cultural property belongs.

References

Abrahams, R.D. (1987). 'An American Vocabulary of Celebrations', in A. Falassi (ed.), *Time Out of Time: Essays on the Festival*. Albuquerque: University of New Mexico Press, 173–83.

Armstrong, E. [1990](2002). *Before Copyright: The French Book Privilege System 1498–1526*. Cambridge: Cambridge University Press.

Arnold, R. (1999). 'Are Performers Authors?' *European Intellectual Property Review* 21, 464–9.

---

75   Note 8 *supra*, 65–7.

76   See, e.g., J.R. Slaughter (2011). 'Form & Informality: An Unliterary Look at World Literature', in R. Warhol, *The Work of Genre: Selected Essays from the English Institute*. English Institute in Collaboration with the American Council of Learned Societies, http:// quod.lib.umich.edu/cgi/t/text/text-idx?c=acls;idno=heb90055, 177–240.

77   See Flessas, n 3 *supra*; and K.A. Carpenter, S. Katyal and A. Riley (2009). 'In Defense of Property', *Yale Journal of Law* 100–204.

Bently, L. and B. Sherman (2009). *Intellectual Property Law*. Oxford and New York: Oxford University Press, 3rd edn.

Blake, J. (2000). 'On Defining the Cultural Heritage', *International and Comparative Law Quarterly* 49, 61–85.

Carpenter, K.A., S. Katyal and A. Riley (2009). 'In Defense of Property', *Yale Journal of Law* 100–204.

Durkheim, E. [1912](1954). *The Elementary Forms of Religious Life*. Glencoe: Free Press.

Falassi, A. (1987). 'Festival: Definition and Morphology', in A. Falassi (ed.), *Time Out of Time: Essays on the Festival*. Albuquerque: University of New Mexico Press, 1–10.

Flessas, T. (2003). 'Cultural Property Defined, and Redefined as Nietzschean Aphorism', *Cardozo Law Review* 24, 1067–97.

Giorgi, L. (2009). 'Between Tradition, Vision and Imagination: Literature(s) in Search of a Festival', in J. Segal and L. Giorgi (eds), *European Arts Festivals from a Historical Perspective*. EURO-FESTIVAL Project: European Arts Festivals and Public Culture, Deliverable 2.1, WP2 Main Report, July 2009; http://www.euro-festival.org/publications.html, 30–52.

Giorgi, L. (2008). 'Literature Festivals: Literature (Festivals) as a Subject of Sociological Inquiry in Search of Cosmopolitanism', in M. Sassatelli (ed.), *European Public Culture & Aesthetic Cosmopolitanism*. EURO-FESTIVAL Project: European Arts Festivals and Public Culture, Deliverable 1.1, WP1 Main Report, October 2008; http://www.euro-festival.org/publications. html, 95–110.

Guerzoni, G. (2009). 'L'impatto economico dei festival: un'annosa prospettiva di ricerca', *Economia della cultura* 19.

Handler, R. (1991). 'Who Owns the Past? History, Cultural Property and the Logic of Possessive Individualism', in B. Williams (ed.), *The Politics of Culture*. Washington: Smithsonian Institution Press.

Lawrence, D. (1987). 'Rules of Misrule: Notes on the Doo Dah Parade in Pasadena', in A. Falassi (ed.), *Time Out of Time: Essays on the Festival*. Albuquerque: University of New Mexico Press, 123–36.

Macmillan, F. (2002a). 'Copyright and Corporate Power' in R. Towse (ed.), *Copyright and the Cultural Industries*. Edward Elgar Publishing, 99–118.

Macmillan, F. (2002b). 'The Cruel ©: Copyright and Film', *European Intellectual Property Review* 483–92.

Macmillan, F. (2008). 'The UNESCO Convention as a New Incentive to Protect Cultural Diversity', in H. Schneider and P. van den Bossche (eds), *Protection of Cultural Diversity from a European and International Perspective*. Mortsel: Intersentia.

Macmillan, F. (2010). 'Many Analogies, Some Metaphors, Little Imagination: The Public Domain in Intellectual Space', *Pòlemos* 2, 25–44.

Macmillan, F. (2013). 'The Protection of Cultural Heritage: Common Heritage of Humankind, National Cultural "Patrimony" or Private Property?' *Northern Ireland Legal Quarterly* 64, 351–64.

Macmillan, F. (2014). 'Arts Festivals: Property, Heritage or More?' in K. Bowrey and M. Handler (eds), *Law and Creativity in the Age of the Entertainment Franchise*. Cambridge: Cambridge University Press.

Mazdon, L. (2006). 'The Cannes Film Festival as Transnational Space', *Post Script* 25:2, 19–30.

Nordmann, S. (2009). 'A History of Cultural Festivals in Europe', in J. Segal and L. Giorgi (eds), *European Arts Festivals from a Historical Perspective*. EURO-FESTIVAL Project: European Arts Festivals and Public Culture, Deliverable 2.1, WP2 Main Report, July 2009; http://www.euro-festival.org/publications. html, 19–29.

Miles, M.M. (2008). *Art as Plunder: The Ancient Origins of Debate About Cultural Property*. New York: Cambridge University Press.

O'Grady, A. and R. Kill (2011a). 'Exploring Festival Performance as a State of Encounter', Unpublished paper, May 2011.

O'Grady, A. and R. Kill (2011b). 'Environments for Encounter and the Processes of Organizing for Interactivity and Performative Participation within the Festival Space'. Conference on *Visuals and Performativity: Researching Beyond Text*, Segovia, Spain, May 2011.

Santoro, M., J. Chalcraft and P. Magaudda (2008). 'Music Festivals: An Interdisciplinary Literature Review', in M. Sassatelli (ed.), *European Public Culture & Aesthetic Cosmopolitanism*. EURO-FESTIVAL Project: European Arts Festivals and Public Culture, Deliverable 1.1, WP1 Main Report, October 2008; http://www.euro-festival.org/publications.html, 77–93.

Sassatelli, M. (2008). 'Public Culture, Cosmopolitanism and Festivals', in M. Sassatelli (ed.), *European Public Culture & Aesthetic Cosmopolitanism*. EURO-FESTIVAL Project: European Arts Festivals and Public Culture, Deliverable 1.1, WP1 Main Report, October 2008; http://www.euro-festival. org/publications.html, 15–40.

Segal J. and C. Blumauer (2009). 'Cannes: A French International Festival', in J. Segal and L. Giorgi (eds), *European Arts Festivals from a Historical Perspective*. EURO-FESTIVAL Project: European Arts Festivals and Public Culture, Deliverable 2.1, WP2 Main Report, July 2009; http://www.euro-festival.org/publications.html, 53–82.

Segal, J. (2008). 'Film Festivals', in M. Sassatelli (ed), *European Public Culture & Aesthetic Cosmopolitanism*. EURO-FESTIVAL Project: European Arts Festivals and Public Culture, Deliverable 1.1, WP1 Main Report, October 2008; http://www.euro-festival.org/publications.html, 111–17.

Slaughter, J.R. (2011). 'Form & Informality: An Unliterary Look at World Literature', in R. Warhol, *The Work of Genre: Selected Essays from the English Institute*. English Institute in Collaboration with the American

Council of Learned Societies, http://quod.lib.umich.edu/cgi/t/text/text-idx?c=acls;idno=heb90055, 177–240.

Stapleton, J. 2002. *Art, Intellectual Property & the Knowledge Economy.* Doctoral Thesis, Goldsmiths College, University of London, http://www.jaimestapleton.info/download.htm.

Sulcas, R. (2011). 'Has Beyoncé Stepped Over the Line?' *The Times,* 26 October 2011.

Turan, K. (2002). *Sundance to Sarajevo: Film Festivals and the World They Made.* Los Angeles: University of California Press.

Turner, V. (1974). 'Liminal to Liminoid, in Play, Flow and Ritual', *Rice University Studies* 60.

Vaidhynathan, S. (2001). *Copyrights & Copywrongs: The Rise of Intellectual Property & How it Threatens Creativity.* New York, New York University Press.

Vrdoljak, A.F. (2008). *International Law, Museums and the Return of Cultural Objects.* Cambridge: Cambridge University Press.

Vrettos, A. (2009). 'About the Economic Impact Studies of Arts Festivals', *Economia della cultura* 3, 341–50.

Yeoh, F. (2012). *Copyright Does Not Adequately Accommodate the Artform of Dance.* PhD Thesis, Birkbeck, University of London.

Yeoh, F. (2013). 'The Copyright Implications of Beyoncé's "Borrowings"', *Choreographic Practices* 4:1, 95–117.

Chapter 6

The Artfulness of Design: Copyright and the Danish Modern Inheritance

Stina Teilmann-Lock

Shifts in the relationship between copyright, creativity and cultural heritage affect the formation and dissemination of art and culture in society. Copyright law regulates creative expression by either promoting or restricting it: copyright rules thereby come to contribute to the shaping of a cultural heritage. In this chapter we will consider how the evolution of Danish design in the twentieth century may serve as an indicator of shifting relationships between copyright, creativity and cultural heritage.

Today, under Danish copyright law, design – or rather 'applied art' as it is termed in this context – is defined as a type of subject matter.[1] Copyright in design (in 'works of applied art') has led to numerous conflicts between rivals in the market for such serially produced expressions of creativity as coffee sets, chairs, cutlery, lamps and so forth. In the twentieth century in Denmark and elsewhere, design increasingly came to be recognised as a central and valuable element of national cultures. Arguably, works by some Danish designers constitute the most original expressions of creativity by Danish artists in the twentieth century and by the same token, one of the most substantial contributions to the Modern Danish cultural heritage.[2] As such, to the extent that copyright protection is a societal instrument to promote the public good, it is uncontroversial today, that design should be protected by copyright law on equal terms with the free arts (in the Kantian sense). However, it is also widely recognised that copyright in design should not be used to create monopolies on particular 'forms': chairs with four legs, cylinder-shaped drinking glasses and so forth. Crucially, designs have a double identity and status in society: as works that constitute part of a cultural heritage and as marketable products with everyday functions. To be sure, other

---

1   In this chapter 'design' is used not in its sense in design law which means the appearance of a product – including lines, contours, colours, shape, texture, materials or ornamentation. Rather, 'design' is used to denote a product which is created and authored by a designer but industrially and serially manufactured.

2   Indicative of this were two major Danish museum exhibitions in 2014 celebrating the centenaries of Hans Wegner and Børge Mogensen. See http://designmuseum.dk/udstillinger/arkiv/2014/wegner and http://www.trapholt.dk/udstillinger/udstillingsarkiv/2014/boerge-mogensen-100-aar/.

objects of copyright protection including literature and visual art may also be said
to be works and products at the same time. However in literature and visual art, the
distinction between the 'work' and the 'product' is clearer: the literary text versus
the book and the artistic image (which may be reproduced as postcards and so
forth) versus the unique original. In design the distinction is less clear.

Danish design first came to prominence in the 1950s at home as well as
abroad. Danish design became 'Danish Modern' or 'Danish Design' with upper-
case Ds. Commentators worldwide recognised the originality of works by Danish
designers – Finn Juhl, Hans Wegner, Arne Jacobsen, Kay Bojesen, Børge Mogensen
and others – and the most prestigious international design awards were granted to
Danish designers and design institutions.[3] In the years from 1954 to 1957 'Design
in Scandinavia: an exhibition of objects for the home' visited 24 North American
cities. The exhibition – which showcased items of furniture, glassware, ceramics,
textiles, knitwear and metalwork from Denmark, Sweden, Norway and Finland –
brought international recognition as well as commercial success. The formation
of the very concepts and brands, in particular 'Scandinavian Design', 'Danish
Modern' and 'Swedish Modern' took place in this context.[4]

In the United States 'Danish Design' was acclaimed by some of the most
influential figures of the art world, notably by Edgar Kaufmann, Jr., Director of the
Industrial Design Department at MoMA, New York.[5] Works by Danish designers
were included in the collection of MoMA and shops selling Danish Modern opened
up on prestigious sites, for example 'The Lunning Collection', on Fifth Avenue.
In a similar vein, under the label 'Danish Modern', Danish design entered major
museums and markets in many other countries.[6] Meanwhile in Denmark, the
Danish Modern designers experienced a related success – both in terms of sales
and 'creative' recognition. The designers were endorsed by the Establishment; their
works were installed in public spaces and state offices: railway stations, schools,
hospitals and municipal employment offices were furnished with designer items,
as were many Danish middle-class homes.

---

3   For example, the Danish exhibition co-op, 'Den Permanente', which existed
from 1931 to 1981, received the important award the *Compasso d'Oro Gran Premio
Internazionale* in 1958 while the designer Finn Juhl was awarded, among others, gold
medals and an honorary diploma at the Triennale di Milano and Hans Wegner received the
Lunning Prize. See Fallan (2009, 2014), Guldberg (2011) and Hansen (2006).

4   See Hansen (2006).

5   See Guldberg (2011) and Hansen (2006).

6   See for example the collections of the Victoria and Albert Museum (London), Die
Neue Sammlung (Munich), Design Museum Gent and Musée Des Arts Décoratifs (Paris).

Copyright Protection of Design?

The societal recognition of the value of the artistic expression inherent in design is matched by the recognition by Danish copyright law of the fact that many designed products are the results of personal, creative efforts: it is this that makes them worthy of protection. Design has, in principle, been protected by Danish copyright law since 1908. However, as Danish case law from the first half of the twentieth century reveals, for a long time courts remained hostile to the idea of granting copyright protection to design. The problem was that works of design always have a function; they are always created in order to fulfil a practical purpose: cups to drink from, chairs to sit on, lamps to light up the room. Danish courts found such a utilitarian element incompatible with copyright protection.

By the mid-twentieth century the situation had changed and utility was no longer seen as grounds for excluding design from copyright protection. 'Applied art' was specifically mentioned as an object of protection in the Danish 1961 Copyright Act and the assessment of '*værkshøjde*' – the originality of the artistic expression in a design – was to take place independently of whether a work had a function or not. As a result, a wide range of design works have been granted copyright protection since 1961 including very simple items such as plain cutlery, casseroles, a holder for washing-up brushes, a notice board and so forth.

Essentially, this development gave way to a new problem. In particular, if protection is granted to a form which is – more or less – determined by a function, how does one prevent one designer from obtaining a monopoly on this function? The problem is especially pressing in relation to modern – or functionalistic – design which idealises the idea that 'form ever follows function', as the American architect Louis Sullivan famously phrased it.[7] In other words, how does one secure creative freedom for designers in general (who all work within the same framework of functionality) while also granting them individual copyright protection? Danish courts were always very aware of the urgency of allowing 'fair followers' in the design field. Hence, the practice that evolved in case law was to make the originality requirement proportional to the scope of protection. A low level of originality would provide a narrow protection only. Works of applied art would be protected against close imitations only. This was the law's way of striking a balance between copyright and creativity, to ensure that Danish Design would not be turned into a museum piece but would remain a vibrant and dynamic element of Danish cultural heritage and of the national economy.

Due to recent developments in EU law however, this solution to a never-ending dilemma in relation to copyright in designs is in jeopardy. In the 2011 *Painer* Case – which concerned the degree to which a portrait photograph expresses its 'author's creative abilities' – the Court of Justice of the European Union did not

---

7 Louis H. Sullivan, 'The Tall Office Building Artistically Considered', in *Lippincott's Magazine* #57 (March 1896), 403–9.

allow for inferior protection of any type of original work.[8] That is, the photographer of a standard portrait photograph 'enjoys the same protection as that conferred by copyright on any other work'.[9] The painter of, say, 'Water-lilies' has no stronger protection of his work than that afforded to a photographer who makes a postcard of Monet's painting. Is it then possible for Danish courts to continue the practice of limiting the scope of copyright protection of design to close imitations only?

In the following we will see how the balance between copyright and creativity has been negotiated through the history of copyright in design in Denmark. Statutory developments as well as a number of landmark cases involving design will be studied. And it will be considered what may be the effect, in the context of design, of a harmonised copyright protection as prescribed in *Painer*.

Artistic Rights in Danish Design

In an amendment of 1908 to the Danish Act on Authorial and Artistic Rights it was specified that copyright protection was to be extended to artistic works with a practical use and made with the aim of mass production.[10] In line with a number of other European countries – including France, Germany and Britain[11] – the Danish parliament decided that design, or 'applied art', should be granted a legal status similar to the fine arts. This development in the law may be understood in the context

---

8   Eva-Maria Painer v Standard Verlags GmbH and Others (C-145/10), cf. paragraph 99.

9   http://curia.europa.eu/jcms/upload/docs/application/pdf/2011-12/cp110132en.pdf

10   Six years before, the Danish Parliament had intended to make works of applied art eligible for copyright protection. Thus in the 1902 Act on Authorial and Artistic Rights it had been stated that: 'An artist has, according to the restrictions of this Act, the sole right to publish or sell or let be published or put up for sale reproductions of his original work of art or of parts of it. This is so when the reproduction requires mediating artistic work as well as when the reproduction takes place by purely mechanical or chemical means' (Lov om Forfatterret og Kunstnerret, 19 December 1902, § 24 (as amended by the 1904 law)). However, the amendment did not work according to intention. A 1907 ruling by the Danish Supreme Court made this clear. The case concerned alleged infringement of the copyright in a Royal Porcelain blue-fluted china coffeepot designed by Arnold Krog. The Supreme Court decided against the plaintiff on the grounds that their coffeepot 'according to its description as ordinary industrial ware, the foremost purpose of which is practical usage, cannot be considered a work of art in the sense wherein this expression is used in the Act of 19 December 1902 § 24'. Ibid., 620 That is to say the Supreme Court decided that there was no provision in the 1902 Act to grant copyright protection to design insofar as design is made 'for practical use with the aim of mass production. Lov om Forfatterret og Kunstnerret af 19de December 1902, 621.

11   Copyright protection of applied art had been introduced in France with the Law of 11 March 1902 and in Germany with the Law of 9 January 1907. The British Copyright Act 1911 was to include 'works of artistic craftsmanship' as objects of copyright protection.

of a new self-awareness among designers exercised by for example, members of the British Arts and Crafts Movement and later the *Deutsche Werkbund*, and the increased political awareness in many countries of the value of design as a tool for nation-building and economic growth. (This is evident in the series of World Fairs that began with The Great Exhibition in the Crystal Palace in London in 1851.) Thus in 1908 § 24 of the Danish Copyright Act was revised so as to specify that:

> According to this Act, original artistic works intended to be prototypes for industrial art and handicrafts, as well as the objects created on the basis of such works, are to be considered works of art whether or not these are produced individually or in a larger quantity. The right according to this Act is valid for any type of reproduction, when it requires mediating artistic work as well as when the reproduction takes place by purely mechanical or chemical means, and whether or not the reproduction takes place with a purely artistic purpose or with an industrial purpose or to serve a practical use.[12]

New to the definition of a copyrightable 'work of art' was that it might be something which had been created with 'an industrial purpose' or to 'serve a practical use'. This broadening of the definition of a 'work of art' in Danish copyright law was reaffirmed by the Danish Copyright Acts of 1912 and 1933. Yet, the copyrightability of design remained uncertain all through the first half of the twentieth century.[13] This may well be seen as caution on the part of Danish courts: there was great awareness of the danger of granting monopolies to anything that was 'naturally and technically motivated by the material and the intended use' as the Danish Supreme Court formulated it in a decision of 1935 in which copyright protection was denied to Marcel Breuer and Mart Stam's iconic tubular steel cantilevered chairs S 32, S 64 and S 33.[14] The decision is remarkable: Breuer and Stam are counted among the most original designers of the Bauhaus and the chairs remain classics of modernist design. Three years earlier, in 1932, the German *Reichsgericht* had found the chairs worthy of copyright protection. Even so, the Danish Supreme Court did not consider the chairs to be 'original artistic works

---

12 Amendment to the Act on Authorial and Artistic Rights of 28 February 1908.

13 Many pieces of design were denied protection during this time (see for example U. 1935.692H, U.1935.695H, U.1935.699H, U.1954.170Ø, U.1960.762SH and U.1956.237H) and the items that were found worthy of protection repeatedly had an element that was purely decorative (see U.1913.760 (silver jewellery from Georg Jensen), U.1924.251H (a bottle opener in the shape of a sea horse) and U1930.376Ø (a lamp designed by Poul Henningsen where the 'decorative' base was found copyrightable). Particularly the Supreme Court was hostile towards awarding copyright protection to design. Thus when the Royal Porcelain Factory, in 1926, was involved in a second copyright suit over Arnold Krog's coffee pot (the very design that had occasioned the revision of §24 in the Copyright Act – see note 10) the Supreme Court vote in favour of copyright protection was carried by the narrowest margin: 5–4,.See Schmidt (1989), 58.

14 U.1935.695H

destined to be prototypes for industrial art'[15] as went the definition of design as objects of artistic copyright according to Danish copyright law.

Similar lines of reasoning continued in Danish courts in the decades that followed. In a Supreme Court ruling of 1956, the test of whether a feature was technically or artistically motivated was applied again. However, this ruling came to effect a change in Danish copyright statutory law.[16] The lawsuit involved charges for copyright infringement as well as for breach of marketing law and the plaintiff lost on both.[17] It concerned a hand-operated bread slicer by the royal Danish cutlery maker Raadvad. A recognised visual artist, Ove Larsen, had been commissioned by Raadvad in 1933 to design the slicer which consisted of a wooden tray to place the bread on and a guillotine-style movable part in iron shaped as a semi-circle with a blade across. On the iron part the name Raadvad and the royal seal was added in low relief following the curve of the semi-circle. In 1952 the Raadvad company discovered that a copy of the bread slicer was being marketed by a Copenhagen ironmonger. The defendant's bread slicer was a copy of the plaintiff's in all respects except for the sculpted name and royal seal. Court-appointed experts – such distinguished figures as Mogen Koch and Erik Herlov – maintained that the Raadvad bread slicer possessed such qualities as to render it an 'original intellectual work'.[18] In the explanatory statement presented to the Supreme Court the experts explained that:

> Our estimation is based on the fact that the visual artist Ove Larsen by his drawing and the model created on the basis thereof has clearly demonstrated a deliberate and independent design of the cast end-piece: thus the design – apart from being made with regard for the function – is artistically determined.[19]

The experts considered the design of the bread slicer to be the result of aesthetic choices on the part of its designer. Accordingly, in their opinion, the likeness of the defendant's bread slicer could not be explained away by reference to functional necessity. However, the majority of the Supreme Court judges disagreed. Five out of seven judges maintained that

> Considering that the bread slicer is a sheer work tool – in which the artistic design that has been carried out on part of the tool is of rather ancillary significance compared to the practical purpose – it cannot be considered an

---

15   Lov om Forfatterret og Kunstnerret af 26. April, 1933, § 24.

16   U.1956.237H

17   In relation to the charge for breach of good marketing practice, the Supreme Court found that consumers would not confuse the two bread slicers as the name of Raadvad did not appear on the defendant's bread slicer.

18   Ibid., 240

19   Ibid.

object of industrial art as defined by the Act on Authorial and Artistic Rights §
24 (3).[20]

In this ruling, the practical purpose of the bread slicer was weighed against
any artistic expression in it; by this measure the artistic element was in effect
overruled by its function. This way of reasoning on the part of the Supreme Court
was probably what led to the specific pointing out of 'applied art' as subject matter
by the Danish Copyright Act of 1961.[21] The object of protection was defined by § 1
of the 1961 Act as follows:

> The person creating a literary or artistic work shall have copyright therein, be it
> expressed in writing or in speech as a fictional or a descriptive representation,
> or whether it be a musical or dramatic work, cinematographic or photographic
> work, or a work of fine art, architecture, *applied art*, or expressed in some other
> manner [italics added]. [22]

No doubt remained as to the decision of the Danish parliament to make design
protectable by copyright. However, there was also great appreciation of the need
for open competition on the market for design products. This was the political
premise laid out for Danish courts in 1961.

In a larger perspective the *Raadvad* ruling and the 1935 ruling concerning
Marcel Breuer and Mart Stam's cantilevered chairs are indicative of a practice by
Danish courts in the first half of the twentieth century, where the notion of 'function'
was used to exclude certain works of applied art from copyright protection (see
also footnote 13). The artistic idiom of functionalism – the industrial, anti-
ornamental and de-individualised expression of functionalist furniture – added
extra complexity to the situation. Importantly, this practice may be seen as a way
for courts to strive to sustain a balance between creativity and copyright coverage.
Yet this practice was made unworkable by the 1961 Danish Copyright Act.

The 'Narrow' Scope of Protection

Soon after the new copyright act had been passed by the Danish parliament,
the Supreme Court heard a case concerning a set of steel cutlery designed by a
renowned Danish Modern designer.[23] Kaj Franck had designed a set of cutlery –
marketed under the name *Scandia* in Finland and under the name *Langelinie* in

---

20   Ibid., 240f. The remaining two judges considered the end piece of the bread slicer
to be artistically designed in a way as to make it a protectable original work under the
Danish copyright act.
21   See Schovsbo, Rosenmeier and Petersen (2013), 100.
22   Lov om ophavsret til litterære og kunstneriske værker af 31. maj 1961
23   U.1961.1027H

Denmark – for the Finnish cutlery manufacturer Hackman & Co. The cutlery was an all steel simple design in mirror finish, its main characteristic being the grooved surface of the handle on some of the pieces. Hackman became aware of two sets of cutlery named *Rio* and *Kongedybet* produced by the Danish company C. Thaysen & Co that bore striking resemblance to the *Langelinie* set. In particular, the two sets had grooved handles very similar to that of *Langelinie*. Therefore, Hackman & Co filed suit for copyright infringement and for breach of competition law, and after it had been heard by the Maritime and Commercial Court, the case went on appeal to the Supreme Court. Court-appointed experts were called to evaluate the originality of Kaj Franck's cutlery and to determine the degree of similarity between the sets. The experts were unequivocal in their evaluation of the originality of the *Langelinie* set:

> The groove design is not in itself new and original. However Kaj Franck has been accomplished enough to give this familiar motif a characteristic modern form. Accordingly, the court-appointed experts maintain that the cutlery set designed by Kaj Franck is an original work of art.[24]

Moreover, the experts added that

> In modern design it is rarely the details that render something an original work of art. Rather, what is aimed for in modern design is the creation of a harmonious unity. Kaj Franck's cutlery set is an independent artistic work in that the groove design makes up a harmonious element of the overall effect of the cutlery set and because there is a well-calculated balance between the form and dimensioning of all elements.[25]

In this way the experts argued that Kaj Franck had used a known pattern in a distinctive way and thereby created an original work – in accordance with modernist aesthetics. In addition, the experts argued that the defendant's two sets of cutlery were so (infringingly) similar to Kaj Franck's work as to make it likely that the engraver working for the defendant had in fact been provided with instructions to create a set of cutlery similar to *Langelinie*.[26]

The court only partly agreed. The Supreme Court confirmed – like the first court – that the *Langelinie* set was an 'original work protectable by copyright'.[27] Yet, the fact that the grooved design was 'neither new nor original' meant that there would be no protection against use by other designers of this motif.[28] This was at one time an affirmation of the 'low' originality requirement that exists to

---

24   Ibid., 1029
25   Ibid., 1030
26   Ibid., 1030
27   Ibid., 1030
28   Ibid., 1032

this day in Danish copyright law and of the limited scope of protection that comes with it. Thus in the case of the *Langelinie* set, protection would apply only to the 'total artistic effect achieved by the presentation and juxtaposition of details'[29] in the work. Such was the principle outlined by the Supreme Court: that the 'low' originality requirement for design must have as its concomitant a 'narrow' scope of protection.

Over the years this principle has become the basis for the development of the doctrine that only a 'close imitation' of a functionalist design would amount to copyright infringement. Thus, in a number of relatively recent Supreme Court rulings concerning design, the principle was applied and reaffirmed. In 2001 in a case that concerned Peter Opsvik's Tripp Trapp High Chair produced by Stokke since 1972, it was found that the so-called 2-Step Chair marketed by a rival furniture maker, Tvilum Møbelfabrik, was such a 'close imitation' that it infringed the copyright in the Tripp Trapp, which was (of course) an 'original work'.[30] The defendant's chair was a close imitation although it had a number of features – including curved sides, various cross pieces and a curved stiffening piece – which the Tripp Trapp chair lacked.

In 2002, the principle that only 'close imitation' amounts to infringement in functionalist design was applied again in a Supreme Court decision. This time the case concerned a modernist design icon which may well be said to belong to a class of world heritage designs: Arne Jacobsen's 'Ant chair' from 1952. Following the 2001 Tripp Trapp decision it was likely that the decision would be in favour of the plaintiff, the furniture company Fritz Hansen, which produces and holds the license to the Ant chair. However, Fritz Hansen lost its case against the defendant, Dan-Form Aps, the producer of the alleged copy, the 'Jackpot chair'. The Danish Supreme Court found no infringement.[31] The Ant was found to be an original work and as such the 'origin' of the many stackable moulded plywood chairs that are made today. However, according to the Supreme Court judges 'the Ant is most accurately defined by the distinct back', and, as the Jackpot chair did not share this feature it was not found to be an infringing copy.[32]

---

29 Ibid.

30 U.2001.747H

31 The *Ant* case was initially heard by the Copenhagen Maritime and Commercial Court where the plaintiff had been successful. The Court emphasised that the judgment must rest on a comparison of the overall impression. As the argument of the first court went: 'It is of no consequence that the chairs differ in a number of ways – particularly as regards, in the Ant, the characteristic "milling-out" of its back, which has been omitted in the Jackpot chair – in that the differences are insignificant in relation to the overall evaluation which reveals that the chairs share the same appearance and lines. No element has been added to the Jackpot chair to make its design go further than the design of the Ant and the Jackpot chair appears simply as a designerly reduction of the internationally renowned design of the Ant. By producing and selling the Jackpot chair, defendant has, therefore, infringed paragraph 2 of the Danish Law of Copyright' U.2002.1715/2H, 1726.

32 U.2002.1715/2H, 1728

In 2003 the Danish Supreme Court decided that there was no infringement of Jens Møller-Jensen's 'Albertslund lamp' from 1963.[33] The lamp is a classic of modern design and one of the greatest commercial successes of the manufacturer, Louis Poulsen & Co. Louis Poulsen sued the company David Super Light A/S for infringement of the copyright in the Albertslund lamp in four of the latter company's lamps. There was no doubt as to the copyrightability of Møller-Jensen's lamp: originality lay in 'the overall effect arising from the very simple idiom characterised by strict, precise geometric lines'.[34] Yet, there was no copyright infringement as the four lamps by the defendant 'according to an overall evaluation were not such close imitations as to infringe the copyright in the *Albertslund* lamp'.[35]

The rulings confirm the view that copyright in design should not prevent the use of particular forms and motifs by designers. As such they are in accordance with an overall principle – that copyright in design should exist to serve a general good – that of promoting creativity and sustaining (access to) cultural heritage and not to advance the individual market positions of design companies. This highlights the distinctiveness of copyright law as a regulator of designers' work. For example, the criterion of infringement in copyright is that there is substantial similarity between an original work and a 'copy'; the intention and use made of the copy by its originator is without significance. Furthermore, copyright protection may include protection of the designer's moral rights – that is of his or her right of paternity and right of integrity. The status of designs as 'works' and as 'products' means that legal disputes often give rise to charges for copyright infringement as well as for breach of good marketing practice (as mentioned in the discussion of cases above). And, unlike in copyright law, the evaluation of infringement in marketing practices law is based on a test where the use by the alleged infringer of the alleged copy is taken into consideration. Thus, under the Danish Consolidated Marketing Practices Act it is stipulated that

> Traders subject to this Act shall exercise good marketing practice with reference
> to consumers, other traders and public interests.[36]

And further that

> Marketing in respect of consumers' economic interests may not be designed to
> significantly distort their economic behaviour.[37]

In this way, restrictions on the uses of design relate only to situations where the design is marketed as a product and not to the use of the design in its capacity

---

33   U.2003.1219H

34   Ibid., 1230

35   Ibid.

36   Consolidated Marketing Practices Act, Act no 58 of 20 January 2012, section 1.

37   Ibid., section 1(2).

as a piece of cultural heritage by other designers in their creative practice. By contrast, when a design is protected by copyright such uses would usually require permission from the rights holder – unless the scope of protection is narrow.

There is often an inherent logic – developed over the years – in national systems of legal protection to prevent unwanted consequences: one such is the doctrine in Danish copyright law that only a 'close imitation' of a functionalist design would amount to copyright infringement. Such inbuilt 'safety measures' are precisely what is at jeopardy if Danish courts are to follow *Painer*. It would disrupt the balance between copyright and creativity, cultural heritage and economic vitality.

Design as Cultural Heritage

The cultural heritage constituted by designed objects is reinterpreted not only by new generations of designers. It may also constitute an object for artistic commentary. Thus, in 2006, the artist group Superflex launched their work Copy Right which is made up of a large number of legal copies of the Ant chair trimmed to be exact copies of the Ant:

> A Replica chair of the renowned *Ant Chair* by Danish architect Arne Jacobsen from 1953 is manually modified in an attempt to correct and hereby make it more similar to Jacobsen's original design. Hence, mass-produced imitations of a design classic are turned into unique pieces.[38]

By this gesture – in the tradition of Duchamp – Superflex turned items of practical use into a work of free art. And they managed to do so without litigation being brought against them.[39] This may be the first time: Superflex has a long record of legal actions against their works because they create what they term SuperCopies. For example in the project *Supercopy Factory* from 2007 a silk screen-printing facility is used to print the text SUPERCOPY on counterfeit objects supplied by visitors to Superflex's 'Copy Shop'. This is a process in which 'a copy product is turned into a Supercopy – a new original'.[40] This work occasioned an injunction against Superflex and a ransacking of their studio.

Another work, the *Biogas PH5 Lamp* (2002) was a modification of Poul Henningsen's original PH5 lamp from 1953 – an icon of Danish Modern and a much celebrated piece of Danish twentieth-century cultural heritage. As explained by Superflex, the idea of this work was to bring the best of Danish Design to

---

38   http://www.superflex.net/tools/copy_right

39   The artists had informed Fritz Hansen in advance and the company made no objections to the art work.

40   http://superflex.net/tools/supercopy_factory

people living in rural areas with no access to electricity.[41] The exhibition where the work was first displayed was nearly closed after threats of legal action from Louis Poulsen & Co, the manufacturer and rights holder of the PH5 lamp.

This sort of artistic commentary only consolidates the importance of the designed pieces as pieces of cultural heritage.

For over a century Danish courts have strived to maintain a balance between creativity and copyright. It has been done, first, by not allowing that which is 'technically determined' to be protected and, later, by granting protection against 'close imitations' only. However, if this is no longer feasible after the *Painer* case, what is to be expected? There seems to be no way of resolving the problem that arises from the fact that in any design the form is always if not entirely determined by its function. And therefore, too rigid an interpretation of protection – and too broad an interpretation of copying – would have the undesirable effect of stifling creativity by creating monopolies on coffee pots, cutlery, stackable chairs and so forth. In *Painer* the Court of Justice of the European Union decided that if something is a 'work' then 'its protection is not [to be] inferior to that enjoyed by any other work'.[42] However, in the case of design its protection *has* to be inferior. From a non-legal perspective (we might call it common sense) it seems obvious that all works are not created equal and do not need equal protection: a Monet is not the same as a postcard, and a designer coffee-pot is not the same as a copied pot.

References

Fallan, Kjetil (2009). 'Heresy and Heroics: The Debate on the Alleged "Crisis" in Italian Industrial Design around 1960', *Modern Italy* 14:3, 257–74.

Fallan, Kjetil (2014). 'Milanese Mediations: Crafting Scandinavian Design at the Triennali di Milano', *Konsthistorisk Tidskrift/ Journal of Art History* 83:1, 1–23.

Guldberg, Jørn (2011). 'Scandinavian Design as Discourse: The Exhibition "Design in Scandinavia"', *Design Issues* 27:2, 41–58.

Hansen, Per H. (2006). *Da Danske Møbler blev Moderne*. Odense: University of Southern Denmark.

Schmidt, Per Håkon (1989). *Teknologi og Immaterialret*. Copenhagen: GAD.

Schovsbo, Jens, Morten Rosenmeier and Clement Salung Petersen (2013). *Immaterialret. Ophavsret, Patentret, Brugsmodelret, Designret, Varemærkeret*, 3rd edn. Copenhagen: Jurist- og Økonomforbundets Forlag.

---

41   http://superflex.net/tools/biogas_ph5_lamp
42   Paragraph 99.

Chapter 7

Who Owns *Uncle Tom's Cabin*? Literature as Cultural Property

Peter Schneck

[W]e fundamentally misunderstand the very concept of property if we focus primarily upon a Western model of exclusive individual and corporate ownership ... . Property plays many roles in societies; it makes itself manifest in ideologies, multiple legal systems, social relationships, social practices, and in the interrelationship between these ... . Surely, the very topic of cultural property demands greater critical reflexivity with respect to property's diverse forms ... .

Rosemary Coombe (2009: 14–15)

Introduction

While certainly not an exclusive invention of the early modern era, the idea that ideas can be owned and claimed as property came to play a decisive, even essential role in the emergence and formation of the modern state and its subjects. Moreover, the institution of intellectual property as a legal concept at the beginning of the eighteenth century had a crucial impact on the ever expanding purview of capitalist forms of propertisation and exchange from the realm of the tangible to the intangible which continues to haunt contemporary debates about globalisation, ownership and cultural identity. Thus, for instance, Caren Irr (2001) has argued that intellectual property, especially in the form of literature, 'has a historically original role' because it prefigured 'the treatment of a wide array of the new economy's most valuable products':

> literature as intellectual property, in earlier phases of capitalist development, operated first as a homology for mercantilist means of accumulation and then as a synecdoche for industrial expansion; in the context of globalization, literature as intellectual property operates proleptically. (Irr, 2001: 774)

If literature – or more precisely the notion that literature could be a form of property – in this way prefigured modern legal, economic, and even political concepts and theories of subjectivity, personhood, ownership and freedom, the concept of literary property does not simply present a specific way of thinking about ownership in regard to the incorporeal, the evanescent, the transient, the immaterial or the imaginative, indeed, the *geistige Eigentum*: the property of the 'spirit'. Rather, literary property comes to stand in for an essential condition of modern proprietary relations: A way of conceptualising property – of living and realising ownership – which trades in (quite literally) the objective reality of an object owned for the experience of subjectivity by way of imaginary identification, i.e., a form of fantasmatic ownership which could be described both along the lines of spiritual and psychological possession and desire. Thus one particular feature of the uncanny 'proleptic' modernity of literary property is its co-emergence and complicity with a speculative economy which couples desire and investment and, at the same time, disconnects appropriation and the sense of property from actual possession. During the seventeenth and eighteenth centuries, property itself became increasingly virtualised (and mobilised) and the more it came to rely on the market of exchangeable, abstract value, symbolised and secured by various forms of documents, the less it was geared towards an actual object of value (i.e., 'real property'). As Martin Kayman has commented:

> the development, through the seventeenth and eighteenth centuries, of government debt, lottery tickets, insurance policies, bonds or shares in joint-stock companies, options for their future purchase or sale, bills of exchange, discount bills, endorsable bearer bonds, and promissory notes or bank notes, as well as the generalized increase in the importance of contracts, testified to the fact that property was undergoing a profound change. Rather than the natural solidity of land, property was increasingly taking the form of signifiers of abstract value, paper bearing promises of future expectations, whose reality at the moment was only imaginary, and whose value was defined not by substance or use, but by a deferred closure, or by the price for which it could be sold, or people could be persuaded to believe it might later fetch. In sum, then, the new regime installed by the Glorious Revolution was that of a constitution subordinate to the rule of law, a law based in 'real property', in which citizens engaged increasingly in the commercialization of signifiers of imaginary realities. For obvious reasons, the literary was to prove paradigmatic of the new forms of property and the book trade was to become both materially and symbolically a significant context for the commerce in such properties (Kayman, 1996: 767–8).

The rise to dominance of this speculative economy and the exchange of abstract values also had major consequences with regard to the cultural conception of property itself – most obviously in the sense that property became ever more 'fluid' as it could be won and lost in much less time than before, also meaning more and more that property ceased to be the most obvious and reliable indicator for historical and genealogical entitlement. Another way of putting this would be to state that property turned from a discourse about valuable objects into a discourse about valuable claims, i.e., discursive investments into future profits within an economy based on the rhetoric of promise, trust and creditworthiness.

More importantly perhaps, in the global market economy which emerged during the seventeenth and eighteenth centuries, the increasing dimension of speculative exchange also encouraged or even enforced the conceptual convergence of separate categories of property. In the expanding speculative economy of early modern capitalism, the specific features of property are abstracted from their use value in favour of their exchange value within the larger logic of speculation in a transnational, global market. The flourishing triangular trade of slaves, molasses and commodities between Africa, colonial America and the European Continent, presents an obvious example of how the abstraction of property from its specific objects worked to mobilise the property form in a global market of exchanging 'goods', no matter whether these goods were raw resources, manufactured items or human beings.

The increasing convergence and subsequent transformation of property concepts in the wake of the expansion of capitalist speculation was certainly not without conflicts and tensions, and arguably one of the most symptomatic conflicts with regard to legal and moral limitations of proprietary relations was the conflict about slavery in the US which culminated in the Civil War. Yet while it certainly dominated public debate, the contested issue of slavery was only one within the larger struggle over the definition of ownership and property rights which also included the question of copyright and literary property.

As legal historian Stuart Banner (2011) has observed, Americans are 'eager to claim ownership' – these claims have always been haunted by the 'troublesome question: what does it mean to own something?'. I would like to rephrase and revise Banner's troublesome question by focusing on literature (and culture) as 'something' that can be owned, possessed and claimed as individual but also as collective property. What haunts the claim for literary property, I will suggest, is its unstable and unsecure status within the larger processes of propertisation, commodification, and exchange. So my question will not be 'what does it mean to own literature' but rather '*how* can we own literature?' There are several answers to this question and my attempt here will be to demonstrate that these answers are related to each other, in fact, they are co-dependent, even where it would not appear so on first sight. I will therefore use the term 'literary property' as a radical or even transgressive notion, meaning both ownership *in* literature (i.e., literature as a form of property, whatever that may entail) and ownership *through* literature (i.e., literature as a form of owning or claiming something as property). This expansive understanding of 'literary property' aims at drawing the two different dimensions of literary ownership or appropriation closer together and – for want of better terms – I will refer to them as 'internal' and 'external' form(s) of ownership, respectively. In a second step, I will try to analyse the particular relationship between the two dimensions – the actual or objective sphere of 'real' property relations on the one hand and the imaginary, fictitious representation or dramatisation of these relations on the other – in order to come to a better understanding of their entanglement.

I will therefore tackle the question in my title, 'Who owns *Uncle Tom's Cabin*?', from three different angles: After a rather brief look at the question of property and ownership *in* the text, the central part of my discussion will deal with Harriet Beecher Stowe's various struggles to claim and protect *Uncle Tom's Cabin* as her own exclusive property – a struggle that is beset by conceptual tensions and moral ambivalences.

These tensions and ambivalences will then be reviewed and discussed using a Hegelian perspective on freedom and religion and the particular role of property with regard to legal personhood and social recognition. This reading is especially encouraged by the observation that the main conflict in Stowe's novel results from the unresolvable conflict between the abstractions of legal form (especially property versus person) on the one hand, and the concrete experience of violent repression, suffering and injustice on the other – through which abstract law becomes actualised, i.e., objectified as a reality. The inherent conflict between abstraction and actualisation also informs Stowe's struggle for authorial control and ownership and thus links the internal and external negotiation of proprietary relations concerned with the question 'who owns *Uncle Tom's Cabin*?'

In a concluding step, I will talk about a specific consummating moment of *cultural* appropriation at the end of the nineteenth century which helped to transform Stowe's work into a collective form of cultural property as an exemplary literary achievement of nineteenth-century American culture. The major argument in my closing discussion will be that the very idea that literature could (or should) be regarded as a form of national cultural property presents an uneasy correlation between Lockean and Hegelian notions of ownership and property. On the one hand, this correlation of essentially antagonistic concepts allowed for the successful introduction of an international framework on literary copyright (i.e., the 1886 Berne convention, and in the US, the Chace act of 1891) based on the idea of the protection of national cultural property. On the other hand, however, the very success of the model of protection it helped to introduce has gradually eroded the correlation itself, and the antagonism between the two understandings of ownership has come back to haunt contemporary discussions about copyright and cultural property.

Owning Uncle Tom

Since its first serial publication in the abolitionist newspaper *The National Era* between June 1851 and April 1852, and its subsequent book publication in March 1852, *Uncle Tom's Cabin* has been both highly praised and admired, severely criticised and attacked, as well as imitated, satirised, ridiculed and reviled by its readers. Critics have found it superior in morals and wanting in aesthetic expression – as well as morally ambivalent and highly effective in its affective, melodramatic strategies. All these positions, no matter how shifting and contradictory over time, have established a resonating space for the novel's various cultural meanings which has lasted until our own time.

Thus, in one of the many contemporary editions (from 2001), the preface (by Jane Smiley) calls *Uncle Tom's Cabin* 'the most important American literary document of the nineteenth century ... it is undeniably a hot property, and it has been almost too hot to handle since the day it was published' (Smiley, xiii).

Smiley uses the term 'property' quite on purpose since, as she well knows, Stowe's novel most and above all presents a literary document of nineteenth-century notions of property and ownership. Most obviously, of course, in its treatment of slavery as an institution based on the status of people – African-American slaves – as legal property owned by white slaveholders.

While the question 'who owns Uncle Tom' may be easily answered by referring to the names of the various owners who claim Uncle Tom as property, it is also obvious that the central concern of the novel lies less in the 'who' and much more in the 'how': slavery is not a homogeneous or stable system of ownership and there are obvious distinctions in the way proprietary rights and relations are realised. The comparison of these different forms of ownership is strategic for it allows Stowe to trace the decline and gradual perversion of an ideal form of 'sentimental possession' (cf. Merish, 1996) into an irresponsible and abusive as well as physically and morally destructive form of absolute ownership.

What Stowe clearly found the most troubling and indeed morally abhorrent and inacceptable aspect of slavery as a system of ownership is the transfer of title and possession – and thus the forced displacement and alienation of persons – made possible by this form of ownership. In other words, for Stowe, Uncle Tom's scandalous status as property is characterised less by the simple (but fundamental) fact that he is owned, but rather by the fact that he can (and will) be sold. The latter condition is obviously contingent on the first; but what is more, it also introduces a split or difference *within* the concept of property and the notion of ownership. It actually suggests that property exists in more ways than one, in the sense that the concept may be realized in two rather different manners: on the one hand, complete or full ownership, which is realised through extensive identification with and responsibility for one's property, and on the other hand we find proprietary relations in *Uncle Tom's Cabin* which are characterised by alienation rather than identification. Property rights here are reduced to the rights of buying and selling objects, i.e., the contractual rights of commercial exchange. What distinguishes the two perspectives on property is precisely the degree of abstraction or actualisation, respectively, which defines the particular property.

Consequently, the opening scene of the novel presents a sales talk in which the main protagonist is introduced only *in absentia* both as a human person, and as a profitable purchase. But the scene not only defines Uncle Tom as 'living property' (Stowe, 2001: 46), it also sets the plot in motion by turning Uncle Tom into *movable* living property. The mobility of human property in fact is the major driving concern of the novel's investigation of the system of slavery, both in the form of enforced removals through the selling and reselling of slaves down south, and in the form of the escape of fugitive slaves to the North.

Both types of movement are of course tied to each other in a dialectics that makes each the preliminary cause but also the inevitable consequence of the other. A cruel logic that characterises slavery as a system of ownership aimed at the maximisation of profits – yet also the logic that informs the melodramatic action of the novel ensuring the high interest and affective engagement of its readership.

The difference between movable and immovable property is crucial here for two related reasons: First, it marks both a distinction in forms of property and their inherent complicity. The sale that sets the living property and the events in motion is meant to avoid the loss of other more valuable objects, indeed, the master's house and home. Moreover, it also deprives Uncle Tom of his cabin, again signalling the enforced separation of movable from immovable 'property' that is at the centre of the novel's concern.

Second, the difference between the two types of property in the novel also marks an increasing tension between conventional and emergent cultural as well as legal notions of property throughout the nineteenth century. The conventional understanding of property was dominantly 'physicalist and absolutist', as Kenneth Vandevelde has argued in his seminal article on the transformation of property during the nineteenth century:

> [A]t the beginning of the nineteenth century, property was ideally defined as absolute dominion over things. Exceptions to this definition suffused property law ... [e]ach of these exceptions, however, was explained away. Where no 'thing' existed, one was fictionalized. Where dominion was not absolute, limitations could be camouflaged by resorting to fictions ... . The result was a perception that the concept of property rested inevitably in the nature of things and that the recognition of some thing as the object of property rights offered a premise from which the owner's control over that thing could be deduced with certainty. (Vandevelde, 1980: 328–9)[1]

In contrast, the 'new' concept of property, which emerged during the nineteenth century, was both less physicalist and less absolute:

> By the end of the nineteenth century, [the] conception of property as absolute dominion over things had become fatally anachronistic, and was supplanted by a new form of property. This new property had been dephysicalized and thus consisted not in rights over things, but of any valuable right. The new property had also been limited. It consisted not of an absolute or fixed constellation of rights, but of a set of rights which were limited according to the situation'. (Ibid., 357)

---

1   See also Grey (1980) on the disintegration of property.

The idea of property as a 'bundle of rights' that concerns the relation between persons rather than the relation between persons and things was of course not entirely new – it had been around at least since the end of the eighteenth century. Yet only by the end of the nineteenth century had it gradually been developed into the dominant concept of property.

Vandevelde's assessment of the gradual transformation of the Blackstonian concept of absolute dominion over things and based on the relation between persons and material objects into a Hohfeldian notion of property as a bundle of rights which fundamentally concerns relation between people has been criticised – among others by Jeanne L. Schroeder – as being based on a reductive misreading of Blackstone. As Schroeder maintains, Blackstone was fully aware of the 'intersubjective nature' of property and he did not merely 'present property as an immediate, binary subject-object relation' (Schroeder, 2005: 164). For Schroeder the intersubjective dimension is at the heart of Blackstone's concept of property as a *right*:

> Blackstone not only is aware but expressly states that the concept of dominion can only be understood as the right of one individual in relation to other individuals. Blackstone recognizes property as objective, not only in the sense of relating to an object but also in the sense of being generally enforceable against the relevant community of legal subjects. That is, Blackstone does not simply describe property as power over a thing, as Vandevelde suggests. (Ibid.)

As Schroeder furthermore points out, Blackstone's concept of property was also not

> limited to rights to physical things ... [i]ndeed, Blackstone makes it very clear that he uses the word 'thing' not in the sense of *physical things* but as objects of property. Such objects are defined in the negative – as that which are not human. ... An 'object' is external – in the sense of other than – the 'subject'. (Ibid.: 165, emphases in the original)

Schroeder does not question that notions of ownership and property did indeed change radically over the course of the nineteenth century. Her point is rather that the shift in perspective in legal theory from the objective to the intersubjective nature of property 'represses' the former aspect in favour of the latter. Thus her criticism is an important reminder not only that proprietary relations always entail an objective *and* an intersubjective dimension but also, and more significantly, that the transformation of property during the nineteenth century which Vandevelde and others have described cannot be simply understood as a shift from one paradigm to another, but rather as a consequential rearrangement or renegotiation of an already established but nevertheless constantly shifting correlation between the objective and the intersubjective dimensions of property. This rearrangement in turn must be understood as a reaction to a 'crisis within the existing paradigm'

(Schroeder, 2005: 162) rather than as a complete makeover of the Blackstonian concept of 'absolute dominion'.

In regard to *Uncle Tom's Cabin*, it will appear obvious even from a cursory reading that the novel in various ways reflects both the gradual transformation as well as the crisis of the dominant property paradigm. Indeed the novel explicitly attempts to reveal the interdependence and mutual enhancement of the objective and the intersubjective dimensions of property which characterise and sustain the system of slavery (as a proprietary order but also as an economy). For Stowe, concrete material possession as absolute dominance (e.g., over the slave's physical body) is not different from or opposed to the abstraction of human labour which allows for its alienation within a larger system of capitalist exchange: they are indeed two faces of the same coin. The complementary nature of the two forms of property as contingent forms of subordination and submission is also registered on the level of emphatic resonance, since Stowe carefully draws parallels between direct physical abuse and bodily harm and the emotional pain and suffering inflicted by the separation and selling of 'living property'. For Stowe's readers then, ownership as defined by slavery is characterised (and compromised) both by excessive forms of absolute dominance (physical harm) and by its subjection to the abstract forces of the market which 'perverts' the cruelty of direct personal possession even more.

The intersubjective dimension of property in *Uncle Tom's Cabin* is not reduced to the problem of abstraction and alienation alone. In fact, Stowe radically expands the intersubjective aspect of property in the sense that all social relations in the novel are in one way or another impacted, afflicted and in this way determined by that particular 'species of property' as Francis Lieber called the peculiar institution in one of his troubled communications about slavery with his wife (qtd in Keil, 2011: 55). Moreover, the discourse of ownership in the novel embraces and thus connects all forms of real and imaginary forms of possession: slaves and servants, houses and cabins, beliefs and ideas, God and the soul, countries and nations and, obviously, rights. Owning and being owned is paramount within the general social and cultural logic which the novel portrays; in fact *Uncle Tom's Cabin* presents a 'labyrinth of property concerns', as Stephen M. Best has succinctly remarked (2004: 115). Freedom thus is not a matter of escape from slavery either by refuge or redemption, it is ultimately a matter of proprietary relations which, as Stowe argued in her closing commentary, simply 'feel right' (Stowe, 2001: 632).

Who Owns Uncle Tom's Cabin?

While the economic success and cultural resonance of Stowe's novel were certainly exceptional, it was of course not only the sheer number of copies that were sold until the end of the Civil War which ensured the novel's strong effect and its huge national and international audience. Once the book had been published – which happened even before its serial run was finished because of the extraordinarily high public demand – its life as a cultural property unfolded in manifold ways, as image, object, sound and performance, creating what could be called the *Uncle Tom* effect – or, in the phrase of a more recent critic, the 'Uncle Tom Epidemic' (Buinicki, 2006: 76).

As I will sketch out later, the novel's status as an acknowledged national cultural property was established only after the Civil War, when *Uncle Tom's Cabin* had already become a household name or a familiar brand, signifying both the acknowledgement of American literature within an international context and the effectiveness of literature as an agent of historical change and progress.

The sheer versatility and unlimited potential of the ways in which the novel's familiarity could be used to market and sell any cultural product not only nationally, but also internationally, made the question of literary property and ownership a rather urgent one for Stowe. As Melissa Homestead (2005) and Martin Buinicki (2006) have argued in similar ways, it is precisely the unprecedented success of *Uncle Tom's Cabin* that made it a pivotal point within the debate about literary property rights and international copyright laws in nineteenth-century American culture. It also helped to bring about a change in the perception of literary property and copyright that increasingly centred on the interest and the rights of the author as original creator and proprietor of the literary work. As Buinicki has stated, after the publication of *Uncle Tom's Cabin*, 'American authors were finally prominent in the discussions of copyright, and Harriet Beecher Stowe's success put her firmly in the center of the debate of over literary property rights' (Buinicki, 2006: 65).

And yet, it was moral argument rather than economic interests or legal reasoning that eventually convinced Congress to pass the International Copyright Act in 1891 – an argument that is closer to the sentiment of Stowe's novel than to the way in which its author tried to argue for and protect her own literary property rights.

In 1853, only one year after the initial book publication of *Uncle Tom's Cabin*, the Philadelphia publisher F.W. Thomas began to publish a German translation of the novel in the German American newspaper *Die Freie Presse.* (published in 1864 as a book under the title *Onkel Tom's Hütte, Oder, Leben unter den Verstossenen*). Given the strong abolitionist leanings among the 100,000 Germans living in Philadelphia, this was a shrewd business move – to which Stowe reacted quickly by taking legal action to protect her property rights. What is most remarkable about this reaction, as Melissa Homestead has noted in her comprehensive discussion of the ensuing case, is the fact that Stowe had not only filed for copyright for the novel already before its serial publication, she had also already registered copyright for a German translation in her own name in 1852.

The arguments that Stowe's lawyers presented before the court, however, carefully avoided any reference to the potential economic disadvantages that Stowe would suffer. Rather, they insisted on the natural foundation of Stowe's interests in her own creation:

> An author is the 'creator', the efficient cause of a thing … . In respect to a book,
> he is a creator of the ideas – the thought – the plan – the arrangement – the

figures – the illustrations – the argument – the style of expression. The exclusive
right to sell these is what is secured by copyright. The right is original, inherent;
a right founded on nature ... a right which stands on better ground and is more
deeply rooted than the right to any other property whatever. Now, a translation is
an infringement of this right. (qtd in Homestead, 2005: 121)

This argument in favour of an absolute right was clearly recognised by the
following comment on the case:

As for absolute moral right, we see nothing in the nature of things to limit the
ownership of the author. It is his [*sic*] work and ought to be the essential right of
the case ... (qtd in Homestead, 2005: 120)

As Melissa Homestead has shown rather convincingly, the argument for the
moral absolute right of the 'author-creator' that Stowe's lawyers brought forward
emphasised a romantic idea of the 'author as creating an intentional object and
owning that object in its immaterial form' (Homestead, 2005: 122) – despite the fact
that Stowe had repeatedly denied such authorial powers of creation, for instance,
when she asserted that 'the Lord himself wrote [*Uncle Tom's Cabin*], and I was but
the humblest of instruments in his hand' (qtd in Homestead, 2005: 106, n. 4).

In his decision against Stowe, the court eventually rejected both the notion of
the 'incorporeal nature of literary property' (Curtis in Homestead, 2005: 122) and
the claim for absolute possession. Insisting that the author's right 'consists only in
a right of copy', Judge Grier famously argued:

By the publication of Mrs. Stowe's book, the creations of genius and
imagination of the author have become as much public property as those of
Homer or Cervantes. Uncle Tom and Topsy are as much publici juris (i.e. public
property) as Don Quixote and Sancho Panza. All her conceptions and inventions
may be used and abused by imitators, play-rights and poetasters. They are no
longer her own – those who purchased her books, may clothe them in English
doggerel, in German or Chinese prose. Her absolute dominion and property in
the creations of her genius and imagination have been voluntarily relinquished.
(qtd in Buinicki, 2006: 77)

The comparison of the two positions clearly shows an inversion of the two
aspects of the transformation of the concept of property during the nineteenth
century: while Stowe's lawyers insisted on an absolute right over incorporeal
property, Judge Grier argued that Stowe's right as an author are limited precisely
by the physical object, the copy. Therefore he concluded: 'A translation may, in
loose phraseology, be called a transcript or copy of her thoughts or conceptions, but
in no correct sense can it be called a copy of her book' (qtd in Buinicki, 2006: 77).

Judge Grier's decision has some very obvious relations to the anti-abolitionist
criticism of Stowe's novel during the 1850s, and as some important recent re-

readings of the case have emphasised, there is an obvious connection between the debates about slavery and the debates about copyright and literary property.[2] This is certainly not all too surprising, given that both debates are about the nature and limits of property rights. That the issue of slavery was in fact to be decided on the grounds of property rights and their constitutional priority, would also become the rationale behind the Supreme Court's ruling in the famous *Dred Scott* case in 1857 – a case that had drawn considerable attention and to which Stowe had already responded in her second novel about slavery *Dred: A Tale from the Dismal Swamp* (1856).

The particular way in which the two debates on property converged in Stowe's suit against the German translation in *Die Freie Presse* is a strong reminder that during the ante-bellum period the conflict about notions of property rights always involved the question of moral legitimacy: questions of property were not only legal or political, but also moral questions. Thus when Stowe filed her suit, her claim for the extension of her proprietary rights to include the work of others (the German translator and his publisher) was seen in clear opposition to her criticism of slavery as a deeply immoral and cruel system of ownership aimed at the exploitation of slave labour. Accusations of Stowe's moral hypocrisy were of course a recurring element in the writings of anti-abolitionist critics, who argued that Stowe herself was exploiting the work of slaves by using their experience as a source for her (immorally high) income without any recompense.

The suit against *Die Freie Presse* seemed to prove the truth of such accusations, and it eventually harmed Stowe's reputation – especially among the German audience in Philadelphia – an audience that was for the most part pro- rather than anti-abolitionist. But in the case of the German critic's reaction another moral argument reinforced the accusation of Stowe's greed and hypocrisy: the suit was seen as an attempt to enforce a monopoly in regard to translations of original works, which appeared especially outrageous since Stowe's own German translation appeared to be inferior to the translation Thomas had provided.

In one of the most critical commentaries on Stowe's copyright suit in the German press, the accusation of moral hypocrisy links the literary property suit with Stowe's particular sentimental abolitionism. In particular, Stowe's refusal of a financial settlement offered by Thomas enraged the German correspondent: 'Thus does an American abolitionist propagate her teachings. Will we ... finally realize that this abolitionism, at least in the whining, pietistical abolition of Mrs. Stowe,

---

2   This relation is made most obvious by the fact that Judge Grier was also a strong supporter of the Fugitive Slave Act. Grier's decision against Stowe, as Gene Andrew Jarrett remarks, 'indicates his ideological resistance to the anti-slavery praxis affirmed by *Uncle Tom's Cabin* and rejected by the Fugitive Slave Law'. As Jarrett concludes '[t]he case also supports the scholarly contentions of Lovalerie King and Stephen M. Best that law has generally mediated the relation between race and property, that copyright law has likewise mediated the more specific relationship between racial representation and literary property' (Jarrett, 2011: 134, 135).

is a humbug and a money business, like Barnum's sea tiger and Tom Thumb?' (qtd in Homestead, 2005: 129).

Two of the most detailed discussions of Stowe's copyright suit by Melissa Homestead and Martin Buinicki that I have already referred to above, carefully and convincingly reveal the important connections between the abolitionist debate on property in slaves and the debate on international copyright and literary property in nineteenth-century American culture.

Yet, while they do not explicitly say so, their research also clearly suggests that the conjunction of the two debates in the overall rhetoric of possession and ownership that framed existing notions about property as absolute dominion versus as a bundle of rights, also effectively harmed the position of American authors and publishers in favour of extended international copyright protection in 1850s until the end of the Civil War. Given the high visibility of Harriet Beecher Stowe as an outspoken abolitionist and also an extremely successful writer, the opponents of international copyright legislation in the US could successfully use her as an example to frame the international debate on literary property by reference to a highly charged conflict on the national level. Taking a stance on literary property and international copyright thus inevitably involved a stance on the issue of slavery and abolitionism – a factor that most likely had a detrimental effect on the pursuit of international copyright protection in the US, at least until the end of the Civil War.

'Property, Reputation, and Education': A Hegelian Digression

The accusations of the pro-slavery critics that Stowe's suit against the German translation was not about protecting her 'natural' rights as an author but a hypocritical attempt to capitalise on the work of others and monopolise her own, obviously reveal more about their own notions about the essential economic function of property rights than they could actually convey about the specific motivation and interest which made Stowe persue legal action. And despite the convincing arguments brought forward by Homestead and Buinicki, even today most readers would probably agree that her motives and interests must have been predominantly pecuniary. While it would be counterintuitive, if not even counterfactual, to deny any such pecuniary motives, the absence of any counter argument or alternative explanation appears a bit surprising. Even Stowe's admirers did not put forward any argument which would have supported the convergent rather than contradictory nature of her literary arguments about property law and her legal arguments about literary property. Of course, it is difficult to determine whether the arguments for the author's natural right brought forward by Stowe's lawyers were also genuinely her own, but it is obvious that Stowe was in favour of more extensive copyright protection, regardless of the specific argumentation in the case about the German translation.

But there is enough evidence in the novel itself that would allow for a reading of both the fictional and the legal argument along the same lines, in particular with regard to property assessed not simply in terms of economic value, but as a necessary precondition for social recognition. In order to do so, however, one first has to take a different perspective on Stowe's notion of property and look at its particular function in Hegelian terms. Attempting to read *Uncle Tom's Cabin* with Hegel in mind does not mean to suggest that Stowe's argument about property could be completely aligned with Hegel's complex discussion of property and personhood in the *Philosophy of Right* (1821), nor that, indeed, Stowe's specific representation of the intersubjective 'logic' of proprietary relations actually owes anything to Hegel's philosophy. Nevertheless, there are some important points of convergence in interest and motivation as well as a remarkably similar insistence on the necessity of property for the ethical actualisation of subjective will and freedom. Of course, one could easily read Stowe's novel in Hegelian terms from the perspective of the earlier *Phenomenology of the Spirit* (1807), and particularly with regard to the well-known Master-Slave dialectic, yet this would effectively reduce the extended discourse on property in *Uncle Tom's Cabin* to the discourse on slavery.[3] More essentially, it would also obscure the logical connection between the two works in regard to Hegel's major concern, that is, the relation between religion and politics, as Angelica Nuzzo has recently observed.[4] Arguably, the question about the relation between religion and politics, or rather the function of religion in the political culture of the nation, is also a central concern for Stowe. Thus, *Uncle Tom's Cabin* presents a strong reaction to the fundamental ethical problems resulting from political and legal prescriptions with regard to property laws and rights connected to slavery and the escape of slaves. As is well known, Stowe wrote *Uncle Tom's Cabin* in response to the 1850 fugitive slave act, her novel thus must be regarded as a political as much as a literary intervention in the public sphere. The political and public aspect of the text has been acknowledged by Stowe's admirers and critics alike, and both in her concluding remarks and her subsequent publication of *A Key to Uncle Tom's Cabin*, Stowe herself made a point

---

3   In his recent discussion of the pitfalls of such a reductive use of Hegel's metaphor see Gerard Aching, who has argued that reading 'the master-slave dialectic as either a struggle between two individuals or a struggle between two forms of consciousness with the subject has important theoretical and methodological consequences ... '. While the former reading thus tends to overlook the self-reflective struggle for resistance within subjective consciousness, the latter tends to de-contextualise these struggles from their specific historical conditions and circumstances. As Aching maintains 'the master-slave dialectic does not end with a life-and-death struggle that liberates the slave but describes moments of compromised freedom made possible by the unsettling work of reflection that constitutes the zero point of resistance' (Aching, 2012: 912, 916).

4   'Hegel's reflection on these issues dates back to his early philosophical works ... leading up to the 1807 *Phenomenology of Spirit*. However, it is in the *Encyclopedia* ... and the 1821 *Philosophy of Right* that Hegel reaches his mature systematic organization of the questions pertaining to the connection between politics and religion' (Nuzzo, 2013: 3).

of her social and political motives in writing the novel. Literature thus is only the medium for Stowe to make her arguments public, to elicit a response and to encourage sympathy for and action on behalf of her abolitionist agenda. However, the fact that it is literature through which Stowe attempts to impact public opinion, this is more than just a matter of articulation, argument and persuasion. What the discourse about literary genius and originality radicalises (and thereby wants to conceal or even negate) is actually an inherent trait of all forms of literature: literary 'creation' as a form of work or labour always entails an act of acquisition and appropriation. Literature is not made from nothing, it needs language as its basic material from which it takes a selection of elements, forms, structures etc. in order to compose a 'work'. From this perspective, literature as property is accrued before it is invented or created as art. Of course, such an approach may do less to invalidate than to further specify the aspect of originality, and one could still argue, as Stowe's lawyers did, that her composition, her characters, her plot lines, her settings are all her own creation and thus to be protected by authorial rights as her property.

The problem with this specification is that it acknowledges property only in its individualistic dimension, and what remains unacknowledged or even negated is the intersubjective function of property in general, and literary property in particular. This obviously is also how Judge Grier interpreted the claims of Stowe's lawyers – as an attempt to exclude others from partaking in her work and thus to monopolise the public sphere for individual profit.

Yet, similar to the accusations from the pro-slavery critics, Grier's absolutist reading reduces Stowe's novel to property in the legal sense, which means it abstracts from the individual act of creating property – the work – and looks at Stowe's novel simply as a published, that is public, piece of property. From this perspective the process of radical original creation is merely inverted; in a similar act of magical de-creation, *Uncle Tom's Cabin* becomes part of the material basis of literature and culture, and has ceased to be literary property since it belongs to everyone in general and no one in particular.

Both arguments, however, fail to acknowledge that literature as property is an act of articulation not merely in the artistic or aesthetic sense; literary property as property in the Hegelian sense is also and more fundamentally an act through which the self articulates and actualises her will in the world. That is, from a Hegelian perspective, property is not something that comes into existence by the interaction of individuals with their natural environment, either through an act of first occupation or by mixing of human labour with natural resources. In contrast to Lockean and utilitarianist notions of property rights, as Jeanne Schroeder notes, Hegel denies that property rights could be said to exist in the state of nature, in fact, 'property is intersubjective and, as such, cannot precede society' (Schroeder, 2005: 461). Hegel's perspective on property thus can be read as a critique of the premises of natural rights approaches to property (including literary property), as Schroeder explains:

Hegel begins with liberalism's starting point: the autonomous free individual located within a hypothetical 'state of nature'. Such 'natural' freedom is negative, abstract and, therefore, merely potential. To be actual, freedom must become positive and concrete. This can only occur through intersubjective relations (i.e. within society). To restate this in a slightly different way, rights cannot exist in the state of nature because they are intersubjective in nature. As Wesley Newcomb Hohfeld so famously articulated, rights, duties, powers and immunities can only be understood as existing insofar as they can be asserted and enforced against other persons. Similarly, Hegel defined the creation of rights as the first step individuals take in their attempt to escape the lonely autonomy of the state-of-nature in order to actualize their freedom through intersubjective relations. (Schroeder, 2005: 461)

It is this character of property as an essential means for the articulation and actualisation of the free will within an intersubjective context that may be seen to align Stowe's obsessive and expansive negotiation of the 'labyrinth' of contrasting and conflicting notions of possession and ownership in *Uncle Tom's Cabin* with her own struggle for the rights to her literary property. From a Hegelian perspective, the argument against slavery at the core of Stowe's novel thus may be grasped in its most expansive form: as an abominable violation of the slaves' physical integrity, their human dignity and their natural rights to life and liberty, the system of slavery furthermore also essentially corrupts and denies the ethical actualisation of the 'freedom' not only of their masters, but even within society and culture at large. Yet while the unethical perversion and general instability of proprietary relations in *Uncle Tom's Cabin* are thus strong indicators for the lack of legal and ethical order, they are also clearly what characterises social relations in the first place. The mutual determination of social and property relations does not simply affect the realm of intersubjectivity; it effectively defines it as the space in which social identity is negotiated through claims of ownership and acts of appropriation. These negotiations run through the complete gamut from physical to symbolic violence, from complete negation of the other by the slave master to the self-negation of the slave. While there may be social spaces that appear to be free from violence, as with middle-class homes and families, they nevertheless become affected by it – most obviously through the fugitive slaves appearing at their doors for help and shelter.[5] Again, in order to understand the central problem of proprietary relations within Stowe's novel, it might be helpful to look at the

---

5   Lori Merish has made a convincing argument about Stowe's deployment of a notion of 'Loving ownership' and 'sentimental property' based on Christian middle class values which was meant as a counter model to the prevailing notion of slaves as a 'tool' (Merish, 1996: 18). The idealisation of these forms of proprietary relations does not, however, secure them from corruption or the pressure of political or legal actions. While it is obvious that the humanity of the slave might be actualised in some proprietary relations while completely negated in others, it is a matter of debate whether this is a difference in kind or in degree.

function which property assumes in Hegel's *Philosophy of Rights*. For Hegel, property rights are essentially a means through which the necessity of property for the actualisation of the free will of the self becomes mutually acknowledged. In this way property not only sustains the individual as a matter of survival but also the individual's recognition by others (and by herself) as a person. The 'self as abstract will', as Costas Douzinas remarked,

> claims to be essential reality, but the existence of external ... objects, and our dependence on external reality contradicts this. The self, therefore, needs to appropriate external objects – it must own property. The self becomes particularized and concrete ... through ownership. Potentiality becomes actuality. (Douzinas, 2002: 388–9)

Thus property 'is a necessary moment in the struggle for recognition'; the will of the self is no longer abstract, 'it takes determinate existence'. Yet without the recognition by others, individual possession would be insecure, the actualisation of the free will would be constantly endangered. Only through the mutual recognition of property rights can possession help to realise the determinate existence of the free will. 'In the legal universe that Hegel describes', Douzinas concludes, 'property is a pre-condition of the recognition of others. The right to property is the right to have rights and to be recognized as a (legal) person' (Ibid.). This inherent connection between social recognition and property rights is another essential aspect of Stowe's understanding of the intersubjective function and effect of different forms of possession and ownership in the novel. In one explicit remark in her final commentary she states that 'this country has already seen examples of men, formerly slaves, who have rapidly acquired property, reputation, and education' (Stowe, 2001: 633–4), thus emphasising that the acquisition of property and the social acknowledgement of personal achievement are not only interdependent, but also representative and essential for the actualisation of the freedom of the former slaves.

Mutual social recognition thus is as crucial a factor for Stowe's understanding of the essential function of property as it is for Hegel's, and from this perspective the specific work of *Uncle Tom's Cabin* may be described as a fundamental critique of insufficient and dysfunctional notions of property as an end in itself by way of contextualising their detrimental intersubjective effects.[6] That does not

---

In other words, sentimental property relations are still property relations; no matter how 'human' a slave is considered to be, she remains a 'human' slave.

6 'When Locke makes property rights first, it is because they are the end to which everything else is means. When Hegel puts them first it is because in their immediate form as the minimal mode of human freedom they are in radical need of correction and completion through contextualizing' (Westphal, 1992: 31).

'All political and social orders are inextricably involved in the formation of subjects and the constitution of the conditions for their self-determination. But liberal theorists

mean that Stowe's understanding of property is Hegelian – far from it – but it also rejects the idea that her notion of property could be reduced to a Lockean or utilitarian framework.

The struggle for recognition was certainly also a driving force behind Stowe's attempts to secure greater copyright protection for her work – which at the end of the nineteenth century eventually turned out to be successful largely due to a different rhetoric of recognition, the recognition of literature as cultural property.

Recognising Literature as Cultural Property: Owning the Cabin

From our contemporary perspective on literary property and copyright, Stowe's suit against the German translation of her novel may appear like a slightly anomalous episode within the larger, more dominant trend towards a more extensive notion of authorial rights and the protection of literary ownership that succeeded in the years after the Civil War. Thus, in 1870 translations were included into the rights protected by copyright, and in 1891 Congress finally passed the International Copyright Act thereby overcoming the long held public opinion against such legislation which had been largely fuelled by the fear that American publishers would suffer and American readers would have to pay higher prices for their books.

What is notable, however, is the significant change in perspective and in rhetoric after the Civil War with regard to the issue of literary property. While questions about distribution, availability and economic effects are relegated to the background of the debate, the discussions in the last three decades of the nineteenth century are dominated by the notions of cultural achievement, the existence and sustenance of a national literature, as well as the desire for mutual international acknowledgement. What had been regarded as a discussion at the international level, now became a matter of national interest. As Catherine Seville has stated in her discussion of Anglo-American copyright relations: 'What remains striking is

---

obdurately refuse to properly acknowledge this, regarding the state as a necessary evil and the paramount threat to freedom. Since they also identify freedom with property and consumer choice, they help to legitimate and secure the manipulation, subjugation, and domination of individuals by economic managerial power, all in the name of "liberty".' (Maker, 2013: 66). Stowe's criticism of property as an absolute form of dominion and her negotiation of proprietary relations as intersubjective, i.e. social and ethical relations, somehow can neither be fully captured or described by a Lockean nor a Hegelian account of the relation between freedom and property. This points to an uneasy perspective on property, to put it mildly, resulting from the realisation, also inscribed into *Uncle Tom's Cabin*, that property has both empowering and disempowering aspects, and moreover, the power which the control of property may help to wield may encourage unethical choices and decisions. The problem, as Deak Nabers has argued at length, is obviously that Stowe in contrast to Hegel does not see the state as a structure which would ensure the actualisation of freedom as ethical life. The Lockean notion of 'natural freedom' thus cancels out the ethically enabling function of the state and the legal system.

the extent to which the American advocates of international copyright identified it as a matter of national significance, and linked it to national pride' (Seville, 2010: 42).

With reference to this development, the changing reception of *Uncle Tom's Cabin* in the years before 1893 – when Stowe's copyright finally expired and Uncle Tom indeed became public property – is instructive as well.

In my conclusion I thus want to briefly talk about the cabin and what kind of ownership it may signify or suggest. For even though the novel after all is titled for the cabin and not for its owner, the cabin tends to be regarded as a given, merely a place of temporary habitation that Uncle Tom is forced to leave behind.

The cabin, however, stands as the first, and probably most significant space of education, of communal exchange and most of all of literacy. It is not only the space where Uncle Tom, 'the hero of our story', as Stowe tells us (Stowe, 2001: 31), is finally introduced to the reader as a central actor; the hero moreover is placed in the midst of a mixed community of black and white characters, engaged in various activities of reading, writing and exchanging ideas, thus establishing a scene of sentimental, evangelical education that finally culminates in the reading and interpretation of the 'last chapters of revelation' (Ibid.: 43).

As Barbara Hochman has written: 'Throughout *Uncle Tom's Cabin* scenes of reading underscore the power of literacy, especially Bible reading, as both a moral force and a practical skill – a skill systematically denied to African Americans in slave culture' (Hochman, 2006: 91). Hochman is certainly not the first to notice this, yet her discussion of the post-Civil War reception of Stowe's novel will help me to conclude my own sketchy narrative of *Uncle Tom's Cabin* as property and culture with a final moment of appropriation – translating Stowe's literary property into a collective cultural property. This final appropriation happens at the very moment when Stowe's proprietary rights finally expired and *Uncle Tom's Cabin* entered the public domain.

For the Columbian Exposition World Fair in 1893, the Connecticut Board of Lady Managers organised a Harriett Beecher Stowe display as the centrepiece of the Connecticut women's exhibit in the Women's Building library. The Stowe display presented mainly objects like a portrait of the young writer, a marble bust, a huge mahogany bookshelf with glass-encased shelves and an inkstand made of silver that showed 'two slaves freed from their shackles' (qtd in Hochman, 2006: 84).

The bookshelves housed a full set of Stowe's collected works that had been exclusively printed and bound for the display at the fair. The collection was surrounded by a total of 42 copies of *Uncle Tom's Cabin* – all translations of the original English edition in various languages. In addition, Stowe's supplementary volume *A Key to Uncle Tom*, as well as the first and the last editions of *Uncle Tom's Cabin* (from 1852 and 1889, respectively) to be published while her copyright was still valid, were also prominently displayed. None of the books, however, could be touched physically or be read at the fair: the exhibit effectively transformed the literary property into a cultural object, as well as into an object of cultural veneration.

The display thus expressed in visual terms the changed perspective on Stowe's novel that developed during the later decades of the nineteenth century. As Hochman notes, the objective of the particular design of the Stowe exhibit fell in line with the attempt of her publishers (Houghton and Mifflin) to reach new audiences before the copyright would expire. Thus the 1889 edition emphasised the status of the novel as world literature and as a historical document, while downplaying its sentimentalism, as well as its moral and political objectives. Most of all, *Uncle Tom's Cabin* was presented as an effective agent within a larger story of continuous political, social and cultural progress. As Hochman states: 'publishers and editors of the nineties sought additional grounds for claiming the cultural significance of Stowe's text. ... *Uncle Tom's Cabin* represented not only America's literary coming-of-age but also its moral, political, and cultural maturity' (Hochman, 2006: 85).

As Hochman also points out, a closer look at the later nineteenth-century editions of the novel – especially those that her publishers produced in order to fill 'as many market niches as possible' (Winship, 2010: 330) – reveals some significant revisions in regard to those scenes from the story that were highlighted by the illustrations of the respective editions. While the illustration in the 1852 edition repeatedly emphasised scenes of reading and writing as well as scenes that showed African-American slaves as active agents in their liberation and education as citizens, the late nineteenth-century editions present the slaves as meditative, passive subjects that are not acting out their own destiny but have simply become objects for the scrutiny of a historically distant observer. In Hochman's words, these 'illustrations of *Uncle Tom's Cabin* offered an image of slave culture that memorialized – but also perpetuated – the cultural divide between African Americans and the contemporary white reader' (Hochman, 2006: 97). As a result the 'black figures are like museum exhibits'; like Stowe's books they have been turned into 'objects on display' (Ibid.: 98).

It is somewhat ironic – an irony of the more bitter sort – that this final appropriation of Stowe's novel as a work of genius, a national icon and an example of the superior achievements of American culture in general established *Uncle Tom's Cabin* as a cultural property only at the expense of its particular properties as literature. The cultural and communal necessity of sentimental reading and its communication across generational and racial divides which form the core of Stowe's argument for literary propriety, had been completely obscured and made irrelevant by the transformation of *Uncle Tom's Cabin* into a visible monument, thus restoring and reassuring full and absolute possession of Stowe's novel as collective property.

A Short Conclusion

To return to my beginning: In a proleptic reading of the history of literary property in the US, as suggested by Caren Irr, the acknowledgement of authorial rights and intellectual property by the 1891 Chace Act and the final recognition of *Uncle Tom's Cabin* as a central literary achievement and national cultural property does not just present 'two sides of the same coin'. What is achieved is less the successful consolidation of a particular notion of 'national' literary and cultural property and more a temporary moment of reconciliation and containment of antagonistic notions of individual and collective ownership. Paradoxically, it is the very success of a nationally grounded international framework for the protection of literary property which today has made its inherent antagonisms increasingly problematic and ever more difficult to contain and reconcile. Thus the increasing 'Americanization of intellectual property rights', as Eva Hemmungs Wirtén has described the 'relentless pursuit of ownership' (Hemmungs Wirtén, 2003: 85) which has become a major point of contention in contemporary disputes about copyright issues, destabilises the – already – shaky balance between individual rights and public interest: the absolutism of the idea of exclusive ownership and control increasingly cancels out the ideal of creativity for collective rather than individual ends, that is, the very idea of cultural property as a form of collective partaking and identification. In consequence, both the idea and the ideal of literature as national cultural property becomes more and more untenable as the work of authors is produced for international global markets, and it remains to be seen whether such counterstrategies as the national digital library in the US or European initiatives like Europeana will be successful in sustaining and renewing a sense of literature as a collective form of cultural property.[7] As Rosemary Coombe has convincingly suggested, the diverse forms of cultural property also demand a 'greater critical reflexivity' (Coombe, 2009: 15) in approaching the concept of property in general, but especially in regard to that most elusive claim of possession: the strange idea that ideas can be owned.

References

Aching, Gerard (2012). 'The Slave's Work: Reading Slavery through Hegel's Master-Slave Dialectic', *PMLA* 127:4, 912–17.

Banner, Stuart (2011). *American Property: A History of How, Why and What We Own.* Cambridge: Harvard UP.

Best, Stephen (2004). *The Fugitive's Properties: The Poetics of Law and Possession.* Chicago: U of Chicago P.

Buchwalter, Andrew (2013). 'Religion, Civil Society, and the System of the Ethical World: Hegel on the Protestant Ethic and the Spirit of Capitalism', in

---

7   See http://dp.la/info/ and http://www.europeana.eu/portal/, respectively.

Hegel on Religion and Politics, Angelica Nuzzo (ed.). Albany: State U of New York P, 214–32.

Buinicki, Martin T. (2006). *Negotiating Copyright: Authorship and the Discourse of Literary Porperty Rights in Nineteenth-Century America*. New York and London: Routledge.

Coombe, Rosemary J. (2009). 'The Expanding Purview of Cultural Properties and their Politics', *Annual Review of Law and Social Science* 5:18, 1–20.

Corré, Jacob I. (1997). 'Thinking Property at Memphis: An Application of Watson', in *Slavery & the Law* (ed.) Paul Finkelman. Madison: Madison House, 437–51.

Douzinas, Costas (2002). 'Identity, Recognition, Rights or What Can Hegel Teach Us about Human Rights?' *Journal of Law and Society* 29:3, 379–405.

Grey, Thomas C. (1980). 'The Disintegration of Property', in *Property* (ed.) J. Roland Pennock and John W. Chapman. NY: NY UP, 69–85.

Harris, Cheryl I. (1993). 'Whiteness as Property', *Harvard Law Review* 106, 1709–89.

Hegel, G.W.F. (1984). *Lectures on the Philosophy of Religion* (trans. R.F. Brown, P.C. Hodgson, J.M. Stewart). Berkeley: U of California P.

Hegel, G.W.F. [1821](1986). *Naturrecht und Staatswissenschaft im Grundrisse: Grundlinien der Philosophie des Rechts. Werke in Zwanzig Bänden* (ed.) E. Moldenhauer and H.M. Michel. Frankfurt a.M.: Suhrkamp, Vol. 7.

Hemmungs Wirtén, Eva. (2003). 'Life, Liberty and the Relentless Pursuit of Property Rights: the "Americanization" of Intellectual Property Rights', *American Studies in Scandinavia* 35, 85–94.

Hesse, Clara (2002). 'The rise of intellectual property, 700 B.C. – A.D. 2002: an idea in the balance', *Daedalus – Journal of the American Academy of Arts and Sciences* 131:2, 26–45.

Hochman, Barbara (2006). '*Uncle Tom's Cabin* at the World's Columbian Exposition', *Libraries and Culture* 41:1, 82–108.

Homestead, Melissa J. (2005). *American Woman Authors and Literary Property, 1822–1869*. Cambridge: Cambridge UP.

Jarrett, Gene Andrew (2011). *Representing the Race: A New Political History of African American Literature*. New York: New York UP.

Kayman, Martin (1996). 'Lawful Writing: Common Law, Statute and the Properties of Literature', *New Literary History* 27, 761–83.

Keil, Hartmut (2011). '"That Species of Property": Francis Lieber's Encounter with Slavery and Race', in *Paths Crossing. Essays in German-American Studies* (ed.) Cora Lee Kluge. New York: Lang, 55–83.

Irr, Caren (2001). 'Literature as Proleptic Globalization, or a Prehistory of the New Intellectual Property', *The South Atlantic Quarterly* 100:3, 773–802.

Maker, William (2013). 'Religion and the Dialectic of Enlightenment', in *Hegel on Religion and Politics* (ed.) Angelica Nuzzo. Albany: State U of New York P, 59–77.

Merish, Lori (1996). 'Sentimental Consumption: Harriet Beecher Stowe and the Aesthetics of Middle-Class Ownership', *American Literary History* 8:1, 1–33.

Nabers, Deak (2007). 'Shadows of Law: Melville, Stowe, and the Government of Liberty', *Law Culture and the Humanities* 3, 102–26.

Nuzzo, Angelica (2013). 'Introduction' in *Hegel on Religion and Politics*. Albany: State U of New York P, 3–13.

Ostergard, Robert L., Jr. (1999). 'Intellectual Property: A Universal Human Right?' *Human Rights Quarterly* 21:1, 156–78.

Penningroth, Dylan C. (2003). *The Claims of Kinfolk: African American Property and Community in the Nineteenth-Century South*. Chapel Hill: U of North Carolina P.

Plumpe, Gerhard (1979). 'Eigentum – Eigentümlichkeit: Über den Zusammenhang ästhetischer und juristischer Begriffe im 18. Jahrhundert', in *Archiv für Begriffsgeschichte* (ed.) Hans Georg Gadamer and Joachim Ritter, Vol. 23. Bonn: Bouvier Verlag Herbert Grundmann, 175–96.

Rose, Carol M. (1994). *Property and Persuasion: Essays on the History, Theory, and Rhetoric of Ownership*. Boulder, San Francisco, and Oxford: Westview Press.

Schroeder, Jeanne L. (1998). *The Vestal and the Fasces. Hegel, Lacan, Property, and the Feminine*. Berkeley, U of California P.

Schroeder, Jeanne L. (2005). 'Unnatural Rights: Hegel and Intellectual Property', *U of Miami Law Rev* 60, 453–504.

Seville, Catherine (2010). 'Nineteenth-century Anglo-US Copyright Relations: The Language of Piracy versus the Moral High Ground', in *Copyright and Piracy: An Interdisciplinary Critique* (eds) Lionel Bently, Jennifer Davis and Jane C. Ginzburg. Cambridge: Cambridge UP, 19–43.

Siegrist, Hannes, and David Sugarman (eds) (1999). *Eigentum im internationalen Vergleich (18.-20. Jahrhundert)*. Göttingen: Vandenhoeck & Ruprecht.

Smiley, Jane (2001). 'Introduction' in *Uncle Tom's Cabin*. New York: Modern Library, xiii–xxi.

Stowe, Harriet Beecher [1852](2001). *Uncle Tom's Cabin*. New York: Modern Library.

Vandevelde, Kenneth J. (1980). 'The New Property of the Nineteenth Century: The Development of the Modern Concept of Property', *Buffalo Law Review* 29, 325–67.

Westphal, Merold (1992). *Hegel, Freedom and Modernity*. Albany: State U of New York P.

Williams, Robert R. (2013). 'The Inseparability of Love and Anguish. Hegel's Theological Critique of Modernity', in *Hegel on Religion and Politics* (ed.) Angelica Nuzzo. Albany: State U of New York P, 133–56.

Winship, Michael (2010). 'The Library of Congress in 1892: Ainsworth Spofford, Houghton, Mifflin, and Company, and *Uncle Tom's Cabin*', *Libraries and Cultural Records* 45:1, 85–91.

PART III
Creativity, Authorship, Copyright and the Public Domain

Chapter 8

Pirates, Librarians and Open Source Capitalists: New Alliances in the Copyright Wars

Martin Fredriksson

'Say hello to your new librarian'

On 28 June 2012 the Swedish Library Association published a full page ad in one of the country's largest newspaper, *Dagens Nyheter*, where an elderly man in a three-piece suit is looking sternly at the reader under the heading 'Say hello to your new librarian'. The ad declares that 'There is a silent revolution going on in our public libraries. Not long ago, libraries were independent. Free to select, buy and recommend literature and factual books from amongst all the books that were in print. Then came the e-book'. The Library Association criticises the publishers' strict control over the distribution of e-books, particularly their refusal to release new titles to the libraries and their rigid price policies. The ad states that while the e-book is a wonderful opportunity for libraries, it is both an opportunity and a threat for publishers: 'E-books are potential cash cows – provided that the threat of libraries' independent choices and purchases are eliminated'. Here the libraries' aim to freely and publicly disseminate culture and knowledge is in contrast to the commercial interests of the publishers who threaten to take control over the libraries: 'Your new librarian likes money more than books and owns a large publishing company' (Svensk Biblioteksförening, 2012).

This is not a unique Swedish debate. Over recent years, the *European Bureau of Library, Information and Documentation Association* (EBLIDA) has been running a similar campaign that tries to draw attention to how the control that the publishers impose on the e-book format prevents the libraries from fulfilling their obligation to 'guarantee free access to content, information and culture for all European citizens' (EBLIDA, 2013). EBLIDA points to how the licensing of e-books controls the libraries' acquisition policies, but also how it violates users' privacy by collecting and storing personal user data and limits their access to the material since it restricts how, where and on what devices an e-book can be consumed (EBLIDA, 2012). In an American context similar initiatives have been taken, for instance by the campaign 'e-books for libraries' (http://ebooksforlibraries.com).

Figure 8.1   'Say hello to your new librarian', The Swedish Library
              Association (Svensk Biblioteksförening)

The library organisations' interest in copyright issues is not limited to e-books. Librarians have mounted the barricades against extensive copyright legislation several times in the past. In her book *Terms of Use* Eva Hemmungs Wirtén points out that few 'institutions are as affected by the threats now waged against the public domain and the increased permission culture that proliferates in its wake as libraries'. She goes on to discuss how libraries and affiliated organisations were among the most vocal opponents against the limitations to the public domain imposed by the American Copyright Term Extension Act (CTEA) of 1998 (Hemmungs Wirtén, 2008: 128). In 2005 the respected British institution, The UK Royal Society for the Encouragement of Arts (RSA), issued 'The Adelphi Charter on creativity, innovation and intellectual property', which called for a limitation to the expansion of copyright law which threatens creativity and the public domain (RSA, 2005). A few years later similar initiatives were taken by the Australian Library and Information Association (ALIA) which took a stand against the copyright implications of the Australia-United States Free Trade Agreement (AUSFTA). The Australian copyright scholar Lynn Spender argues that the positions of RSA and ALIA represent 'the spread of support for copyleft principles in the upper echelons of the legal, scientific and artistic establishments' (Spender, 2009: 124).

This scepticism towards copyright expansionism is a consequence of the library's basic function. As Siva Vaidyanathan points out in his book *The Anarchist in the Library*: 'Libraries are leaks in the information economy. As a state-funded institution that enables efficient distribution of texts and information to people who can't afford to get it commercially, the library pokes holes in the commercial information system' (Vaidyanathan, 2004: 123). As such the library is, just like the pirate, at conflict with the content industries that constantly attempts to fill such leaks with the help of stricter copyright legislation and harsher implementation.

This chapter starts from the assumption that libraries are, if not piratical, then at least articulate some of the conflicts over authorship, copyright and access to knowledge that have come to underpin the debates on piracy and copyright since the 1990s. Piracy and copyright has been a recurring theme politicised throughout history (c.f. Fredriksson, 2009, 2012, 2014; Johns, 2009). The clash between intellectual property and freedom of information – sometimes referred to as the copyright wars – was intensified by the proliferation of file-sharing technologies that followed in the wake of Napster, and the expansion of intellectual property rights that caught on in the 1990s. The conflicts intensified even more in 2006 when Swedish authorities initiated a prosecution against the internationally acknowledged file-sharing site The Pirate Bay, partly at the request of American media companies (Burkart, 2013; Fredriksson, 2013; Rydell and Sundberg, 2009). Over time these debates over enclosure and access to knowledge have given rise to a growing popular resistance against what is perceived as copyright expansionism: a legislative development towards enclosure and privatisation of culture and information. Today this pirate movement can be said to stretch from hardcore 'hacktivists' such as Anonymous to national political parties – so-called Pirate

Parties – that seek parliamentary representation in order to protect the freedom of speech, access to information and rights to privacy in a digital world.

The first part of this chapter will discuss the intersections between apparently disparate actors such as the pirate movement, libraries, and academia and how they relate to semi-commercial actors offering free access to information such as Google Books. This section partly draws on research interviews from an ongoing project about pirate parties in the United States, Europe, and Australia.[1] The second part of the chapter asks whether actors like The Pirate Bay and Google Books can be regarded as new kinds of libraries, and how we in that case define a library: if it is just an institution that provides access to as much information as possible or if it also fulfils other functions. Eventually the text widens the scope and frames the discussion about libraries and access to information within the context of a new logic of open source capitalism. Here the increased use of cloud storage and data mining problematises the debates about free access to information as user data emerges as the new commodity that is extracted, shared and exploited in the information society.

The Pirate, the Librarian and the Open Source Capitalist

The first Pirate Party was formed in Sweden in 2006, largely as a reaction to the police raid and following prosecution against The Pirate Bay, and the implementation of stricter copyright laws. Similar initiatives were soon taken in several other countries and they all shared a common focus on access to knowledge and protection of privacy in a digital society (Burkart, 2013; Fredriksson, 2013, 2015). It should come as no surprise that members of the Pirate Party have shown great enthusiasm for the librarians' cause. The president of the youth branch of the Swedish Pirate Party, Gustav Nipe, expresses a deep concern over the e-book issue and claims that he is looking towards librarians for mutual support. Aligning with the libraries is not only an attempt to gain public credibility, it is also fully consistent with the pirate movement's fundamental views on information politics:

> I've noticed that the same discussion that took place when they introduced the public libraries 100 years ago is going on again today. 'If people will be able to borrow books for free no one will want to buy them'. It is the same

---

1   The material mainly consists of semi-structured interviews but also includes information material such as websites and party programs. All interviewees play important roles in their local Pirate Party community, but these roles differ significantly due to the heterogeneity of the pirate parties. Although two of the interviewees are members of the European Parliament, and thus professional politicians, the vast majority are amateurs, dedicating their spare time to party work. The project is funded by Riksbankens Jubilemsfond [The Swedish Foundation for Humanities and Social Sciences]. For a more detailed account of this project see (Fredriksson, 2013, 2015).

argumentation ... But then the politicians took a stand and said that it is important for people to be able to borrow books. There is an educational ideal that is more important than the publisher's right to make even more money. But now it's not so much a political issue anymore. (G. Nipe, interview, 1 November 2012)[2]

The same historical comparison is made by the Swedish Pirate Party's secretary, Jan Lindgren (J. Lindgren, interview, 10 October 2012), and this strong identification with libraries is also evident in many national Pirate Parties. Zacary Adams Green of the New York Pirate Party, for instance, talks at length about the social importance of public libraries and the need to form alliances with librarians, and he concludes that 'The Pirate Party is basically "The Library Party". The Pirate Bay *is* a library' (L. Brunner and Z. Adams Green, interview, 2 April 2012).

The parallel between file-sharing networks and libraries is often evoked by copyright critics, and Adams Green refers to a widely shared blog-post he wrote for the Pirate Party founder Rick Falkvinge's website which compared The Pirate Bay to New York Public Library:

> The way media piracy works is that one person or group purchases a work, and then shares it with millions of other people. This supposedly deprives the author or artist of those millions of people's money. One group has acquired over 50 million media items, and makes each of them available to approximately 20 million people – which must be a tremendous hit to creative professionals' wallets. This notorious institution is called the New York Public Library. (http://falkvinge.net/2012/12/07/the-pirate-bay-is-the-worlds-most-efficient-public-library/)

The blog-post goes on to argue that The Pirate Bay is an even larger library, but the 'reason that The Pirate Bay is offensive, and the New York Public Library is not, is because of its efficiency' (Adams Green, 2012).

The idea that the internet is in itself basically a library, and as such the largest and most efficient one ever made, is common among many pirate activists, who see the internet as the ultimate medium of enlightenment and regard any attempts to control its flow of information as limitations to free speech and the public access to knowledge. In this regard, file sharing, particularly through

---

2   Nipe's reflections are only partly historically accurate. Initially it was mainly the book sellers who felt threatened when the public libraries began to spread in early twentieth-century Sweden: the publishers were on the contrary happy for the expanding market that the libraries provided. In the shadow of the financial crisis and the falling book revenues of the 1930s, the publishers however became more sceptical and joined the sellers and authors in a common demand for an embargo on public lending of new titles (Svedjedal, 1993: 543 ff). Although this demand was turned down in favour of a general lending fee to authors, it reflects a tendency of publishers to look towards the libraries and other alternative forms of distribution as a scapegoat when the market is failing.

the BitTorrent protocol, is often conceptualised as the ultimate technology of information exchange as it is free and egalitarian, and relies on mutual exchange of information between collaborating individuals rather than on centralised, top-down distribution of content from producers, corporations or authorities to passive consumers. File sharing is thus articulated not as a matter of entertainment but as a tool of enlightenment and education. Jay Emerson from the New York Pirate Party describes this very vividly when he talks about how he discovered the magnitude of academic literature that had been posted on The Pirate Bay:

> I wasn't thinking outside of the box at that time. I was thinking music and movies. But then when the books came into it, that was a different moment. Then I was thinking to myself. These books … . The whole purpose of the university back in the days was to send your kids off to it because that's where they had the libraries, the education, the expertise. That is no longer the case … everybody should have access to the education and the knowledge of all those books … it's a humanitarian effort to get that out there (J. Emerson, interview, 21 April 2012)

A cornerstone of the pirate ethos, as it is expressed by most Pirate Party members, is thus that information technology has huge potential to promote public education by creating virtually unlimited and universally accessible digital libraries, but that this is stifled by too restrictive copyright laws.

Just as the pirate ideologists tend to articulate values and positions that are traditionally well established in the library sector, they also draw on a belief in openness and free dissemination of scientific knowledge that has a long tradition in academia. These freedoms are often perceived as under threat by current policies and there are legions of examples of how an expanding IP-regime stifles research, for instance through the proliferation on gene patents (Boyle, 1996; Halbert, 2005). In his foreword to J.D. Lasica's book *Darknet: Hollywood's War against the Digital Generation*, Howard Rheingold sets out with a reflection on his own experience as a scholar and author:

> If you look at my earlier books … you might notice that there are more quotes and longer quotes, than in my most recent book, *Smart Mobs*. The explanation for that is that 'fair use' – the fundamental scholarly tradition of building upon the (accurately attributed) work of others (?) – has been chipped away by large 'content owners'. (Rheingold, 2005: vii)

This suggests that academics and ideologically dedicated file-sharers might share a common experience of having their freedom of expressions limited by copyright law.

In this regard the pirate agenda seems to align with the interest of academics who defend the right to share and use knowledge against attempts at commodification, privatisation and enclosure from the copyright industry. Lately this position has also gained ground in mainstream research politics as both EU and many national research councils have begun to require that the research they fund is made available in open access. The access to scientific knowledge and the freedom of research is also a high priority among the pirate parties, and they often speak of the need to make publicly funded research available in open access. In a European context this basically becomes an endorsement of the existing policies, such as in the Manifesto of the United Kingdom Pirate Party: 'We support the existing government policy that all academic research funded or partially funded by the taxpayer via the UK Research Councils is published under a CC-BY license' (*Manifesto*, Pirate Party UK, 2012: 39).

The Pirate Party's position on open access illustrates Lynn Spender's claim that the pirates' 'valuing of the commons is parallel to the desire of many academics, software developers, public interest groups and librarians who are part of an "information commons" movement' (Spender, 2009: 151). That the pirates, the professors and the librarians seem to be closing ranks against the threat of the copyright industry is seen as a response to a privatisation of a wide range of previously communal resources, such as traditional or academic knowledge, which is often conceptualised as an enclosure of the information commons (Boyle, 1996; 2003; Hess and Ostrom, 2006). As Christine Schweidler and Sasha Costanza-Chock attest: 'As the enclosure of knowledge encroaches further into all spheres of life, transnational movements increasingly integrate IP resistance into their agenda. At the same time, commons-based alternatives to IPRs, many of them self-consciously modeled on FOSS, are becoming more widespread' (Schweidler and Costanza-Chock, 2009: 23). This could be regarded as a mainstreaming of IP issues on both sides of the fence: while intellectual property rights are included in an increasingly wide range of sectors and more and more kinds of resources are defined as intellectual property, a wider range of social movements are also forced to take a stand on IP-related issues (cf. Halbert, 2005).

IP policies thus affect many people who in different ways depend on access to information, and thus pirate activists, librarians and academics protecting their intellectual freedom have ended up in the same camp, opposing the copyright industry's attempts to privatise growing parts of the public domain. In the struggle against copyright enclosure, the proponents of open source culture have also made occasional alliances with parts of the emerging tech industries, which largely thrive on open access to content. The entertainment and the technology industry are often seen as two opposing business models where the entertainment industry strives to maintain and extend its control over information through intellectual property while companies like Google, Youtube and Facebook make money from distributing user-generated material or content that is for other reasons in the public domain (Jacobsson, 2012; Fredriksson, 2015). This became particularly evident in the protests against the proposed bills Stop Online Piracy Act (SOPA) and Protect Intellectual Property Act (PIPA) which were rejected by the American Congress in early 2012 due to massive protests. Digital rights activists were alarmed by what was perceived as limitation of free speech, and tech companies like Google and

Mozilla joined the protests since they objected to the restrictions and liabilities for user-generated content that the legislation would impose on them. In an interview with the *New York Times*, Stephen Dodd, head of the Motion Picture Alliance of America and one of the bills' sponsors, also discussed this as a conflict between Hollywood and Silicon Valley (Cieply and Wyatt, 2012; Fredriksson, 2015).

Google's commitments to the principles of public access to knowledge, and the potential conflicts with the content industry that this creates, became apparent when it decided to go into the library business by launching Google Books in 2005. The basic idea was that Google would – eventually – scan and digitally publish all books ever printed. The copyright holders were given the possibility to opt out and copyrighted works were only published in parts, but the project nevertheless met hard resistance from publishers and authors who claimed that Google violated their rights as copyright holders. Within a short time, court cases were filed and in 2011 a court ruling halted Google's efforts (Helft, 2011a). This is hardly surprising and comes across as a conflict between a copyright industry that thrives on enclosure – i.e. on protecting its copyrights and monopolising and selling content – and a technology industry that provides free content but makes money on additional services.

What is a Library?

It appears that many actors are laying claims to the title 'library' and the legitimacy that comes with it. New York Public Library, Google Books and The Pirate Bay can be said to represent three different kinds of libraries: *the public library* funded and organised by public institutions, schools and universities in accordance with existing copyright laws; *the private library* funded and organised by a private company that negotiates (but not necessarily opposes) existing copyright laws; *the pirate library* organised by collectives of users – swarms if you like – who attest to their own rules and usually disregard existing copyright laws.

These relate to each other in different ways. The pirates clearly identify with the public libraries, partly as a strategy to draw on the respectability and legitimacy that they provide, but also because many of them see the file-sharing revolution as a contemporary extension of the educational project that was initiated with the public libraries in the nineteenth century. At the same time the Swedish Library Association's e-book campaign shows that the libraries can also borrow rhetoric from the pirates. The worst problem that libraries face when handling e-books is not the selection process but the costs. This partly depends on the model of payment where publishers charge the same prices for old and unattractive titles as they do for new ones, which makes it expensive for the libraries to keep a large stock of less popular e-books. It is also largely caused by the fact that the libraries get no state funding for e-books in the same manner as they do for printed books, and are left to pay the publishers out of their own pockets (Lindberg, 2011).[3] The problems with the economy of e-books thus depend both on the relation to the publishers and to the state, but the latter is toned down in the information folder that the Library Association issued with its e-book campaign, where the demand for a state-funded compensation for lending of e-books is just briefly mentioned as one among eight demands (Svensk Biblioteksförening, 2012). Although the Library Association's most important demand is directed against the state, the campaign focuses on the antagonism with the publishers in a way that ties in with the dichotomy between the content industry and the users which had been established during the copyright wars. So, it could be argued that it is not only the pirates who look to the libraries for legitimacy, but also the libraries that can, at least in this case, lean on pirate rhetoric to make an impact.

In its turn, Google Books also tries to present itself as a kind of library: on the website, they trace Google's history back to 1996 when Sergey Brin and Larry Page were developing technologies for Stanford University Library – technologies that would lead not only to Google Books, but to the very core of the Google empire: the PageRank algorithms (http://books.google.com/googlebooks/about/history. html). The libraries' reactions to Google Books have, however, been ambiguous. A number of large university libraries have allowed Google to scan the collections and some librarians, like Michael A. Keller at Stanford University Library, welcome Google's initiative (Helft, 2011b). Others, such as Robert Darnton, head of Harvard University Library, discard Google Books as a commercial endeavour in a sphere that should remain public and object to what they perceive as a potential privatisation of a common literary heritage (Helft, 2011b). The very existence of Google Books has inspired authorities in America and Europe to take similar initiatives, such as the Digital Public Library of America (http://dp.la/) or EU's Europeana (http://www.europeana.eu/portal/). In the end nevertheless, Google has contributed to the revitalisation of the world of public libraries.

Judging by these examples, the sphere of libraries appears to be expanding as new actors are being said to offer similar services to those of the public libraries. This however gives rise to the more fundamental question of what a library actually *is*. If a library is defined simply by its function to make books and other sources of information available, then both The Pirate Bay and Google Books can certainly be regarded as libraries. However, traditionally, a library has not only offered access to content, it has also made a careful selection of what content to offer and set down rules for how and where that content can be accessed. When actors like The Pirate Bay and Google Books claim to provide the same services but without the selection and the restrictions, it questions whether the selection

---

3 Every time someone lends a printed book at a public library the state compensates the copyright holder with a standard fee according to a general agreement. No such agreement exists for e-books which means that the libraries themselves have to pay the fee of 20 SEK (around 2 Euro) per e-book loan that the central distributor of e-books, Elib, demands.

and restriction have only been a technical limitation or if it is one of the library's operational functions: if providing a carefully assorted selection of literature and a space to enjoy it in is not also a part of the library's assignment.

This is where The Pirate Bay differs from conventional libraries. The efficiency of The Pirate Bay largely rests on what could be described as a crowd-sourced practice of acquisition – i.e. on anyone being welcome to contribute whatever content they like. With a base of more than 6 million registered users from all over the world (http://thepiratebay.se/), this of course enables a huge quantity of material that can hardly be matched by any conventional or remotely legal library. What The Pirate Bay does not provide, however, is the quality control that the stricter requisition policies of conventional libraries have ensured. From a libertarian position this is often cherished as eliminating the gatekeepers to ensure a new, and freer distribution of information: the website boasts that 'The only time The Pirate Bay removes torrents is when the name does not match the content – you should know what you are downloading' (http://thepiratebay.se/about). The same ideological premises also legitimise the plethora of pornography that litters the website and alienates large user groups.

There is however, a wide heterogeneity of piracy practices and The Pirate Bay is not at all representative of all kinds of file-sharing networks. Hungarian copyright scholar Balázs Bodó points out that The Pirate Bay is only 'the public face of file sharing: beyond them there is a whole network of *closed, private trackers* that lurk in the depths of dark-nets' (Bodó, 2014). Bodó argues that such alternative networks also impose strict rules of exchange that often reflect those of conventional IP regimes, but tend to be more efficient. In closed file-sharing networks, the users are often given access to a ratio of downloads partly based on how much uploaded material they contribute to the community. As Bodó points out, copyright holders can sometimes be rewarded with extra credits for allowing their works to be available, and an internal economy tends to be created on those networks. File sharing is thus not necessarily free from norms and gatekeepers, nor is it always free of charge. This means that the large bulk of file-sharing networks actually perform the very same act of selection and regulation as traditional libraries do, and they even impose the same kind of artificial scarcity as e-book licensing when they deliberately construct technological limitations to the flow of information in order to uphold an economic system. Compared to open sites like The Pirate Bay, the private trackers may better resemble how a conventional public library works – with the fundamental exception that they are not actually public.

Changing Modes of Enclosure

These examples show how actors that in various ways distribute information try to relate to each other and negotiate different positions in a new information economy. Although the role of the library may be under reconsideration, the library as such still seems to serve as a point of reference, at least in an ideological and rhetorical sense where the title 'library' carries the legitimacy of serving the public good. The question is, who is best equipped to fulfil the task of the public library in a digital age? Is Google Books really the best that the information society can offer those who want free and universal access to literature without being solicited by digital pimps? And just how free is the content offered by the open source capitalists?

Google tries hard to position itself within a discourse of free culture, and draws on values and principles both from the hacker movement and academia. The logic of the PageRank algorithm strongly resembles traditional academic citation analysis and Google's commercial success has been related to its reliance on practices and norms that have guided the libraries for a long time (Caufield, 2005). James Caufield concludes that if previous search engines were littered with ads and their results highly biased by sponsored links, then Google 'insisted on the simplicity of the user interface, a practice recognized in the library community as a means of facilitating access. ... Thus Google's site design and advertising decisions were made with a view to improving access rather than maximizing immediate profit' (Ibid.: 563). The key word in this sentence is of course 'immediate', for even though Caufield concludes that Google's commercial success largely depended on the fact that the company adopted traditional library values such as access to information and neutral selection processes, he attests that 'Libraries also provide a public good, and library values have developed in the context of service, usually public service. It is crucial to identify those library values that cannot be embodied in privately held search engines' (Ibid.: 569).

As Caufield suggests, it is necessary to ask under what logic different kinds of libraries operate. In this regard Google's commitments to free access to culture and information can be regarded in relation to what Peter Jacobsson calls 'the openness industry'. The term is a response to the widely used 'copyright industry' and refers to a new kind of business model that has emerged around the commercial exploitation of open source programming and user-generated content: a model that relies on openness, rather than enclosure, as a media industrial logic (Jakobsson, 2012). The openness industry is not a countermovement to the neoliberal process of commodification that the copyright industry represents, but instead a business strategy to better exploit what is not commodified as intellectual property: 'A more open policy in regards to intellectual property also means that the emerging intellectual commons on the Internet can be merged into the market and exploited by new and alternative business models' (Jakobsson and Stiernstedt, 2012: 53).

This new business model radically changes the way the internet works. Rasmus Fleischer, activist and academic, points out that in the 2000s, the internet turned us all into archivists when new technologies for file sharing and cheap devices for data storage allowed common users to store, organise and share large quantities of information. The defence for file sharing, in its most ideological form, is not only about access to information but about protecting everyone's right to create their own archives in collaboration with equal peers. This is a radical potential of the internet that is eroded by centralised data storing in the so-called 'cloud' (Fleischer, 2013: 41). David Lametti argues that the widespread implementation of streamed media and cloud storage, where content is increasingly hosted on central servers rather than on the users' private devices, is a strategy for technology companies to maintain control over the use and distribution of media and information. The cloud thus enforces a centralised use of culture and technology as it 'prevents users from participating in the Internet as creators, collaborators and sharers' (Lametti, 2012: 197). Lametti calls this 'Enclosure 3.0': a technological shift with 'the potential to disempower Internet users and conversely empower a very small group of gatekeepers' (Ibid.). This mode of control actually surpasses the enclosure enforced though intellectual property rights since 'the structure of the Cloud makes control over content possible to a degree unmatched by these various legal measures' (Lametti, 2012: 225).

The creation of economic value in the knowledge information thus resides not only in producing or owning content. With the expanding field of amateur producers and the rich availability of open access material, a growing body of information is actually already available and produced for free. The challenge is how to make that information searchable and easily accessible. This pushes the borders of the digital commons debate that previously tended to regard enclosure and accessibility as a simple binary opposition: either content is available or it is unavailable. As the three examples discussed in this chapter show, accessibility is not such an uncomplicated concept. There are various modes of accessibility, particularly when we are trying to access such vast materials as the New York Public Library, The Pirate Bay or Google Books offer, which cannot be accessed without structured catalogues. In this regard access to knowledge is not synonymous with unlimited access to content, but rather a matter of who owns the technologies of accessibility: who controls the catalogues that shape the user's choices and patterns of consumption. Furthermore, these catalogues go both ways: they register not only the content they offer to the user, but also the user and the usage itself.

The debates about copyright enclosure has understood enclosure as limiting access to culture and information, but the changing discussions about cloud storage and data mining imply that enclosure can mean free access to information, not only for individual users but first and foremost for the new media corporations. Because even though the so-called Web 2.0 might break down the barrier between users and producers – creating a new group of 'produsers' – it comes in no way close to overcoming the divide between 'produsers' and those who own and control the technological platforms where the products are distributed. Instead of paying for access to content most users get accustomed to a system where content is free but comes at the price of privacy.

Copyright expansionism and the enclosure of the information commons must indeed be opposed. Most of us would like information to be free, and few of us would like a publisher for a librarian. In this chapter I have discussed how not only digital rights activists, but also librarians, academics and many others have come to realise that too extensive IP regimes harm that freedom. At the same time there are good reasons to question what freedom actually means and where the frontiers of enclosure are progressing. We should ask ourselves if we really want *all* information to be free for *anyone* to use for *any purpose*, and remember that the price we pay for access to information differs depending on where we obtain it. Because the meaning of public is not only about public *accessibility* but also about public *accountability* – not only *what* the library serves but about *who* it serves; and as this chapter has tried to illustrate: serving information *to* the public is not necessarily the same as *serving the public*.

References

Adams Green, Zaquary (2012). 'The Pirate Bay is the World's Most Efficient Library', Falkvinge & co. on Infopolicy. http://falkvinge.net/2012/12/07/the-pirate-bay-is-the-worlds-most-efficient-public-library/

Andrejevic, Marc (2007). *iSpy: Surveillance and Power in the Interactive Era.* Lawrence: University Press of Kansas.

Bodó, Balasz (2014). 'Set the Fox to Watch the Geese: Voluntary IP Regimes in Piratical File-sharing Communities', in Martin Fredriksson and Jame Arvanitakis (eds), *Piracy: Leakages from Modernity.* Sacrament, CA: Litwin Books, 177–94.

Boyle, James (1996). *Shamans, Software and Spleens: Law and the Construction of the Information Society.* Cambridge, MA: Harvard University Press.

Boyle, James (2003). 'The Second Enclosure Movement and the Construction of the Public Domain', *Law and Contemporary Problems* 66: 33, 33–74.

Burkart, Patrick (2013). *Pirate Politics.* Cambridge, MA: MIT Press.

Caufield, James (2005). 'Where did Google get its Value', *Portal: Libraries and Academy* 5: 4, 555–72.

Cieply, Michael and Edward Wyatt (2012). 'Dodd Calls for Hollywood and Silicon Valley to Meet', *New York Times* 19 January 2012.

EBLIDA (2012). 'EBLIDA Key Principles on the Acquisition of and Access to E-Books by Libraries', 22 October 2012. http://www.eblida.org/Special%20Events/Key-principles-acquistion-eBooks-November2012/GB_English%20Version%20Key%20Principles.pdf (accessed 17 February 2014).

EBLIDA (2013). 'The Right to E-read: An E-Book Policy for Libraries in Europe', 13 June 2013. http://www.eblida.org/about-eblida/the-right-to-read-task-force-on-e-books.html (accessed 17 February 2014).

Fleischer, Rasmus (2013). 'Nätets kontrarevolution', *Tapirskrift.* Stockholm: Axl Books, 15–38.

Fredriksson, Martin (2009). *Skapandets rätt: Ett kulturvetenskapligt Perspektiv på den Svenska Upphovsrättens historia.* Göteborg: Daidalos.

Fredriksson Martin (2012). 'Piracy, Globalisation and the Colonisation of the Commons', *Global Media Journal: Australian Edition* 6: 1.

Fredriksson, Martin (2013). 'An Open Source Project for Politics: Visions of Democracy and Citizenship in American Pirate Parties', in James Arvanitakis and Ingrid Matthews (eds), *The Citizen in the 21st Century*. Witney: Inter Disciplinary Press, 201–13.

Fredriksson, Martin (2014). 'Copyright Culture and Pirate Politics', *Cultural Studies* 28.

Fredriksson, Martin (2015). 'The Pirate Party and the Politics of Communication', *International Journal of Communication* 9: 909–24.

Halbert, Debora J. (2005). *Resisting Intellectual Property Law*. New York: Routledge.

Helft, Miguel (2011a). 'Judge Rejects Google's Deal to Digitize Books', *The New York Times*, March 22, 2011. http://www.nytimes.com/2011/03/23/technology/23google.html?ref=technology (Accessed 19 March 2014).

Helft, Miguel (2011b). 'Ruling Spurs Effort to form Digital Public Library', *The New York Times*, 3 April 2011. http://www.nytimes.com/2011/04/04/technology/04library.html?pagewanted=1&_r=2&ref=technology (Accessed 19 March 2014).

Hemmungs Wirtén, Eva (2008). *Terms of Use: Negotiating the Jungle of the Intellectual Commons*. Toronto, Buffalo, London: University of Toronto Press.

Hess, Charlotte and Elinor Ostrom (eds) (2006). *Understanding Knowledge as a Commons*. Cambridge: MiT Press.

Jakobsson, Peter (2012). Öppenhetsindustrin, Örebro: Örebro universitet. http://oru.diva-portal.org/smash/get/diva2:482726/FULLTEXT02.pdf (Accessed 19 March 2014).

Jakobsson, Peter and Fredrik Stiernstedt (2012). 'Reinforcing Property by Strengthening the Commons: A New Media Policy Program?' *TripleC* 10: 1, 49–55.

Johns, Adrian (2009). *The Intellectual Property Wars from Gutenberg to Gates*. Chicago and London: The University of Chicago Press.

Lametti, David (2012). 'The Cloud: Boundless Digital Potential or Enclosure 3.0?'. *Virginia Journal of Law and Technology* 17: 3, 190–243.

Lindberg, Niclas (2011). 'E-böckerna ruinerar biblioteken', *SVT*, 21 November 2011. http://debatt.svt.se/2011/11/21/e-bockerna-ruinerar-biblioteken/ (Accessed 30 April 2014).

Rheingold, Howard (2005). 'Foreword', in J.D. Lasica, *Darknet: Hollywood's War Against the Digital Generation*. Hoboken, NJ: John Wiley & Sons.

RSA (2005). *Adelphi Charter on Creativity, Innovation and Intellectual Property*. http://a2knetwork.org/sites/default/files/workshop_kit/APVol43-Adelphichartertext.pdf (accessed 12 March 2014).

Rydell, Anders and Sam Sundberg (2009). *Piraterna: De svenska fildelarna som plundrade Hollywood*. Ordfront: Stockholm.

Schweidler, Christine and Sasha Costanza-Chock (2009). 'Common Cause: Global Resistance to Intellectual Property Rights', in Dorothy Kidd, Clemencia Rodriguez and Laura Stein (eds), *Making Our Media: Mapping Global Initiatives Toward a Democratic Public Sphere*. Creskill, NJ: Hampton Press.

Spender, Lynn (2009). *Digital Culture, Copyright Maximalism and the Challenge to Copyright Law*. Sydney: University of Western Sydney.

Svedjedal, Johan (1993). *Bokens samhälle: Svenska Bokförläggareföreningen och svensk bokmarknad 1887–1943*, vol. II. Stockholm: Svenska Bokförläggareföreningen.

Svensk Biblioteksförening (2012). 'Säg hej till din nya biblitekarie': http://www.biblioteksforeningen.org/wp-content/uploads/2012/08/Folder-Sag-hej-120907.pdf (Accessed 17 February 2014).

UK Pirate Party (2012). Manifesto: http://www.pirateparty.org.uk/sites/default/files/Manifesto2012.pdf

Vaidhyanathan, Siva (2004). *The Anarchist in the Library: How the Clash Between Freedom and Control is Hacking the Real World and Crashing the System*. New York: Basic Books.

Chapter 9

Copyright, Creativity, and Transformative Use

Kim Treiger-Bar-Am[*]

Introduction

Creativity relies upon copying and changing prior works. Authors and artists are influenced by and respond to earlier elements of cultural heritage. Sir Isaac Newton claimed that if he had seen further, it was because he had stood on the shoulders of giants. As Justice Story wrote, in literature, art and science, nothing is truly new.[1] Copies and changes abound.[2] It may be said that all expression is at some level borrowed – or copied. Understanding creativity as based on copying does not require adopting a postmodernist view deconstructing the concept of authorship.[3] Rather, *all* authors, including those whose authorship involves borrowing and indeed copying from others, should be allowed to develop their creativity.

The purpose of copyright is to foster creativity. As can be seen from the title of the UK Statute of Anne and the US Copyright Clause, copyright is designed for the 'Encouragement of Learning' and 'the Progress of Science and useful Arts'.

---

* I wish to thank Helle Porsdam for her review and invaluable encouragement in the preparation of this chapter.

1 *Campbell v. Acuff-Rose*, 510 U.S. 569, 575 (1994) ('For as Justice Story explained, '[i]n truth, in literature, in science and in art, there are, and can be, few, if any, things, which in an abstract sense, are strictly new and original throughout. ...' (citation omitted). As Ralph Waldo Emerson wrote: '[A] man is a ... selecting principle, gathering his like to him wherever he goes. He takes only his own out of the multiplicity that sweeps and circles around him ... . [T]here never was an original writer'. Thomas MacFarland (1985), *Originality and Imagination* 14–16.

2 Examples may be brought from works in the visual arts by Rembrandt following Da Vinci, Picasso following Velasquez, Manet following Renaissance and ancient Greek artists; in literary art by Shakespeare and Hans Christian Andersen; and in music works inspired by Bach's Fugues. See Leslie Kim Treiger-Bar-Am (2006a), 'Adaptations with Integrity', in Helle Porsdam (ed.), *Copyright and Other Fairy Tales: Hans Christian Andersen and the Commodification of Copyright*.

3 Michel Foucault (1979), 'What is an Author'?, in Josue V. Harari (ed.), *Textual Strategies: Perspectives in Post-Structuralist Criticism*; Martha Woodmansee and Peter Jaszi (1994) (eds..), *The Construction of Authorship: Textual Appropriation in Law and Literature*.

Yet despite copyright's purpose, copyright law restricts the copies and changes necessary for creativity. The copyright-holder's distribution right prevents the production of *copies*; the author's moral right under copyright prevents *changes* to works; and the copyright-holder's right to derivative works prevents *copies with changes*. Can copyright doctrine nevertheless protect the creativity of authors who copy and change the so-called 'original' works of the 'primary' authors they follow?

One method of allowing creativity is the provision of a defence to claims of copyright infringement where expression makes *transformative use* of prior expression. Within its fair use doctrine, US law provides a defence for transformative use. In recent analysis of US case law, the transformative use of a work has been called the central factor upon which courts rely in considerations of fair use.[4] UK law has been said to recognise a fair use defence, and can be seen to include doctrinal developments supporting transformative use as well. This chapter explores courts' analysis of the transformative use defence in particular in the context of appropriation art, defined as 'the more or less direct taking over into a work of art a real object or even an existing work of art'.[5]

It is shown here that in their analyses of the transformative use defence, courts engage a hermeneutic analysis which is also used in free speech cases and in the art world. The hermeneutic method interprets works by examining the three elements of Author, Reader and Text. In each of the areas considered – copyright doctrine, free speech case law, and aesthetic theory – the focus has shifted towards the Reader. Given the focus on the Reader's understanding of the meaning of the appropriation artist's copies of and changes to previous artwork, the law is able to accept transformative use of works in copyright. Creativity may thus be protected.

The second section of this chapter sets out the legal understanding of transformative use in UK law, and the third section, in US law. The discussion in the fourth section turns to hermeneutic analysis, exploring the method of court consideration of free speech claims in the US. The fifth section returns to the transformative use defence under US law, where a similar hermeneutic court method is seen. It is put forward that with this method of analysis courts are able to accept transformativity in appropriation art. While copyright doctrine has increasingly restricted creativity, the hermeneutic method utilised by courts

---

4   Neil Weinstock Netanel (2012), 'Making Sense of Fair Use', *Lewis and Clark L. Rev.* 15:3, 715. See also Michael D. Murray (2012), 'What is Transformative? An Explanatory Synthesis of the Convergence of Transformation and Predominant Purpose in Copyright Fair Use Law', *Chi.-Kent J. Intell. Prop.* 11, 260; Matthew D. Bunker (2002), 'Eroding Fair Use: The "Transformative" Use Doctrine After *Campbell*', *Communication Law and Policy* 7. See also Joseph P. Liu (2003), 'Copyright Law's Theory of the Consumer', *B. C. L. Rev.* 44, 397, 420–21 (defending viewing, even without transformative use).

5   This definition of appropriation art by the Tate gallery is cited in *Cariou v. Prince*, 714 F.3d 694 (2d Cir. 2013), cert. denied, 186 L. Ed. 2d 946 (2013). The case is further discussed below, see notes 109–11, 124–8.

considering the transformative use defence may enable copyright law to further its goal of encouraging and promoting creativity.

UK Copyright Law

UK copyright law includes a 'substantial part' doctrine, which on some views allows transformative use. Moreover, UK copyright law allows a fair use defence, of which commentators have seen transformative use as an element. Finally, courts evaluating moral rights claims under copyright appear to utilise a judicial test termed here the minimal-maximal test, which allows the protection of transformative uses. Together, these three doctrines may allow copies and changes upon which creativity depends.

Substantial Part

The substantial part doctrine may be seen as protecting transformative use. UK copyright law restricts acts of copying to the 'work as a whole or any substantial part of it'.[6] Where the subsequent work does not retain a substantial part[7] of the prior work, the secondary work is protected: as long as what has been taken from a prior work has been changed enough so that no 'substantial part of the plaintiff's work survives in the defendant's work', a defence will stand.[8] Thus in effect, the law allows a change – or what may be termed a transformation – to the prior work.[9] Sir Hugh Laddie called this use of the substantial part doctrine a 'device' for the protection of transformative use,[10] suggesting that a court will find that no substantial part has been taken *because* of the alteration to the material, in order

---

6   UK Copyright, Designs and Patents Act, 1988 ('the Act' or 'UK Act') Section 16(3) (a). Compare this Section of the UK Act with factor 3 of the US fair use test, regarding substantial similarity. 'Substantial part' is also a term used in the United States copyright doctrine, for example by the House Report on 17 U.S.C.A. Section 107 (House Report no. 94–1476), and in Section 108(e).

7   Laddie wrote that the test asks whether a substantial part of the skill, knowledge, labour or judgment – 'i.e., originality' – was taken. Sir Hugh Laddie, Peter Prescott, Mary Vitoria, Adrian Speck, Lindsay Lane (2000) (eds..), The Modern Law of Copyright and Designs (3rd edn) at 3.137, 3.57–74.

8   W.R. Cornish and D. Llewelyn (2003), *Intellectual Property: Patents, Copyright, Trade Marks and Allied Rights* (5th edn) at 11–09. See also Lionel Bently (2009), in Geller and Nimmer, *International Copyright Law and Practice* UK: 34-section 2[3][a].

9   Laddie et al., (2000) at 3.139.

10   Ibid., at 3.134. See also Ibid., at 4.42.

to protect transformative use.[11] For instance, the law 'smiles on' parodies, which are given 'latitude'.[12]

In *Designers Guild Ltd. v. Russell Williams (Textiles) Ltd.*, Lord Scott essentially acknowledged transformative use when he said that with altered copying, if 'the alterations are sufficiently extensive it may be that the copying does not constitute an infringement at all'.[13] Even where there is direct evidence of copying, 'the differences between the original and the copy may be so extensive as to bar a finding of infringement'.[14]

Laddie recognised that a change of context can be transformative under copyright doctrine. Removing material from its context may effectively destroy its originality, so that no substantial part is taken.[15] In borderline cases, it may make a difference how much further skill and labour the defendant bestowed on his own work so as to give it original character; it is a question of fact and degree.[16]

An alternative view was taken in *Williamson Music Ltd. and Others v. The Pearson Partnership Ltd.* and *Schweppes Ltd. v. Wellingtons Ltd.*[17] There the courts found that if it takes a substantial part from the primary work, the secondary work's originality does not excuse that work's use of the primary work. It is said that the point is not how much is new, but how much was taken. Nevertheless, Laddie's analysis arguably may still be maintained, supporting a transformative use defence.

While in his comments for the Hargreaves review Professor Lionel Bently called Laddie's view 'valiant', and indicated the 'restrictive interpretation of "substantiality"' in developments in UK and EC law,[18] he nevertheless suggested a provision that

> would not focus on how much was taken, but what was added and whether
> there was, as a result of what was added, a transformation of what was taken.

---

11   Ibid., at 4.54 (where use is considered fair, the formal legal conclusion would be that no substantial part of claimant's work had been taken).

12   Ibid., at 3.142.

13   *Designers Guild Ltd. v. Russell Williams* (Textiles) Ltd. [2001] F.S.R. 11, at 131 para. 64. See infra n. 18 for a restrictive interpretation of this case.

14   [2001] F.S.R. at 131 para. 65.

15   Laddie et al., (2000) at 3.139.

16   Ibid., at 4.55. See also supra n. 7, on Laddie's discussion of labour and skill in this regard.

17   *Williamson Music Ltd. and Others v. The Pearson Partnership Ltd.* [1987] F.S.R. 97; *Schweppes Ltd. v. Wellingtons Ltd.* [1984] F.S.R. 210. See Michael Spence and Leslie Kim Treiger-Bar-Am (2007), 'Private Control/Public Speech', in Katja S. Ziegler (ed.), *Human Rights and Private Law: Privacy as Autonomy*.

18   Lionel Bently (2011), 'Exploring the Flexibilities Available to UK Law', *Hargreaves Review of Intellectual Property and Growth* at C(1)(81). Bently offered a restrictive view of Designers Guild in Bently (2011). Compare text at n. 13.

In effect, compilations comprising small takings that are synthesised into a new work would be permissible.[19]

The Hargreaves Review of 2011, commissioned and endorsed by the UK government, suggested making fuller use of limitations and exceptions under EU law, in order to update copyright law in the digital age.[20]

Fair Use Defence

In addition to the substantial part doctrine, a fair use defence may allow transformative use under UK law. UK copyright law provides a defence for 'fair dealing', as set forth in Section 30 of the UK Copyright, Designs and Patents Act 1988 ('the Act', or 'UK Act'). In addition to that statutory defence, courts are said to examine the 'object and purpose' of the use of a work, thus protecting the fair use of a copyright work.[21] Laddie has put forward the analysis of UK case law that shows fair use considerations of copyright claims.[22] While the development of a fair use exception in UK law is currently considered to be restricted given the EC Information Society Directive 2001/29/EC ('European Directive'), the constraints on exceptions and limitations imposed by the Directive have been considered overestimated.[23] Professor Bently commented that the UK review of limitations and exceptions is '[c]learly ... interested in the development of a "fair use" exception .... My own view is that a real case can be made for the desirability of such a defence'.[24]

It is noteworthy that also in the European Directive the fairness of use is of concern. Criticism and review are listed among the permissible exceptions or limitations to rights of reproduction and communication, conditioned upon 'fair practice'. According to the Directive, 'quotations for purposes such as criticism or review' may be permitted:

> provided that they relate to a work or other subject-matter which has already been lawfully made available to the public, that, unless this turns out to be impossible, the source, including the author's name, is indicated, and that

---

19 Bently (2011) at C(1)(92).

20 See Final Report, Review, paras. 5.24–5.38: http://www.ipo.gov.uk/ipreview-finalreport.pdf

21 Laddie et al., (2000) at 3.134.

22 Ibid., at 4.54.

23 'Article 5 of that Directive only constrains the application of exceptions in national law with respect to the reproduction right, the communication right and the distribution right ... [which] leaves scope for some flexibility in national law for arrangements/adaptations, and translations'. Bently (2011) at A(2).

24 Ibid., at B(4–5).

their use is in accordance with *fair practice*, and to the extent required by the specific purpose.[25]

I submit that in fact courts should expressly allow transformative use pursuant to a fair use defence. The law should allow as fair use the taking of a substantial portion of a copyright work, where it has been transformed.[26]

Moral Rights, and Meaning

Finally, it is submitted that the moral right can be understood to allow transformative use. The UK Act allows authors the moral right of integrity to prevent infringing modifications to works, labelled derogatory treatment.[27] While the Act does not explicitly allow a fair use defence to moral rights,[28] in considering claims of an infringement of the integrity right courts use a textual evaluation comparing the primary and modified works I term a minimal-maximal test, which can be seen as allowing transformative use.[29] Where the allegedly infringing modifications are significant and constitute transformative use of the primary work, the claim of infringement of the moral right is not upheld.[30]

---

25   European Directive Article 5(3)(d)(emphasis added). See Bently (2011) at B(2) (d)(30).

26   Leslie Kim Treiger-Bar-Am (2007), 'Authors' Rights as a Limit to Copyright Control', in Fiona Macmillan (ed.), *6 New Directions in Copyright*, 368.

27   'Derogatory treatment' is defined as addition to, deletion from or alteration to or adaptation of the work which amounts to 'distortion or mutilation of the work or is otherwise prejudicial to the honour or reputation of the author or director'. UK Act Section 80.

As the US moral rights provision set forth in Section 106A of the US Copyright Act entitled the Visual Artists Rights Act ('VARA') 1990 is limited, the discussion here addresses only the UK moral rights protection.

28   Fair dealing is an exception to the moral right of attribution pursuant to the UK Act 79(4)(a), but not to the moral right of integrity preventing infringing modifications.

By contrast, under US law fair use is defined as an exception to moral rights, VARA Section 106A. The Australian Law Reform Commission took note of concerns about the possible adverse effects on the moral rights of creators from a transformative use exception. See Australian Law Reform Commission, Copyright and the Digital Economy, at 10.43.

29   The substantial part doctrine in copyright and the minimal-maximal test under moral rights function similarly, regarding copies and changes, respectively.

Michael Spence writes that the potential remedy to a claim of infringement of the integrity right, of a notice explaining that a work has been modified, may be seen as a commitment to allowing transformative use. The notice would declare that the relevant speech is no longer that of the original creator, but of the modifier. Spence and Treiger-Bar-Am (2007).

30   Also where modifications are minimal, infringement is not found, see *Pasterfield v. Denham* [1999] F.S.R. 168; *Tidy v. Trustees of the Natural History Museum* [1995] 39 I.P.R. 501 (Ch). Only modifications falling into a middle ground are found infringing, see, e.g., *Morrison Leahy Music Ltd. v. Lightbond Ltd.* [1993] E.M.L.R. 144 (modifications found

For example, the court protected maximal changes in *Confetti Records v. Warner Music U.K. Ltd.*[31] *Confetti Records* involved the defendant's modification of a music track transferred to it by the plaintiffs, on a compilation album. While the claim of infringement of the author's integrity right failed in that the treatment was not held to be derogatory,[32] the court described the process of mixing as one which results in a 'new work'.[33] The possibility appears to be put forward that the defendants' work would have risen to this level.

UK courts considering moral rights claims have also recognised that multiple meanings can be given to a work, thus supporting the notion of a transformation of meaning. In *Confetti Records*, the court examined the meaning of the modification to a rap superimposed upon garage music. The court described it as a 'faintly surreal experience of three gentlemen in horsehair wigs examining the meaning of such phrases as "mish mish man" ',[34] and wrote that meaning is not necessarily fixed and singular, but is open to different interpretations. Moreover, in *Pasterfield v. Denham*, the court cited an earlier decision in finding 'the "one meaning rule" strange', thus affirming the possibility of multiple meanings.[35]

Thus while UK law has not expressly recognised a transformative use defence, transformations may be allowed. The use of earlier works is sometimes permitted where the use is not of a substantial part of the earlier work; a fair use defence may be evolving; and moral rights claims are not upheld where the change to a work creates a new work. It is submitted that transformative use should be considered fair use, and termed as such directly.

US Copyright Law

The transformative use defence has been recognised by US courts more expressly than in the United Kingdom. This section begins by examining the transformative use defence, and then distinguishes it from the derivative rights doctrine. In the following section the transformative use defence is compared with certain elements of the US free speech doctrine.

---

potentially to occupy the infringing middle ground were sent for a factual determination at trial).

31   [2003] E.C.D.R. 31.

32   The court found that the words of the rap overlying the primary composition were hard to decipher (see infra text at n. 34), and that there was no proof of distortion.

33   [2003] E.C.D.R. 31 at para. 7.

34   Ibid., at paras 151, 156.

35   [1999] F.S.R. 168 at 184 (citation omitted). See infra text at nn. 124–8, on courts' recognition of the Readers' role in defining the meaning of a work.

Transformative Use under Copyright

In the US Supreme Court case *Campbell v. Acuff-Rose*, involving 2 Live Crew's parody *Pretty Woman* of Roy Orbison's song *Oh, Pretty Woman*,[36] the Court evaluated the transformative use of the copyright work. The Court developed the transformative use defence, referring to a previous analysis by Judge Leval in an article in the *Harvard Law Review*,[37] and by Justice Story in *Folsom v. Marsh*.[38] In *Campbell v. Acuff-Rose*, the US Supreme Court wrote that:

> ... the goal of copyright, to promote science and the arts, is generally furthered by the creation of transformative works. Such works thus lie at the heart of the fair use doctrine's guarantee of breathing space within the confines of copyright.[39]

The fair use test was developed by courts and then enacted as Section 107 of the US Copyright Act. In determining whether the use of a prior work constitutes fair use under copyright, it asks courts to look to four factors: 1) the character of the use; 2) the nature of the work; 3) the substantiality of the use; and 4) the market effect of the use.[40] Transformative use is a main element of consideration as part of the first factor in the fair use test.[41]

In the *Campbell* case the Supreme Court wrote that an important aspect of the inquiry with regard to the first factor is whether the new work merely 'supersedes' the objects of the original creation, or 'instead adds something new, with a further purpose or different character, altering the first with new *expression, meaning, or message*; ... in other words, whether and to what extent the new work is *transformative*'.[42] The Court also noted that the degree of transformativity is relevant, underscoring that 'the more transformative the new work, the less will be the significance of other factors, like commercialism, that may weigh against a finding of fair use'.[43]

Various forms of transformative use have been recognised by the courts. The digitisation of copyright works has been upheld as transformative use in *Authors Guild v. Google*, as with the thumbnail sketches used in *Kelly v. Arriba* and in

---

36   510 U.S. 569 (1994). The Supreme Court ruled that the Court of Appeals had erred in concluding that the commercial nature of the parody made it unfair, and that the parody copied too much; instead, the Supreme Court noted, a parody may well require conjuring up the original work it parodies.

37   Pierre N. Leval (1990), 'Toward a Fair Use Standard', *Harv. L. Rev.* 103, 1105.

38   9 F. Cas. 342, No. 4901 (C.C.D. Mass. 1841).

39   Campbell, 510 U.S. at 579 (citations omitted).

40   17 U.S.C.A. 107.

41   See Netanel (2012).

42   Campbell, 510 U.S. at 579, citing Leval (1990) at 1111 (emphasis added).

43   Campbell, 510 U.S. at 569.

Perfect 10.[44] Digitisation was also at issue in the use of Grateful Dead photos for historical rather than artistic purposes in *Graham Archives*.[45] Parodies after *Campbell* which discussed transformative use include the use of Leibovitz's photo of Demi Moore by Paramount Pictures for a film promotion with Leslie Nielsen;[46] use of Barbie images by the artist Tom Forsythe;[47] and the 'Wind Done Gone' parody of 'Gone with the Wind'.[48] Judge Leval described transformative use as the creation of 'new information, new aesthetics, new insights and understandings', and gave these further examples of transformative uses: 'Transformative uses may include criticizing the quoted work, exposing the character of the original author, proving a fact, or summarizing an idea argued in the original in order to defend or rebut it. They also may include parody, symbolism, aesthetic declarations, and innumerable other uses'.[49]

Derivative Works

While pursuant to the US statute a *transformed work* is a derivative work over which the copyright owner of the original work has exclusive rights, it is, rather, for *transformative use* that a defence holds to claims of copyright infringement. Significant aspects of the defence may be seen from highlighting the distinction between the derivative rights doctrine and the transformative use defence.

A 'derivative work', over which a copyright owner has exclusive control, is defined as 'a work based upon one or more pre-existing works, such as a translation, musical arrangement, dramatization, fictionalization, motion picture version, sound recording, art reproduction, abridgment, condensation, or any other form in which a work may be recast, *transformed*, or adapted'.[50]

A distinction between *content* and *use* is to be noted. While the exclusive derivative right of a copyright owner goes to the work's *content*, the defendant may raise a defence with regard to her *use* of the earlier work. The derivative rights doctrine prohibits the making of a 'transformed' work, i.e., a transformation of the content of a work; nevertheless, the prior work may be used in a way which lends

---

44   *Authors Guild, Inc. v. Google Inc.*, 954 F. Supp. 2d 282 (S.D.N.Y. 2013); *Kelly v. Arriba Soft Corp.*, 336 F.3d 811 (9th Cir. 2003); *Perfect 10, Inc. v. Amazon.com, Inc.*, 508 F.3d 1146 (9th Cir. 2007) (citations to further case proceedings omitted).

45   *Bill Graham Archives v. Doris Kindersley Ltd.*, 448 F.3d 605 (2d Cir. 2006).

46   *Leibovitz v. Paramount Pictures Corp.*, 137 F.3d 109 (1998).

47   *Mattel Inc v. Walking Mountains Productions*, 353 F.3d 792 (9th Cir 2003).

48   *Suntrust Bank v. Houghton Mifflin Co.*, 252 F.3d 1165 (11th Cir 2001).

49   Leval (1990) at 1111.

50   17 U.S.C. 101, 106(2) (emphasis added). Regarding UK law, Bently writes: 'Protection of a derivative work turns on whether the "skill, judgment and labour" *transforms* the underlying work in a relevant way'. Lionel Bently, in Geller and Nimmer, at UK: 34-section 2[3][a] n110 (emphasis added). Section 16(1)(e) and Section 21 of the Act restrict the adaptation of copyright works. See supra text at n. 19.

it a new expression, meaning or message.[51] In the case of *Castle Rock* discussed further below, where a trivia quiz book regarding the fictional television series Seinfeld was found substantially similar to the original, the court indeed noted the 'potential source of confusion' as to the difference between transformative uses and derivative works.[52]

Commentator Kerry Blasingim writes that it is hard for the art world to come to grips with appropriation art cases since in the usual sense of the word 'transform', the appropriation artist certainly may be said to transform the prior work. In common usage, 'transformative' means a change in composition or structure. Yet as Blasingim notes, the legal definition of 'transformative use' is very different.[53]

Akin to the alternative senses which the terms 'transform' and 'derive' take on, also the term 'appropriation' takes on alternative meanings in copyright law. The latter term is used at times to represent an infringing taking, and at times to indicate an acceptable level of taking. In the *Campbell* case, the Supreme Court referred to appropriation both as an example of infringing copying[54] and as legitimate, as with parody: '[t]he fact that parody can claim legitimacy for some appropriation does not, of course, tell either parodist or judge much about where to draw the line'.[55]

Where is the line to be drawn between infringing copying and legitimate transformative use, in the context of appropriation art? The heart of the test is the evaluation of whether the use alters the original work with new 'expression, meaning, or message'. Before these elements of the test are explored more fully below, the analysis of similar aspects in the related doctrine of free speech is examined.

Free Speech Doctrine

This section explores similarities between the doctrines of free speech and copyright. It is then seen that the judicial method in free speech cases may be termed a hermeneutic analysis, where the elements of Author, Text and Reader are examined. In the following section, it is seen that these same three hermeneutic elements are apparent in courts' analyses of works pursuant to the transformative use defence.

---

51   Anthony Rees (2008), 'Transformativeness and the Derivative Work Right', *Colum. J. L. & Arts* 31, 467.

52   *Castle Rock Entertainment, Inc. v. Carol Publishing Group*, 150 F.3d 132 (2d Cir. 1998) at para. 29 and n9. See infra text at n. 93.

53   Kerry Blasingim and Sebastien Delisle, 'Transformative vs. Derivative in Art Law: *Cariou v. Prince* and the Art Community Response'. ('Blasingim'). http://www. academia.edu/1753470/Transformative_vs._Derivative_in_Art_Law_Cariou_v._Prince_ and_the_Art_Community_Response

54   See infra text at n. 110. Campbell, 510 U.S. at n. 21.

55   Ibid., at 581.

The Two Doctrines Compared

In the US Constitution, the protection of speech under the First Amendment and the protection of an author's literary interests under the Copyright Clause (Clause 8) were adopted together, and research has shown that they arose out of similar concerns of the Founders. That copyright and freedom of expression are in tandem may be seen from the historical roots of the two.[56] Jane Ginsburg has written of the accord between the two constitutional provisions.[57] In *Harper v. Row* the US Supreme Court noted the confluence between the two concepts, when it termed copyright 'the engine of the free expression'.[58] Pamela Samuelson has argued that also in the UK this phenomenon can be seen: the UK Statute of Anne redirected copyright's purpose from censorship towards freedom of expression.[59] In addition to their historical conjunction and purpose, similarities of methodology between the free speech and copyright doctrines may be seen.

Upon both doctrines courts sometimes evaluate the expressiveness of the speech or work at issue. In copyright law the US Supreme Court has ruled that a 'minimal degree of creativity' is necessary for a work to be considered original and protected under copyright.[60] Similarly, in free speech cases the Court has evaluated whether a minimal degree of expressiveness is present, in determining whether the speech will be protected. For example in *Barnes v. Glen Theater Inc.*, the Court questioned whether nude dancing had an element of expressiveness. In that case the Court wrote that there is a 'kernel of expression' in almost every human activity, but that such a kernel is insufficient.[61] In concurrence Justice Souter wrote that 'every voluntary act implies some such idea, and the implication is thus so common and minimal that calling all voluntary activity expressive would reduce the concept of expression to the point of the meaningless'.[62] Given that nude

---

56   Paul Edward Geller (1994), 'Must Copyright be Forever Caught between Marketplace and Authorship Norms?', in Brad Sherman and Alain Strowel (eds.), *Of Authors and Origins*, 164; Jeremy Waldron (1993), 'From Authors to Copiers: Individual Rights and Social Values in Intellectual Property', *Chi-Kent L. Rev.* 68, 842, 857 n. 47.

57   Jane C. Ginsburg (1994), 'A Tale of Two Copyrights: Literary Property in Revolutionary France and America', in Sherman and Strowel (eds.), *Of Authors and Origins*. See also Treiger-Bar-Am (2007).

58   *Harper v. Row*, 471 U.S. 539, 558 (1985).

59   Pamela Samuelson (2002), 'Copyright, Commodification, and Censorship: Past as Prologue – But to What Future?', in Neil Weinstock Netanel and Niva Elkin-Koren (eds.), *The Commodification of Information*, 68.

60   *Feist Publications, Inc. v. Rural Telephone Service Co.*, 499 U.S. 340, 345, 362 (1991).

61   501 U.S. 560, 570 (1991).

62   Ibid., at 581 (Souter, J., concurrence). See Randall P. Bezanson (2009), *Art and Freedom of Speech*, 68–71.

dancing was found to be expressive conduct 'only marginally', the Court upheld the state ban.[63] Both doctrines thus look to creativity, or expressiveness.

The doctrines are further alike in not protecting ideas, but rather expression. In copyright doctrine ideas and expression are distinguished, and only expression is protected, as was determined by US case law as early as 1879, in *Baker v. Selden*.[64] Also in the landmark free speech case of *U.S. v. O'Brien* wherein the US Supreme Court established a test for regulation of symbolic speech, the Court rejected 'the view that an apparently limitless variety of conduct can be labeled "speech" whenever the person engaging in the conduct intends thereby to express an idea'.[65]

Transformation is also seen to be relevant in both doctrines. Ronald Bezanson has written that 'by importing transformation so heavily into fair use, the Court imported the First Amendment into copyright law'.[66] Mark Tushnet has considered both doctrines alongside each other, recalling the transformativity of meaning.[67] Bezanson too considers the transformation of meaning in both doctrines: 'With art and aesthetic speech, the First Amendment concerns seem to turn on ideas of transformation and new meaning drawn from what otherwise would be a mere representation', and in copyright cases such as *Campbell v. Acuff-Rose*, the Court's 'job … was to find new meaning, transformation beyond the original, representation to something else in the minds or senses of the audience'.[68]

While the transformation of a work's meaning under copyright is further discussed below, examples are brought here from free speech case law, such as with the analysis of symbolic speech. In *Texas v. Johnson* the Supreme Court considered whether the meaning of the American flag, a symbol with a variety of

---

63   501 U.S. at 566.

64   *Baker v. Selden*, 101 U.S. 99 (1879); *Donoghue v. Allied Newspapers Ltd.* (1938) Ch. 106 (UK).

65   391 U.S. 367, 376 (1968) (involving the burning of a draft card). Cf. Mark Tushnet (2012), 'Art and the First Amendment', *Colum. J.L. & Arts* 35, 169, 208 (activities covered by the First Amendment 'must somehow teach doctrine or otherwise convey ideas even if they are not expositions of ideas').

66   Bezanson (2009) at 211.

67   Tushnet (2012) at 200–201, 216.

68   Bezanson (2009) at 211; ibid., at 188 (comparing genre and transformation), and generally in Part 3 of his book. See also Randall P. Bezanson (2003), 'Speaking Through Others' Voices: Authorship, Originality and Free Speech', *Wake Forest L. Rev.* 38, 983.

Regarding transformations of meaning in art, see Bezanson (2009) at 272. Moreover, consider Marcel Duchamp's statement that his readymades became the artworks they did because of his choice of the objects, such as with the changing of a urinal into the Fountain: 'Whether Mr. Mutt [Duchamp's exhibition pseudonym in this instance] with his own hands made the fountain or not has no importance. He CHOSE it. He took an ordinary article of life, placed it so that its useful significance disappeared under the new title and point of view …'. Arturo Schwarz (1997), *1 The Complete Works of Marcel Duchamp* 43 (2nd edn) (citation omitted).

meanings, may be altered.[69] A more recent example is the 2010 case of *Kleinman v. City of San Marcos* in the Fifth Circuit, involving the question of whether a painted wrecked vehicle was an expressive work of art: 'Wade sought to transform ... the vehicle into "something that's more respectful of the planet ..."'.[70]

Hermeneutic Analysis in Free Speech Cases

Also common to the free speech and copyright doctrines is the use of hermeneutic analysis. Courts examine three elements of speech or a work, in order to explore its meaning. One element looks to what is shown by the Text itself, as distinguished from the work (*oeuvre*). A second element asks what the Author intended to communicate through the work. The third element relies on the understanding of the work by its Readers, namely the audience viewing or hearing a work. These three elements may be labelled Text, Author, and Reader – or if the order is changed, the elements can be referred to under the abbreviation ART.

The analysis of all three elements in US free speech case law includes case discussion of the determination of when speech is present, namely defining the conditions of speech. In *Clark v. Community for Nonviolence*, the Supreme Court wrote: 'a message may be delivered by conduct that is intended to be communicative and that, in context, would reasonably be understood by the viewer to be communicative'.[71] Charles Collier calls this reliance on the three hermeneutic elements a 'triadic relation among a speaker's intention to communicate a relatively specific message, and an audience's potential understanding of that message'.[72] Bezanson describes it as follows: 'Free speech has historically been premised on a linear process beginning with a speaker who *intends* to express a *message*, which message is in turn *understood* by an audience'.[73]

Hermeneutic analysis for the determination of the meaning of a work has developed from its early concentration on the author's intent. While in the past an author's biography was studied in order to gain a deeper understanding of his intent and therefore the meaning of his work,[74] in more modern times hermeneutics tends to focus on the third element, in what has been called the Reader-reception theory. Michel Foucault and Roland Barthes are early thinkers who put this view

---

69   491 U.S. 397 (1989).

70   597 F.3d 323, 325 (5th Cir. 2010), cert. denied, 131 S.Ct. 159 (2010). The court found the object only minimally expressive, however, in reliance in part on its utilitarian function as an advertisement. The court considered whether the artist's intent to transform the object into an expressive work was sufficient.

71   468 U.S. 288 (1984).

72   Charles W. Collier (2009), *Meaning in Law*, 91.

73   Bezanson (2009) at 81 (emphasis in original).

74   Also with visual art in the modern art period (before postmodern art), the deep unconscious of the creative self was esteemed. See Arthur C. Danto (1999), *Philosophizing Art: Selected Essays*, 75–76.

forward, and many have followed in their paths.[75] The intention view of art has met with criticism, as it is said that the intention view misfits the very nature and value of art, which goes not to the liberty of the artist but to the liberty of the audience engaged in its own ascription of meaning.[76]

First Amendment doctrine follows this shift in focus, from the Author's intention to the Reader's understanding. While the intention view has a 'well-grounded pedigree in First Amendment theory', with both art and speech viewed as an individual act of liberty arising from the intention of the artist or speaker,[77] the Reader is increasingly present. The role of the Reader has come to be central in First Amendment doctrine insofar as the right of the Reader to receive ideas is seen as a right to expression,[78] and courts increasingly recognise the role of the Reader in creating meaning.

For instance in *Barnes v. Glen Theatre, Inc.*, the free speech case discussed above involving nude dancing, all three hermeneutic elements may be seen in the Supreme Court's understanding of expression as communication of a message to Readers,[79] yet the Reader element was in focus in Justice White's call for stronger protection of the expressive act. In his dissenting opinion, Justice White called the nude dancing expressive because of its arousal of emotions on the part of the viewers of the dancing.[80] In libel law the shift towards the Reader can be seen upon comparison between the *New York Times v. Sullivan*,[81] where the Supreme Court focused on Authorial intent, and the later case of *Falwell v. Hustler*,[82] where the Supreme Court expanded its analysis to rely on the view of the reasonable Reader.

The Reader element may also be seen at the forefront of the analysis in *Hurley v. Irish-American Gay, Lesbian and Bisexual Group of Boston*, where the Supreme Court recognised that the meaning of a parade is determined by the audience of spectators viewing it.[83] The Court noted that viewers of the parade, in witnessing the participation of a group, would infer that the organisers of the event supported

---

75   The ramifications of this view for copyright are referred to below, see infra n. 118.

76   Bezanson (2009) at 255.

77   Ibid., at 254.

78   *Board of Education v. Pico*, 457 U.S. 853, 867 (1982).

79   *Barnes v. Glen Theatre, Inc.*, 501 U.S. 560, 581 (1991) (Souter, J., concurring). See supra text at nn. 61–63.

80   Barnes, 501 U.S. at 592 (White, J., dissenting) ('generating thoughts, ideas, and emotions is the essence of communication').

81   376 U.S. 254 (1964) (setting forth the 'actual malice' standard).

82   485 U.S. 46 (1988). See Leslie Kim Treiger (1989), 'Protecting Satire Against Libel Claims: A New Reading of the First Amendment's Opinion Privilege', *Yale Law Journal* 98, 1215, and infra n. 121.

83   515 U.S. 557, 575 (1995) (evaluating how 'GLIB's participation [in the parade] would likely be perceived'), ibid., at 577 (determining how the expression of each unit in a parade 'is perceived by spectators'). See Leslie Kim Treiger-Bar-Am (2006b), 'The Moral Right of Integrity: A Freedom of Expression', in Fiona Macmillan (ed.), *2 New Directions in Copyright*, 149–50.

the group's message. *Hurley* set forth that expression is present where meaning is perceived, even if not conveyed. Mark Tushnet writes that '[t]he resonance between this approach and "reader response" accounts of literature is clear'.[84]

In 2003 the Supreme Court put the Reader in focus in *Virginia v. Black*, in holding that the state of Virginia had reason to protect its African-American citizens from the fear that cross-burning ignites, due to the meaning of cross-burning that has developed over time in Americans' perception.[85] Bezanson writes that the case saw that the construction of meaning of the cross 'resided not in the image, or even very much in the "author's" intent, but in those persons who witnessed the burning of the cross in public view'.[86] In the 2009 case of *Pleasant Grove v. Summum*, the Supreme Court discussed the meaning of a monument, and how viewers' understanding of the work of art and its message varies.[87] The Reader was in focus in the Court's rejection of the respondents' call for the government to expressly adopt the message of the monument it selected.

It is seen below that the use of the three hermeneutic elements of Text, Author and Reader, with an increasing awareness of the role of the Reader, is apparent also in copyright cases considering the transformative use defence.

Transformative Use Re-examined: Hermeneutic Analysis of the Defence

Similar to free speech case analysis, the *Campbell* Court's test of 'expression, meaning, or message' for consideration of transformative use, can be understood as relying upon the hermeneutic elements of Text, Author, and Reader. Here I analyse those three elements, with 'expression' signifying the Text, 'message' signifying the Author's intent, and 'meaning' signifying the Reader's understanding of the creative work, in particular with appropriation art in view.[88] In his article on fair use upon which the *Campbell* Court relied in developing the transformative use doctrine, Judge Leval's language can be seen to signify all three elements of the hermeneutic analysis: 'new information, new aesthetics' as Textual elements;

---

84   Tushnet (2012) at 210, n. 166.

85   538 U.S. 343 (2003). See also Collier (2009) at 120 ('The usage and practices that evolved over time are what gradually bestowed on cross burning its current meaning'.).

86   Bezanson (2009) at 239. Mark Tushnet refers also to the case upholding the statute barring speech in support of terrorist groups, *Holder v. Humanitarian Law Project*, 561 U.S. 1 (2010): '[t]aken together with Hurley and Cohen, Humanitarian Law Project implies that any activity that enough people regard as having some meaning, non-cognitive as well as cognitive, must survive the highest level of scrutiny …'. Tushnet (2012) at 214.

87   555 U.S. 460, 474, 476–7 (2009). See also infra n. 123 (meanings evolve).

88   The use of hermeneutic analysis in art theory may be seen for example where George Dickie writes: 'There are three basic items in the artistic situation: (1) the artist, (2) the art the artist creates, and (3) the audience that experiences the work'. George Dickie (1997), *Introduction to Aesthetics: An Analytic Approach*, 121.

'purpose of the use' such as criticism, as indicating the Author element; and 'new insights and understandings' as Readers' creation of meaning.[89]

The three elements of Text, Author, and Reader are discussed in turn below, and with each category points of caution for its use are noted. The use of the Reader element in the analysis of appropriation art is discussed, as well. It is seen that the courts' shift in reliance on the Reader element in the analysis has enabled creativity's development.

Textual 'Expression'

The examination of the Text is a starting point in courts' analysis of transformative use. Judge Leval's analysis, while referring to all three hermeneutic elements, examines Textual elements in looking to genre, as well as in asking whether the work merely supersedes the earlier work or 'instead adds *something* new', with a 'different *character*' or in 'a different *manner*'.[90]

In the recent federal District Court case in California of *Morris v. Young*,[91] where the British appropriation artist Russell Young used images from Dennis Morris's photos of the Sex Pistols, the court undertook an extensive Textual analysis. The court noted the artist's changing of the hue of the original black-and-white image, and overlaying his own graphics onto the image, including graffiti and a Union Pacific Logo. The court found a possibility of fair use with regard to one of the works at issue, based on artistic transformation of the original photograph.[92]

A further case in point is *Castle Rock Entertainment, Inc. v. Carol Publishing Group*, where in considering the transformative use defence the court conducted a Textual analysis in comparing the Textual differences between the copyright work and the trivia book. The court wrote: 'The SAT's back cover makes no mention of exposing Seinfeld to its Readers, for example, as a pitiably vacuous reflection of a puerile and pervasive television culture, but rather urges SAT readers to "open this book to satisfy [their] between-episode [Seinfeld] cravings"'.[93]

Textual analysis is sometimes considered so important that even Authorial purpose is considered not determinative, without a Textually significant change to the work. In *Infinity Broadcast Corp. v. Kirkwood*, while the court recognised the defendant's claim that the marketing of subscription access to live radio broadcasts

---

89   Leval (1990) at 1111.

90   Ibid., cited in Campbell, 510 U.S. at 579 n. 3 (emphasis added). While derivative works may be identified primarily by Textual elements – regarding the content of the work, as seen above – with transformative use, the Textual analysis is only one element of the analysis.

91   925 F.Supp.2d 1078 (C.D. Cal., 2013).

92   Ibid., at 1089. The court denied summary judgment for the plaintiff in connection with one of the four works challenged in the case, thus requiring a full trial to determine whether the fair use defence could be maintained.

93   150 F.3d at 142.

was 'informative' and thus had a different purpose from the entertainment function of the original, the court found that the difference in purpose alone was insufficient as it merely repackaged the original.[94] Also in *Monge v. Maya Magazines*, the court held that a mere difference in purpose does not necessarily create new aesthetics that are transformative of the previous work.[95]

I indicate two notes of caution here. First, a Textual analysis is not always clear; it is not always a simple children's 'Spot the Difference' test.[96] For example with appropriation art, differences may be difficult to discern. Even with new genres that the art world accepts, the law lags far behind.

Moreover, Justice Holmes in *Bleistein v. Donaldson Lithographing Co.*,[97] put forward an important cautionary note for courts to avoid making aesthetic judgments. So too the UK House of Lords in *George Hensher Ltd. v. Restawile Upholstery (Lancs) Ltd.*[98] warned of the dangers of courts evaluating artistic quality. Yet I believe that the Textual examination undertaken by courts in their evaluation of transformative use is an *aesthetic analysis*, rather than an *aesthetic judgment*. Courts do not make judgments as to whether a transformative use of a work affects the work's quality, or renders an aesthetic improvement. Nor does the transformative use defence require that it do so. The distinction drawn here between aesthetic judgment and aesthetic analysis is however narrow; courts must proceed with their Textual analysis carefully, so as not to run the risk of overstepping the bounds of their role as judges.

Because of these difficulties, courts often turn to and/or act as the Reader, i.e., the audience familiar with a given artistic genre, as the best suited to undertake Textual analysis. The Reader is also relied upon in determining Authorial purpose, as seen below.

Author's 'Message'

As we have seen, while the primary author has an exclusive derivative-works right to transform the *content* of the work, fair use and in particular transformative use is about the purpose of the author's *use* of the work. Courts' analysis of Authorial purpose is central to the evaluation of a transformative use defence. Here the significance of Authorial purpose is reviewed and courts' method of analysis of purpose is analysed, with cautionary notes indicated.

---

94   150 F.3d 104 (2d Cir. 1998), discussed in Rees (2008). See infra n. 101.

95   688 F.3d 1164, 1176 (9th Cir. 2012).

96   Cf. *Pasterfield v. Denham* [1999] F.S.R. 168, 182 (a UK copyright case involving a moral rights claim, in which the court recalled the children's test when it found the Textual differences between the primary and the modified work to be minor).

97   188 U.S. 239, 251 (1903). See also the citation to Bleistein in Cariou, infra n. 128.

98   [1976] AC 64 (HL).

Authorial purpose   Section 107 of the US Copyright Act defines fair use with regard to the *purpose* of the author's use of the copyright work, 'such as criticism [or] comment'. Pursuant to the fair use defence, the first factor for consideration is 'the purpose and character of the use'. In upholding a transformative use defence the *Campbell* Court highlighted the examination of the author's purpose, citing Judge Leval and Justice Story in this regard.[99] In an empirical study of cases considering the transformative use defence, Neil Netanel has noted courts' focus on purpose, rather than on content.[100]

While some courts have found that Authorial purpose without Textual change is insufficient for a finding of transformative use, as seen above, other courts have held the reverse, i.e., that Authorial purpose is central, with or without Textual change. The Ninth Circuit wrote in *Perfect 10* that 'even making an exact copy of a work may be transformative so long as the copy serves a different function than the original work'.[101]

In addition to the Textual analysis in *Castle Rock* and *Morris v. Young* seen above, both decisions included analysis of Authorial purpose. The court in *Castle Rock* rejected the defence insofar as it noted a lack of Authorial purpose appropriate to a finding of transformative use: the SAT's author 'described the trivia quiz book not as a commentary or a Seinfeld research tool, but as an effort to "capture Seinfeld's flavor in quiz book fashion"'.[102] The method of analysis of Authorial purpose in *Morris v. Young* is described below.[103]

Method of analysis of purpose   It is often difficult to discern an author's purpose. In determining the message that the author has put forward, courts have taken evidence of the defendant-artists' statements of purpose.[104] Yet such a judicial method may not suit the methods of the visual artist. A problem presents itself when artists do not verbalise their intention,[105] or do not describe their purpose in words acceptable to a court.

---

99   Campbell, 510 U.S. at 586–7 n. 11 (regarding Text and Reader, as well). See infra nn. 37–38.

100   Netanel (2012). See also Thomas F. Cotter (2010), Minnesota Legal Studies Research Paper No. 10–04, January 20, 2010, *Vanderbilt J. of Entertainment Law* (calling the transformative use test underinclusive and indeterminate, but still suggesting testing purpose).

101   Perfect 10, 508 F.3d at 1165, cited in Rees (2008). See supra n. 94.

102   150 F.3d at 142.

103   See infra text at nn. 112–14. See also the citation in *Morris v. Young* to *Gaylord v. U.S.*, 595 F.3d 1364 (Fed. Cir. 2010) (the Postal Service's distribution of stamps portraying a black-and-white image of the photograph of a Korean War Veterans memorial was held to reflect no purpose beyond that of the primary work: commemorating the Korean War).

104   See Netanel (2012) at 751, 762, 766.

105   On the difficulty of interpreting an author's intentions, see Danto (1999) at 71. Danto writes of Andy Warhol's art that in 'some ways it is perhaps impossible to say what

Copyright infringement claims against appropriation artist Jeff Koons provide an interesting example. An earlier copyright case against him, *Rogers v. Koons*,[106] was decided before the Supreme Court's ruling in *Campbell* adopting the transformative use defence, and was not decided in Koons's favour. In a later case against him, *Blanch v. Koons*, Koons was successful in raising that defence. In *Blanch*, Koons described the purpose of his work, *Niagara*, to the satisfaction of the court. Koons's purposes were seen to be sharply different from plaintiff-Blanch's. Koons knew what to say: 'I want the viewer to think about his/her personal experience with these objects, products, and images and at the same time gain new insight into how these affect our lives'.[107] The court saw Koons's 'commentary on the social and aesthetic consequences of mass media'.[108] It is to be noted that another named defendant in the case was the Guggenheim Foundation; perhaps the exhibit at the Guggenheim of works by Koons, who is now well-recognised, had some effect on the later court ruling.

In the proceedings in *Cariou v. Prince* before the District Court, however, the appropriation artist Richard Prince did not state a purpose to the satisfaction of the court – or did not use the words the court wanted to hear. The lower court did not see the artist as having a purpose respected by law, concluding that 'Prince testified that he doesn't "really have a message" he attempts to communicate when making art'.[109] The District Court saw that Prince intended to emphasise themes of equality of the sexes; highlight the three kinds of relationships in the world, between men and women, men and men, and women and women; and portray a contemporary take on the music scene. But this was not considered sufficient. Prince explained his purpose in the technique of appropriation art as getting 'fact' into his work; the District Court understood this to mean that in his appropriation artwork Prince wanted to tell the truth about Rastafarians, just as the artist Cariou had done in his previous work, and thus that the purpose of the two artists was the same. Commentator Blasingim remarked at the time of the District Court ruling in *Cariou v. Prince*[110] that the art world had difficulty understanding this ruling, as appropriation artist Prince was certainly seen by the art world to have transformed Cariou's work. While the District Court rejected Prince's transformative use

---

his intentions ever were'. 'Regarding Warhol's relation to his own art, Danto concludes: 'I don't think he knew the half of it', but that his achievement, philosophically, was awesome.

Regarding the difficulty of courts' discernment of the meaning of contemporary artworks in copyright cases, see Confetti Records [2003] E.C.D.R. at 151, discussed supra n. 34.

106   *Rogers v. Koons*, 960 F.2d 301 (2d Cir. 1992).

107   *Blanch v. Koons*, 467 F.3d 244, 252 (2d Cir. 2006), citing Koons's affidavit para. 4.

108   Ibid., at 253.

109   784 F. Supp. 2d 337, 349 (2011).

110   Blasingim and Delisle, on Cariou, 784 F. Supp. 2d 337.

defence at trial, that defence was upheld on appeal, where the Circuit Court used a Reader-focused analysis, as seen below. [111]

Also in *Morris v. Young*, the appropriation artist defendant in a copyright infringement lawsuit did not describe his purpose in a manner acceptable to the court. The court rejected the defence of transformative use, as in his deposition the artist 'stated that he does not recall if he was "trying to make a ... particular statement" or offer an opinion when making the Accused Works'.[112] In court pleadings the artist did in fact provide an explanation for his use of the prior work: '"social commentary" on "social norms, values and the like"'.[113] Presumably this addition of an explanation was accomplished with the aid of his lawyers, who knew the legal requirement under the transformative use defence to state purpose. Young stated in his court pleadings that the red tint he applied to 'Sex Pistols in Red' was intended to '"amplif[y] the Sex Pistols punk-rock counter-culture image", and the "grittiness" he applied to "Sex Pistols" was intended to mirror the grittiness of the band members themselves'.[114] The court found however that the latter explanation was insufficient, given the artist's earlier failure to provide the explanation in his deposition, and concluded that Young proffered no credible explanation of his purpose in creating the works.

At times, when the artist has not clearly verbalised his or her purpose for court, the court may supply such a verbalisation. In the Supreme Court's ruling in *Campbell v. Acuff-Rose*, the Court constructed the artists' purpose, according to which the Court upheld the transformative use defence. In *Campbell*, Justice Souter supplied an explanation of what the rap group 2 Live Crew's purpose must have been, in writing its parody. Justice Souter used the kind of language acceptable to a court of law, and judged that purpose transformative.[115] Justice Souter wrote:

> 2 Live Crew's song reasonably could be perceived as commenting on the original or criticising it, to some degree. 2 Live Crew juxtaposes the romantic musings of a man whose fantasy comes true, with degrading taunts, a bawdy demand for sex, and a sigh of relief from paternal responsibility. The later words can be taken as a comment on the naivete of the original of an earlier day, as a rejection of its sentiment that ignores the ugliness of street life and the debasement that it signifies.[116]

---

111   *Cariou v. Prince*, 714 F.3d 694 (2d Cir. 2013). See infra text at nn. 124–8.
112   925 F.Supp.2d at 1082.
113   Ibid.
114   Ibid.
115   The Supreme Court remanded the case for further proceedings in light of the standard it put forward.
116   Campbell, 510 U.S. at 583.

Bezanson critiques the sophisticated description given of 2 Live Crew's purpose, which uses language that the artists might not have chosen to use, if indeed they had chosen to say anything at all.[117]

Thus the purpose of appropriation art may be unclear or unacceptable to a court, or may not be easily put into words by an artist. We have seen cases where appropriation artists provided or failed to provide verbal explanations of their purpose that were satisfactory to the courts, and another where the Court provided the explanation of purpose for an artist considered to have made transformative use of an earlier work. It is seen below that rather than asking the author to supply purpose, or having the court construct one, the Reader may be considered the source of the determination of the artist's purpose. In *Campbell v. Acuff-Rose* the Supreme Court looked to see how the work 'reasonably could be perceived'; this method may aid a court in determining Authorial purpose, as well as a work's meaning.

Readers' 'Meaning'

While in the past an author's biography would be studied to determine Authorial purpose and hence the meaning of a work, in hermeneutic analysis today the Reader is placed in focus. The Reader element is centrally relied upon: the Reader's interpretation of Authorial purpose and the Text is sought, and is used to determine a work's meaning. The shift in hermeneutic analysis in the arts and in free speech doctrine, as described above, has ramifications in the critique of copyright.[118] The shift also has ramifications for courts' consideration of the transformative use defence. It can be seen to facilitate courts' acceptance of the defence as put forward for example by appropriation artists, and as such to facilitate the development of creativity.

Art today is seen as appealing to a 'new or altered perception or understanding' by Readers of a work.[119] Similarly, in evaluating the transformative use defence courts today look to the Reader's understanding of a subsequent work's transformation of what came before it. We can see this approach taken by the Circuit Court in *Leibovitz v. Paramount Pictures Corp.*, where the viewers' perception of the advertisement parodying Leibovitz's photograph was in focus:

> [T]he ad is not merely different; it differs in a way that may reasonably
> be   perceived as commenting, through ridicule, on what a viewer might
> reasonably think is the undue self-importance conveyed by the subject ... .

---

117   Bezanson (2009) at 210.

118   See, e.g., Woodmansee and Jaszi (1994). See also Treiger-Bar-Am (2006b). I have put forward the view that Readers' rights must be balanced with authors' rights in copyright doctrine, in Treiger-Bar-Am (2007).

119   Bezanson (2009) at 253. Regarding art and the transformation of meaning, see supra n. 68.

> Apart from ridiculing pretentiousness, the ad might also be reasonably
> perceived as interpreting the Leibovitz photograph to extol the beauty of the
> pregnant female body, ... and, rather unchivalrously, to express disagreement
> with this message. [120]

With respect to Reader analysis, points of caution are to be noted. The Readers'
view may not accurately judge certain works, as was the case for instance with the
satire written by Jonathan Swift which was believed to be true.[121] Moreover, as
seen above, courts have recognised that the meanings that Readers give to a work
are multiple.[122] The meanings that Readers assign to works also may change, such
as the US Supreme Court wrote in *Pleasant Grove v. Summum*.[123]

Despite these challenges, courts have increasingly looked to Readers to
interpret a work's possible meaning(s). I submit that this movement in court
analysis aids the court in understanding developments in art. The shift in focus to
the Reader indeed facilitated the Circuit Court's understanding of appropriation
art, as may be seen from the ruling on appeal in *Cariou v. Prince*.

Readers' View of Appropriation Art as Transformative Use

In commenting on the District Court's ruling in *Cariou v. Prince*, Blasingim
wrote that art sees the Reader as defining what is transformative, but the law
does not. Blasingim was sceptical that the appropriation art would be allowed
on appeal, writing that '[the] appellate argument – that the test should be applied
post-creation rather than at the time of the taking ... seems to argue that the artist
is not responsible for determining a piece's meaning or how it relates to other
works – which may be true in modern art theory, but not in copyright law'.[124] In
fact on appeal, the Circuit Court accepted the Reader-reception theory and the
view abounding in the art world.

The Circuit Court in the *Cariou* case allowed Prince's appeal, upholding the
transformative use defence for many of his appropriation art works. The court
entered into an extensive Textual analysis of the works, comparing the particular

---

120   *Leibovitz v. Paramount Pictures Corp.*, 137 F.3d 109, 114 (1998).

121   See Treiger (1989). In that article I analysed a difficulty faced in libel law in
protecting satire: libel law poses liability for intent to falsify, and the satirist indeed intends
to state a falsity. A parallel may be seen where copyright law poses liability for copying,
and the misappropriation artist intends to copy. As I argue in both circumstances, authorial
intent must at times take backstage to the Reader's interpretation.

122   See supra nn. 34–5 on multiple meanings, as recognised in Confetti Records and
Pasterfield.

123   555 U.S. at 477. See supra n. 87 (Readers give a work a variety of interpretations).
On the fear of a potential change in the meaning of Central Park resulting from Christo's art
project there, see Leslie Kim Treiger-Bar-Am (2005), 'Christo's Gates and the Meaning of
Art: Lessons for the Law', *European Intellectual Property Review* 389.

124   Blasingim and Delisle. See supra n. 53, and supra n. 110.

elements used in the artists' works and their contrasting styles: the court compared Cariou's 'serene and deliberately composed' works with Prince's 'crude and jarring' works,[125] which were said to bear a different character and aesthetic.[126]

Less credence was given to the Authorial view. Prince's failure to supply a verbalisation of his purpose was excused by the Circuit Court. The Circuit Court criticised the District Court for incorrectly requiring the defendant to show that his work commented on the plaintiff's work: the 'fact that Prince did not provide ... explanations [of his intent] in his deposition ... is not dispositive'; rather, '[w]hat is critical is how the work in question appears to the reasonable observer'.[127]

In its decision, the court explicitly relied upon – and interpreted – the Reader's view. The Court neither gave the plaintiff primary Author control over the work's meaning, nor asked the defendant-Author to state a definite meaning that he gave to the work. The Reader's view that transformative use had been made of the prior works was used by the Court in upholding the defence. The court examined how the works 'may "reasonably be perceived"'.[128] The court thus allowed the Reader to define, and to transform, the meanings of the works.

Thus it may be said that looking to the Reader to interpret a work, such as appropriation art, aids the court in understanding and accepting new artistic developments. Contemporary hermeneutic analysis indeed facilitates the development of authors' creativity.

Conclusion

We have seen that through the transformative use defence courts may protect creativity under copyright law in the US, and may be in a position to do so in the UK as well. In applying the test of transformative use pursuant to US law, courts examine the intent of the defendant-Author, the Textual changes made to the work, and the Readers' understanding of the use of the prior work in the subsequent work. Namely, the message, expression, and meaning of the use are under review.[129] Since *Campbell v. Acuff-Rose*, in US courts' analysis under the transformative

---

125   *Cariou v. Prince*, 714 F.3d at 706.

126   Ibid., at 708; see also ibid., at 710 (examining the substantiality of the portion used).

127   Ibid., at 707.

128   Ibid., at 707, citing Campbell, 510 U.S. at 582, and Leibovitz, 137 F.3d at 113–14. Justice Wallace, in a concurring opinion, suggested that new evidence or expert opinion should be reconsidered on remand, and would allow the District Court to consider Prince's statements. Justice Wallace highlighted the fact that he is not an art expert, and that it is dangerous for a court to be the final judge of the worth of a work of art, citing Bleistein, 188 U.S. 239.

129   The Supreme Court in Campbell referred to 'expression, meaning, or message', 510 U.S. at 579.

use defence all three of the hermeneutic elements of Author, Text and Reader are evident.

Courts ruling on the transformative use defence in appropriation art cases have increasingly relied upon the Reader element in their hermeneutic analysis. This movement in copyright law reflects similar moves in the art world and First Amendment doctrine, where the focus has shifted from the Author's intent to the Reader's response to a work – and the Reader's creation of its meaning. In seeing Readers' acceptance of developments in the art world such as appropriation art, courts have become more open to this art form involving copying and changing, and to its development of meanings. In this way copyright law may allow creativity, and hence move towards its goal of encouraging learning and promoting the arts.

References

Bently, Lionel (2009). 'United Kingdom', in Geller and Nimmer, *International Copyright Law and Practice*. LexisNexis Matthew Bender & Co.

Bently, Lionel (2011). 'Exploring the Flexibilities Available to U.K. Law', *Hargreaves Review of Intellectual Property and Growth*. http://webarchive. nationalarchives.gov.uk/20140603093549/http://www.ipo.gov.uk/ipreview-c4e-sub-bently.pdf.

Bezanson, Randall P. (2003). 'Speaking Through Others' Voices: Authorship, Originality and Free Speech', *Wake Forest L. Rev.* 38, 983.

Bezanson, Randall P. (2009). *Art and Freedom of Speech*. University of Illinois Press.

Blasingim, Kerry and Sebastien Delisle, 'Transformative vs. Derivative in Art Law: *Cariou v. Prince* and the Art Community Response'. http://www. academia.edu/1753470/Transformative_vs._Derivative_in_Art_Law_ Cariou_v._Prince_and_the_Art_Community_Response

Bunker, Matthew D. (2002). 'Eroding Fair Use: The "Transformative" Use Doctrine After Campbell', *Communication Law and Policy* 7: 1.

Collier, Charles W. (2009). *Meaning in Law*. Oxford University Press.

Cornish, W.R. and D. Llewelyn (2003). *Intellectual Property: Patents, Copyright, Trade Marks and Allied Rights* (5th edn). Sweet and Maxwell.

Cotter, Thomas F. (2010). Minnesota Legal Studies Research Paper No. 10–04, 20 January 2010, *Vanderbilt J. of Entertainment Law*.

Danto, Arthur C. (1999). *Philosophizing Art: Selected Essays*. University of California Press.

Dickie, George (1997). *Introduction to Aesthetics: An Analytic Approach*. Oxford University Press.

Foucault, Michel (1979). 'What is an Author?', in Josue V. Harari (ed.), *Textual Strategies: Perspectives in Post-Structuralist Criticism*. Cornell University Press, 141–60.

Geller, Paul Edward (1994). 'Must Copyright be Forever Caught between Marketplace and Authorship Norms?', in Brad Sherman and Alain Strowel (eds.), *Of Authors and Origins*. Clarendon Press, 159–201.

Ginsburg, Jane C. (1994). 'A Tale of Two Copyrights: Literary Property in Revolutionary France and America', in Brad Sherman and Alain Strowel (eds.), *Of Authors and Origins*. Clarendon Press, 131–58.

Laddie, Sir Hugh, Peter Prescott, Mary Vitoria, Adrian Speck and Lindsay Lane (eds.) (2000). *The Modern Law of Copyright and Designs* (3rd edn). Butterworths.

Leval, Pierre N. (1990). 'Toward a Fair Use Standard', *Harv. L. Rev.* 103, 1105.

Liu, Joseph P. (2003). 'Copyright Law's Theory of the Consumer', *B. C. L. Rev.* 44, 397.

MacFarland, Thomas (1985). *Originality and Imagination*. Johns Hopkins University Press.

Murray, Michael D. (2012). 'What is Transformative? An Explanatory Synthesis of the Convergence of Transformation and Predominant Purpose in Copyright Fair Use Law', *Chi.-Kent J. Intell. Prop.* 11, 260.

Netanel, Neil Weinstock (2012). 'Making Sense of Fair Use', *Lewis and Clark L. Rev.* 15: 3, 715.

Rees, Anthony (2008). 'Transformativeness and the Derivative Work Right', *Colum. J. L. & Arts* 31, 467.

Samuelson, Pamela (2002). 'Copyright, Commodification, and Censorship: Past as Prologue – But to What Future?', in Neil Weinstock Netanel and Niva Elkin-Koren (eds.), *The Commodification of Information*. Kluwer Law International, 63–79.

Schwarz, Arturo (1997). *1 The Complete Works of Marcel Duchamp* (2nd edn). Thames and Hudson.

Spence, Michael and Leslie Kim Treiger-Bar-Am (2007). 'Private Control/Public Speech', in Katja S. Ziegler (ed.), *Human Rights and Private Law: Privacy as Autonomy*. Hart Publishing.

Treiger, Leslie Kim (1989). 'Protecting Satire Against Libel Claims: A New Reading of the First Amendment's Opinion Privilege', *Yale Law Journal* 98, 1215.

Treiger-Bar-Am, Leslie Kim (2005). 'Christo's Gates and the Meaning of Art: Lessons for the Law', *European Intellectual Property Review* 27: 11, 389–90.

Treiger-Bar-Am, Leslie Kim (2006a). 'Adaptations with Integrity', in Helle Porsdam (ed.), *Copyright and Other Fairy Tales: Hans Christian Andersen and the Commodification of Copyright*. Edward Elgar, 61–82.

Treiger-Bar-Am, Leslie Kim (2006b). 'The Moral Right of Integrity: A Freedom of Expression', in Fiona Macmillan (ed.), *2 New Directions in Copyright*. Edward Elgar, 127–58.

Treiger-Bar-Am, Leslie Kim (2007). 'Authors' Rights as a Limit to Copyright Control', in Fiona Macmillan (ed.), *6 New Directions in Copyright*. Edward Elgar, 359–76.

Tushnet, Mark (2012). 'Art and the First Amendment', *Colum. J.L. & Arts* 35, 169.

Waldron, Jeremy (1993). 'From Authors to Copiers: Individual Rights and Social Values in Intellectual Property', *Chi-Kent L. Rev.* 68, 842.

Woodmansee, Martha and Peter Jaszi (eds.) (1994). *The Construction of Authorship: Textual Appropriation in Law and Literature.* Duke University Press.

Author Unknown: Last Words

Valdimar Tr. Hafstein

With pirates and Indians and orphans galore, the critical literature on copyright and cultural heritage reads at times like a cross between Oliver Twist and Peter Pan. From literary paternity to piracy, the law is itself littered with colourful metaphors for creativity, property, and appropriation, at times even matching in its poetics the works that fall within its scope. Indeed, copyright sometimes seems to figure the publishing house as a paternity ward while more and more it is making an unwilling orphanage of the archive, the library, and the museum.

The major figure in copyright law, of course, remains that of the author, whose genealogy and coming into being in the eighteenth and nineteenth centuries have been analysed in post-structural detail over the last half-century. The author provides to the law a way to account for creative agency and a metanarrative that assures that texts and images are created once, in one place and at one time by one legal person, and that thereafter they circulate in ways that the law brings under control. As legal persons, authors have both rights and responsibilities: they may be prosecuted for the contents of their works and they may be construed as first owners and beneficiaries of rights and rewards that they legally transfer to the publishing house (or record company, or whatever). The author figure in copyright law thus guarantees the market in cultural goods and justifies the temporary monopoly on the making, selling, and circulation of copies that is at the heart of a business model that has worked well for publishers for the past couple of centuries but has come under threat in recent years.

Authorship is not universal, of course. Neither every expression nor every form of expression is imagined to be the work of an author and not all fall within the scope of protection of copyright law. The outside of authorship is represented by another figure, referred to in the collective singular as the folk: a residual category for texts and music and images that do not fit neatly with the metanarrative that the figure of the author recounts. In the nineteenth century, the folk figured an alternative understanding of creative agency and of the circulation of texts outside of markets.

In a couple of centuries, the eighteenth and the nineteenth, one might say that an anti-Copernican revolution occurred in the cultural field: one that returned man to the centre of his universe, crafting his existence and creating his world. A fundamental shift took place, after which man was not so much created as creative; not so much creature, as creator. Before the eighteenth century, the verb 'to create' was only ever used in conjunction with the divine: 'In the beginning, God created heaven and earth.' Creativity was a divine attribute. It is only in modern times that humans seize this divine spark for their own use – a feat worthy of Prometheus himself (Abrams, 1971: 272–82; *Oxford English Dictionary*, reference terms: 'create', 'creation', 'creative'). The law did not divide the spark equally among humankind, however. Its unequal distribution is expressed in the dichotomy between authorship and folk tradition.

What is and what ought to be the relationship between creativity, cultural heritage institutions and copyright? In the last remaining pages of this book, I will attempt to throw some light on this double question that frames the book and ties together its chapters, and I will build a case for one possible answer. I propose to do so using a genealogical approach, investigating the relation between the figure of the author and the figure of the folk, and eventually exploring a third figure for creative agency: the collector-editor.

*   *   *

The Berne Convention for the Protection of Literary and Artistic Works was signed in 1886. States that join the Berne Union must guarantee the same protection to authors from other signatory countries as their national copyright laws grant to their own subjects (the principle of national treatment), and signatories agree to meet certain minimum standards in their national laws on authors' rights (Ricketson, 1987: 39–80; see also Bogsch, 1986: 295–6). Various treaties on copyright and related rights now complement the Berne Convention, but it is still the primary international convention in the field, with almost universal application, and has been revised a number of times since it was concluded in 1886.

The Berne Union was an exclusive club to begin with: very few countries in what is now referred to as the global South were among its original members. The Convention's reach was extended, however, by article 19, the so-called 'colonial clause', which gave imperial centres the right to include their colonies and protectorates (Olwan, 2013: 43–4). Having wrested their sovereignty from the colonial powers, newly independent states in the 1950s, 1960s and 1970s were therefore 'required to affirm (or denounce) their loyalty' to the Berne Union by declarations of 'continued adherence' (Hemmungs Wirtén, 2010: 537). Amendments to facilitate their adhesion were a major focus of the Stockholm and Paris revision conferences in 1967 and 1971 (see Ricketson, 1987: 81–125; Hemmungs Wirtén, 2010: 296–8; Olwan, 2013: 43–7; and Mezghani, 1986).

In Stockholm, the Indian delegation proposed to add a provision to protect folklore, and a working group was set up to consider the question (Ricketson, 1987: 314; cf. Zografos, 2010: 12–13; *Records of the Intellectual Property Conference of Stockholm*, vol. II: 296). Framed as a topic of special concern to developing countries, the ensuing discussions were groundbreaking inasmuch as folklore had never before seriously been considered an appropriate subject matter for copyright protection, certainly not by a powerful international authority. The Indian proposal met with scepticism. At the end of the day, it was not adopted. In fact, the entire Stockholm conference was a debacle; one participant described it as 'the worst experience in the history of international copyright conventions' (qtd in Hemmungs Wirtén, 2010: 533).

The debate over the international protection of folklore left its mark on the Berne Convention nonetheless. That mark is found in the opaque fourth paragraph added to article 15 in Stockholm in 1967:

> (a) In the case of unpublished works where the identity of the author is unknown, but where there is every ground to presume that he is a national of a country of the Union, it shall be a matter for legislation in that country to designate the competent authority who shall represent the author and shall be entitled to protect and enforce his rights in the countries of the Union.

> (b) Countries of the Union which make such designation under the terms of this provision shall notify the Director General by means of a written declaration giving full information concerning the authority thus designated. The Director General shall at once communicate this declaration to all other countries of the Union (*Berne Convention for the Protection of Literary and Artistic Works*).

The paragraph was drafted by the Stockholm working group that examined the possibility of adding a provision on folklore to the Berne convention. Members of that group had found folklore 'to be extremely difficult to define:'

> Hence the provision applies to all works fulfilling the conditions indicated above. It is clear, however, that the main field of application of this regulation will coincide with those productions which are generally described as folklore (*Records of the Intellectual Property Conference of Stockholm* vol. II: 307–8).

The exact formulation of article 15(4) merits scrutiny. Think about it: so indivisible is copyright from norms of authorship that the Berne Convention can conceive of traditional expression only as the work of an 'unknown author'. In other words, by this reckoning it is not so much the case that H.C. Andersen reworked stories from oral tradition as that oral storytellers repeat the original compositions of Andersen's colleagues in the author's guild, whose names the vagaries of history have separated from the stories that they composed.

This is symptomatic: the concept of creative agency that underpins modern regimes of intellectual property is modelled on solitary genius. Canonised in international law in the nineteenth and twentieth centuries, this Romantic norm has little patience for cultural processes or with expressions developed in a more diffuse, incremental, and collective manner, where it is impossible to fix specific steps like invention or authorship at a given point in time or to assign them to one particular person.

Article 15(4) further stipulates: 'It shall be a matter for legislation in that country to designate the competent authority which shall represent the author and shall be entitled to protect and enforce his rights in the countries of the Union'.

After recasting folklore in terms that are legible under copyright regimes, the special working group in Stockholm realises that something has been lost in translation. They had cast creative agency in traditional expression in the mould of the universal individual subject – the unpublished works of an unknown author. The result was a legal subject with no recourse to representation because it is as void of a real reference as the empty subject 'it' in the phrase 'it's raining'. The convention therefore goes on immediately to fill that empty subject with the will of the state, 'which shall represent the author'.

The Berne Convention illustrates the relationship between copyright and folklore. The paradox that ties the one to the other, while keeping them always apart, has been the ongoing concern of the World Intellectual Property Organization since at least 1967, three years before it was founded. The latest in the series of such efforts, WIPO's Intergovernmental Committee on Intellectual Property and Genetic Resources, Traditional Knowledge and Folklore has been meeting in Geneva since 2001, first to discuss the need for and later to draft an international convention in the field (Groth, 2012). The problem at the heart of its work is that the system of intellectual property protection, which is supposed to encourage creativity and innovation, systematically excludes the knowledge and creativity of a large portion of humanity.

In order to qualify for copyright protection, a narrative, a design, or a piece of music has to be an original creation. Likewise, in order to be granted patent protection, technology and know-how need to pass the test of novelty and involve an inventive step. By means of such criteria, traditional knowledge and expressions are ruled out on principle. No one is entitled to speak for tradition. It is impossible to make a claim to represent it in a way that is legible and logical within the legal regime of copyright.

The solution adopted by article 15(4) of the Berne Convention has not proved helpful – to translate the collective, cumulative, and distributed creative agency of folk tradition by the concept of the 'unknown author' and to grant the state the right to represent that author. The unknown author from article 15(4) is not unknown to us because his identity is lost; the unknown author is unknown to us because he does not exist. He is a legal fiction and as such he was stillborn. Almost fifty years after the Stockholm revision of 1967, only one state, India, has notified WIPO's Director General that it is using the article to protect folklore (Zografos, 2010: 14).

One of the enduring legacies of the Grimm brothers and their contemporaries lies in how they mapped out the domain of collective creativity. Their work inscribed that domain on the scholarly agenda and through the *Kinder- und Hausmärchen* and the countless collections that followed in its wake they helped to make its existence self-evident. It is best understood as a domain within a new discursive regime whose figure is the author. In the eighteenth and nineteenth centuries, a legal regime took shape that complemented this discursive regime: the law of copyright. In this context, we may say that the Grimms helped give a shape to these regimes by devising an instrument (sharper than a letter opener, duller than a scalpel) for carving the discursive field up into authored works on the one hand and non-authored texts on the other.

In order to understand the paradox at the heart of the disputes in WIPO's committee, it is helpful to go back to the time of Herder, the Grimms, their colleagues and contemporaries, and to their legacy, for ultimately the negotiations in Geneva surf on waves that they helped to set in motion. In country after country and language after language, these waves helped reproduce the outlines of the discursive domain of folklore, filling this new category with content in the vernacular, rooting it in national soil, and rendering it relevant for legal practice in state after state.

The concept of creative agency that underpins regimes of intellectual property is based originally on the European fantasy of the melancholy poet or the solitary inventor whose works are completely original. That is a fairy tale in its own right. This Romantic authorship norm is intimately associated with the rise of capitalism. Its historical emergence coincides with the liberalisation of the book trade in Europe and the invention of copyright.

In England, for example, a system of strict censorship was put in place when the printing press first arrived; under the Licensing of the Press Act from 1662 (the last of many), the Stationer's Company had a monopoly on publishing and was made responsible for enforcing that monopoly. Only members of the Company could produce books, and once a member of the Company claimed ownership of a text, no other member was allowed to publish it. This licensing system was replaced in the eighteenth century by a market system. Instead of total monopoly being vested in a few publishers, any publisher could now claim a limited monopoly right in a particular book for a restricted period of time. Invoking this new right, the printer could prevent others from legally copying the book for a given number of years (the number was 14 years to begin with). At the end of that period, the protection expires and the work enters the public domain, which means anyone is free to copy it, distribute it, and use it at will (Rose, 1993; cf. Patterson, 1968).

The public domain did not pre-date copyright; it is not as if before the age of copyright, anyone could print anything. Rather, the public domain came into being with the law of copyright and through the law of copyright. Before copyright laws, the right to copy any and all books in Britain belonged exclusively to printers in the Stationer's Company: there was no public domain.

Moreover, when laws on copyright and authors' rights were formulated toward the end of the eighteenth century, first in Britain, then in France, the German states, and the United States, legislators imposed limits on the kind of work eligible for protection. These limits were measured by the criterion of originality, and they were entangled with an ideal of authorship that was beginning to emerge in this era. The law of copyright placed in the public domain all works that did not fit the individual author-concept of the time and did not measure up to the criterion of originality: this included tales and ballads that men of learning had begun to collect from popular tradition in this same period – for after all this is also when Percy's *Reliques of Ancient English Poetry* (1765) and Macpherson's *Works of*

Ossian (1760–1765) first saw the light of day and Herder's *Stimmen der Völker in Liedern* (1778/9–1807) swept across the European continent (Stewart, 1994; Woodmansee, 1994). The Grimms followed with the *Kinder- und Hausmärchen* (1812/1815), and their colleagues all over Europe cranked out volume after volume of tales, legends, and folklore that nobody owned, traditional grist for the mill of national book industries, circulating in the free textual markets of European states.

The invention of the public domain thus relates directly to the invention of folklore as a category and concept. Folklore and the public domain have been related from the outset – interdependent, coeval, and to a considerable degree co-extensive. This is where the Grimms come in. Their collections, and the collections they inspired, gave substance to the new category of popular tradition and content to the public domain, content that was qualitatively different from authored texts that went out of copyright after a certain number of years, or from classical and ancient texts that pre-dated the copyright regime by a millennium or two. The folktales and legends that the Grimms published and the publications that their work gave rise to were not in the public domain because of *when* they had been published, but because of *how* they were thought to have been created.

Folklore, in fact, came to be defined as such only with reference to norms of originality and ownership intrinsic to authorship and the intellectual property regime. A critical genealogy allows us to understand folklore as a constitutive outside of authorship. Folklore is the non-authored. Better yet, it is the anti-authored. It circumscribes the discursive domain of authorship and defines the criterion of originality. Without folklore, no authorship – or at least it would not have the contours we know and recognise.

Folklore might thus be described as a residual concept. It is brought into being through the formation of authorship and subjectivity, in much the same way as the public domain was brought into being through the formation of intellectual property – as its residue, its precondition, and its product. The formation of folklore as a discursive category is thus to be sought in the rise of possessive individualism in the expressive sphere.

The distinction between authorship and folklore, and the distinction between intellectual property and the public domain, go hand in hand, of course, with social standing and the division of wealth, within society and between societies. The author came into his own as a reflex of the rise of the European bourgeoisie and the ascendance of the bourgeois universal subject. While Romantics elevated bourgeois authors (as well as aristocratic ones, even the odd social climber) to the rank of original geniuses and ratified their private ownership over their works, they also coined concepts like 'folktales' and 'folksongs' to refer to texts supposedly circulating among common people, which, in contrast to novels and books of poetry, were recycled, unauthored, and not owned by anyone.

Thus, creativity and originality were the prerogative of the bourgeoisie, while the masses could only transmit the songs and tales of earlier generations. The art of common people consisted of copies – flawed copies, at that. It took bourgeois authors to create original works of art out of these artless texts of popular tradition: *Kunstpoesie* from *Naturpoesie*; *Kunstmärchen* from *Volksmärchen*.

It is hardly by accident that the Berne Convention always refers to the author as masculine. Thus article 15(4) regulates unpublished works by an unknown author 'where there is every ground to presume that *he* is a national of a country of the Union' and the 'competent authority which shall represent the author ... shall be entitled to protect and enforce *his* rights' (*Berne Convention for the Protection of Literary and Artistic Works*, n.d.; my emphasis). Lurking beneath the author's grammatical gender in the Berne Convention is the notion of literary paternity integral to copyright law. The so-called 'right to paternity' refers to an author's right to claim authorship in his work and to have his authorship duly acknowledged in any publication. Paternity was the most common figure used to represent the author's relationship to his writing in the early modern period, as Mark Rose has shown, and in spite of its awkward fit with the liberalised market in books (in which the author sells his 'brainchild') paternity remains one of the two principal figures (along with real estate) to describe the author–work relation in copyright terms (Rose, 1993: 38–41; Rose, 2002). The metaphor figures the creative process of literary paternity as parthenogenetic. Rehearsing the original divine act of creation, the author creates an original work out of nothing; he is the sole creator of his literary offspring brought forth in a single act of creation (Rose, 2002: 3–5). This asexual form of creation has no use for difference; it disregards the social dimension of creativity and forecloses the possibility of distributing creative agency. Social creativity – collective, cumulative, sexual – is banished from the domain of works of authorship as the regime of authorship carved up the discursive field. Such alternative forms of creative agency were relegated to the residual domain of folklore.

In their reading of literary paternity, Sandra Gilbert and Susan Gubar note that 'because he is an *author*, a "man of letters" is simultaneously, like his divine counterpart, a father, a master or ruler, and an owner: the spiritual type of a patriarch' (Gilbert and Gubar, 2000: 7; emphasis in original). The author's pen is portrayed, in their words, as 'an instrument of generative power like his penis' (ibid.: 6). In the dominant understanding of creativity in the nineteenth century, then, men penned original works; they ruled in the domain of authorship. The place of women was in the constitutive outside of that domain, in its residue: folklore. Women were portrayed not as authors but as gossips (Warner, 1994: 12–65). Their artistry was oral, not literary; they did not create originals, they copied and repeated.

Women, children, and peasants all come together in the folktale as modelled in the *Kinder- und Hausmärchen*: the tale culled from its peasant sources and told in the bourgeois nursery, in the heart of the private sphere, the dominion of women, by a mother or better yet by a grandmother to a group of children. The peasants are naïve and childlike, and so are women. Children are governed by their emotions and defined by their bodies much as women and peasants were portrayed. This imagery is the product of a paternalistic and patriarchal relationship to the subaltern.

All three groups are imagined collectively, rather than individually: unlike the authors of the time, and unlike the editors of folktale collections, storytellers are rarely mentioned by name by the Grimms or in the other collections that took inspiration in theirs. Storytellers figure always as collective sources. At most the area where they live is mentioned. Yet we are led to assume their class and often their gender.

There is an important exception that illustrates this rule. We owe it to the Grimms. Not only did they map the domain of collective creativity, they illustrated the creative agency in that domain. The face of the folk from whom the tales emanate is the face of Dorothea Viehmann, as the Grimms presented her to their readers in 1815 in the second volume of the *Kinder- und Hausmärchen*:

> One of those happy pieces of good fortune was the acquaintance with a peasant woman from the village of Zwehrn near Kassel. Through her we acquired a good part of the tales published here along with a number of additions to the first volume. They can therefore be counted as genuinely Hessian. This woman, still vigorous and not much over fifty, is called Viehmann. She has a firmly set, pleasant face with bright, clear eyes and was probably beautiful when she was young. She has these stories clearly in mind, a gift which she says is not given to everyone. Many people cannot memorize anything at all. She narrates carefully, confidently, and in an unusually lively manner, taking great pleasure in it. (Transl. in Tatar, 2004: 408)

As Heinz Rölleke points out, the Grimms tailored Dorothea Viehmann to suit an idealised image of their contributors, the image that their readers were to carry away with them (Rölleke, 1991: 103). Literally so, as her portrait illustrated the second volume of the tales starting with the second edition of 1819, drawn by the third brother, Ludwig Emil Grimm (ibid.). That Viehmann was in fact the wife of a tailor and came from a Huguenot family hardly matters in this context, nor that many of their other narrators were young ladies from the middle classes.

Dorothea Viehmann died near the end of 1815, but over the next century her name and her image travelled with the Grimms' tales around the world and became synonymous with folk tradition. In 1819, Viehmann's face in Ludwig Grimm's frontispiece was still in part her own, that of the woman in Niederzwehren whom he had sketched in 1814, a year after the brothers came into contact with her. But in 1837, a legend appeared in large print below her portrait in the third edition of *Kinder- und Hausmärchen*. The legend was only one word: Märchenfrau. Her transformation from the individual to the generic, which began 22 years earlier in the first edition of the second volume, was now complete. Hers is the face of the public domain: the face of the folk.

Louis Katzenstein's fabulous image from 1892, 'Die Brüder Grimm bei der Märchenfrau' (Figure E.1), juxtaposes Ludwig Grimm's frontispiece of Viehmann with a famous portrait of the Brothers Grimm and embeds both in a stock scene from visual metafolklore: the scientific collectors, scholars, and editors are portrayed face to face with the folk, sitting in Dorothea Viehmann's home and hanging on her every word, surrounded by well-behaved children and poultry, both listening eagerly (de Blécourt, 2011). These editors occupy an interesting position in between the folk and the author, in the interstices between two discursive domains; one might say in the wound opened up by their division, by the rupture between tradition and modernity. The collector-editor is a certified translator between these domains. He is an adventurer travelling into the hinterlands of tradition to cull its last remaining treasures and carry them back across the ontological borders of modernity.

Figure E.1   'Die Brüder Grimm bei der Märchenfrau', Louis Katzenstein, 1892.

In fact the historical Dorothea Viehmann paid visits to the Grimms and not the other way around. She was the border-crossing adventurer. As far as we know they never set foot in her home (Lauer, 1998: 36–42). As Willem de Blécourt has noted, Katzenstein's illustration 'reflects late nineteenth-century opinion on the activities of the Grimms' (de Blécourt, 2010: 180). Its inverted representation of historical events speaks to the stability of the discursive regime of authorship by the end of the nineteenth century, how firmly the positions of the folk, the author, and the collector-editor had settled by then.

* * *

In an age of file sharing and peer-to-peer networking, of social software and Web 2.0, of mashups and remixes, we need a new language to speak of creative agency. Historically, folklore offered an alternative to authorship: folklore is peer-to-peer, it is collaborative, and it is collective. But the choice between these two options is not satisfactory; we cannot accept it uncritically. We need alternative ways to conceive of creative agency, beyond the figures of the author and the folk. We must come up with ways to imagine creative agency differently and to think in other terms about creative processes that are collaborative, incremental, and distributed in space and time.

Such creative processes are in fact all around us. They are the norm, not the exception. How many people do you imagine wrote that text on the back of your cereal box? Designed the graphic illustration? How many people did it take to create the movie you watched last night? The language of folklore often comes closer to describing creative processes and products than the language of authorship. Neither is accurate, however. Each is based on the exclusion of the other. To construct a new language, we need first to understand the discursive grid we are revising so we do not wind up reproducing the same old discursive antagonisms with merely a new vocabulary. We need an alternative grammar of creativity and a renewed understanding of how cultural expressions circulate.

Here is an idea: How about the collector-editor? Could we model a new understanding of creative agency on the figure of the folklorist? Notwithstanding the immodesty of such a proposal, what possibilities would such an understanding open up? What new perspectives? What if every cultural actor, individual or collective, is acting like the Brothers Grimm when they compiled the *Kinder- und Hausmärchen*? The rapper, the storyteller, the singer, the author, the programmer, the poet, the mashupping contributor to YouTube, the guy cracking jokes at the office party, the student writing a Facebook status in class – everyone, that is? What if we think of culture as a republic of editors – some more (adamant about faithful reproduction or scholarly reconstruction) like Jacob, and others more (inclined to artistic elaboration) like Wilhelm?

We would be taking away from authorship and folk tradition their powerful hold on our imagination because their power depends on their dichotomous relation. By reframing the interstitial position as the central category we challenge the untenable dichotomy that still channels our understanding of creative agency. In redefining the borderlands as the centre, we define the author and the folk as peripheral concepts, as exceptions rather than norms, or, better yet, as labels on either end of a spectrum, with most texts falling not at either end but somewhere in between. And the in-between is the domain of the collector-editor.

Let us return now to the question with which we began, the question with which each of the chapters in this book grapples in its own way: '*What is and what ought to be the relationship between creativity, cultural heritage institutions and copyright?*' What I propose is an alternative model of creativity, in which creative agency is not modelled as individual but as collective or social, where creation is not a single act but a cumulative process, and where the figures of the author and the folk are not mistaken for empirical realities or even used as heuristic models but rather provide two imaginary points on the compass of creative agency; like East and West on the compass, they give a name to cardinal directions with reference to which we can map out different places/texts and describe their relation to one another; East and West are not themselves a place, they describe a relation. The cultural heritage institution is the place in which this relation is mapped out. In this context, the collector-editor stands in for the cultural heritage institution. The *Kinder- und Hausmärchen* of the Grimm brothers may be read as a *pars pro toto* for the archive, the museum, the library. Instead of the collector-editor, we might as well speak of the archivist, the curator, the librarian, all of whom fall somewhere along the spectrum between the author and the folk.

The relationship between cultural heritage institutions and copyright is currently one of exception. Whether through fair use (in the US), fair dealing (in the UK), or the one mandatory and twenty-one optional copyright exceptions in the EU *Acquis*, cultural heritage institutions conduct their work in a narrow loophole in the law that gives legal standing to the categories of authorship (which creates property) and folk tradition (which feeds the public domain). As many authors in this book have brought out in distressing detail, the relationship of exception puts severe limitations on institutions of cultural heritage; it stands between them and the important tasks that society charges them with; it creates unconscionable waste (as in the resource-intensive search for possible rights-holders in orphan works); and it seriously constrains the circulation of culture, the protection of cultural heritage, and the creation of new works. It bears mentioning in this context that the cultural heritage institutions are themselves not innocent of extending these constraints, as it is now nearly standard practice for them to claim a quasi-copyright in their holdings (thus for example the publisher for this book requires that I get permission from holding institutions for reproducing on these pages Katzenstein's illustration from 1892, although the artist died in 1907, long before the term of protection was extended to the current 70 years after the author's death).

If the relationship is currently one of exception, then what remains to be addressed is how it ought to be. The gist of my argument on the preceding pages is that the relationship between copyright and cultural heritage institutions ought to be modelled instead on a revised understanding of creativity as collective, incremental, and distributed. Thus understood, the collector-editor, archivist, curator and librarian actually guarantee the very conditions of creativity. A copyright law that would encourage creativity does not define their practice as an exception. Instead it should be the rule.

References

Abrams, M.H. (1971). *The Mirror and the Lamp. Romantic Theory and the Critical Tradition.* Oxford.

Berne Convention for the Protection of Literary and Artistic Works. WIPO website: Treaties and Contracting Parties. Retrieved 14 August 2013: http://www.wipo. int/treaties/en/ip/berne/index.html

Bogsch, Arpad (1986). 'The First Hundred Years of the Berne Convention for the Protection of Literary and Artistic Works', *Copyright* 22, 291–339.

de Blécourt, Willem (2010). 'Fairy Grandmothers. Images of Storytelling Events in Nineteenth-Century Germany', *Relief* 4: 2, 174–97.

de Blécourt, Willem (2011). 'Metamorphosing Men and Transmogrified Texts. Some Thoughts on the Genealogy of Fairy Tales', *Fabula* 52: 3–4, 280–96.

Gilbert, Sandra M. and Susan Gubar (2000). *The Madwoman in the Attic. The Woman Writer and the Nineteenth-Century Literary Imagination*. 2nd edn. New Haven: Yale University Press.

Grimm, Brothers (1980). *Kinder- und Hausmärchen. Ausgabe letzter Hand mit den Originalanmerkungen der Brüder Grimm*. Ed. Heinz Rölleke. 3 vols. Stuttgart: Reclam, 1980.

Groth, Stefan (2012). *Negotiating Tradition: The Pragmatics of International Deliberations on Cultural Property*. Göttingen: Universitätsverlag Göttingen.

Hemmungs Wirtén, Eva (2010). 'Colonial Copyright, Postcolonial Publics. The Berne Convention and the 1967 Stockholm Diplomatic Conference Revisited', *SCRIPTed* 7: 3, 532–50.

Lauer, Bernard (1998). 'Dorothea Viehmann und die Brüder Grimm. Märchen und Wirklichkeit', *Märchenspiegel* 9, 36–42.

Mezghani, Nebila (1986). 'The Interplay Between the Berne Convention and the Developing Countries in the Evolution of Copyright', *Copyright* 22, 184–91.

Olwan, Rami (2013). *Intellectual Property and Development: Theory and Practice*. Berlin: Springer.

Oxford English Dictionary (1989). Oxford: Oxford University Press.

Patterson, Lyman Ray (1968). *Copyright in Historical Perspective*. Nashville: Vanderbildt University Press.

Records of the Intellectual Property Conference of Stockholm, June 11 to July 14, 1967 (1971). 2 vols. Geneva: WIPO.

Ricketson, Sam (1987). *The Berne Convention for the Protection of Literary and Artistic Works: 1886–1986*. London: Centre for Commercial Law Studies, Queen Mary College / Kluwer.

Rölleke, Heinz (1991). 'New Results of Research on *Grimm's Fairy Tales*', in James M. McGlathery (ed.), *The Brothers Grimm and Folktale*. Urbana: University of Illinois Press, 101–111.

Rose, Mark (1993). *Authors and Owners. The Invention of Copyright*. Cambridge: Harvard University Press.

Rose, Mark (2002). 'Copyright and its Metaphors', *UCLA Law Review* 50, 1–12.

Stewart, Susan (1994). *Crimes of Writing. Problems in the Containment of Representation*. Durham: Duke University Press.

Tatar, Maria (2004). *The Annotated Brothers Grimm. The Bicentennial Edition*. New York: W.W. Norton & Co.

Warner, Marina (1994). *From the Beast to the Blonde. On Fairy Tales and Their Tellers*. New York: The Noonday Press.

Woodmansee, Martha (1994). 'On the Author Effect. Recovering Collectivity', in Martha Woodmansee and Peter Jaszi (eds), *The Construction of Authorship*.

Textual Appropriation in Law and Literature. Durham: Duke University Press, 15–28.

Zografos, Daphne (2010). *Intellectual Property and Traditional Cultural Expression*. Cheltenham: Edward Elgar Publishing.

Index